Apes, Men, and Language

APES, MEN,

NEW YORK

AND LANGUAGE

Eugene Linden

SATURDAY REVIEW PRESS / E. P. DUTTON & CO., INC.

Selections from *The Structure of Scientific Revolutions* by Thomas S. Kuhn are reprinted with permission of the author and the University of Chicago Press. Copyright © 1962, 1970 by the University of Chicago. All rights reserved.

Library of Congress Cataloging in Publication Data

Linden, Eugene.
Apes, men, and language.

1. Chimpanzees—Behavior.   2. Animal communication.
3. Sign language.   I.   Title.
QL737.P96L56   1974   599'.884   74-7060

Published simultaneously in Canada by Clarke, Irwin & Company Limited,
Toronto and Vancouver
ISBN: 0-8415-0343-5
Designed by The Etheredges

To my parents

ACKNOWLEDGMENTS

Without the cooperation and advice of Roger Fouts this book would not have been possible. I would like to thank Harvey Sarles for encouraging me to stick with my unconventional approach to the book's material and for tempering the development of my thinking along the way. David Detweiler gave the manuscript a close reading at several stages during the writing, and my editors, Tom Davis and Susan Schaeffer, offered many valuable suggestions toward pruning some of the denser thickets of prose. Finally, I would like to thank my wife, Madelaine, for her extraordinary drawings that open the book and flood it with light.

CONTENTS

PART ONE

The Chimpanzee in the Temple of Language

CONTENTS

PART TWO

Rehabilitating the Reputation of the Animal Mind

LIST OF ILLUSTRATIONS

LIST OF ILLUSTRATIONS

Introduction

In April of 1967, an infant asked its foster parents to "gimme sweet" and in so doing sent through the behavioral sciences the first tremor of what was to become a massive quake. The event was epochal because the infant was a female chimpanzee, and because she made her request in a human language. Since that time, this chimp, named Washoe, has had increasingly elaborate conversations with a variety of people, including this author. Also since that time, a number of other chimpanzees have been schooled in this language, and some are beginning to use it as a means of communication among themselves. It is the purpose of this book to present what is known so far about the chimpanzee's skills in using language and then to make sense of these achievements.

The nature of these topics demands that they be approached with particular care. The discussion of human language and thought in contrast with a mute and benighted animal world has been an obsession of Western thought—everybody has something to say about it. Within science alone, communication is the object of study among a bewildering variety of disciplines that examine language and animal communication from an equally bewildering variety of perspectives; few of these disciplines share fundamental agreement on what language is. To approach Washoe or language from the particular bias of any one discipline would be to convey the false impression that there is fundamental agreement on the nature of language and a true perspective from which to assess the importance of man-chimp conversation. Before the advent of Washoe, there was fundamental agreement on only one proposition about language: man had it and animals did not.

Instead of setting this book in the agglomerate of notions about language, we will view that Babel of opinions from the new perspective offered by the chimpanzee. By sorting through the aggregate abilities associated with language, we will see how these abilities have been illuminated by the performances of Washoe and her confreres. We will follow Washoe into the temple of language, watch her as she steps on various toes in the behavioral sciences, and then discuss a particular aspect of language when someone cries, "Ouch!" In certain aspects of her language use, Washoe steps on several toes at the same time; in other cases, we find, to further attenuate our metaphor, the same toes in different shoes. Consequently, different characteristics of language that are important to understanding Washoe will be dealt with recurrently throughout the book. These will be expanded upon as they develop and, in turn, are developed by the picture of the chimpanzee's use of a human language.

In Part One, Chapters 1–4 present Washoe and the initial stir she caused in the world of science. Chapters 5–10 describe Washoe's present home, her chimpanzee and human colleagues, and a bold experiment to encourage a colony of chimpanzees to use a human language in daily communication among themselves. Chapter 11 attempts to extract from the foregoing chapters one aspect of behavior, which, given the breakdown of traditional distinctions, might be helpful in understanding some of the manifest differences between man and chimpanzee. Chapters 12 and 13 discuss the future of the work that began with Washoe and the state of an entirely different attempt to communicate with a chimpanzee that began contemporaneously to the work with Washoe. Chapter 14 plumbs the cultural aspects of what it means to be able to talk to another animal.

Part Two, Chapters 15–20, is concerned with the events that led to Washoe and the changes she has signaled in the world of science and in the everyday world of men. I conclude by attempting to describe the origins and nature of the world view in which Washoe is a surprise, in contrast to an emerging world view in which her achievements are no surprise at all.

Part One
The Chimpanzee in
the Temple of
Language

1. The Problem: A Chimpanzee That Swears

In the *Antiquities of the Jews*, Flavius Josephus, the historian of
Roman times, notes that when man was banished from the Garden
of Eden, he lost, among other things, the ability to talk with the
animals. In his account of Genesis, Josephus was reflecting the
belief common among Jews that before the Fall, man could speak
with the animals. The myth of the Fall has been seen as the expression of an ancestral memory of man's original usurpation of
nature's authority; at the time of Josephus, the price of that usurpation was alienation from nature, reflected in the evolution of a
language distinct from that of the other animals. As we all know,
however, this alienation had positive interpretations as well. Just
as it furthered the distance between man and nature, so did it pro-

3

vide man with both the abilities and the moral justification for nature's manipulation. We soon forgot that defiance cost us the ability to speak the language of animals, and, instead, we stressed that they could not speak ours. When cast in this fashion, man's isolation became not a curse but a glory, which carried with it prerogatives to use the world as he wished.

The Bible was spun in an arid region, and it is plausible that such a people, seeing no links between animal and man, would project a philosophical system obsessed with alienation from nature and allowing man great license in its manipulation. Conversely, it is also plausible that other peoples, such as those jungle dwellers who live in proximity to an ascending grade of monkeys and apes that visibly demonstrate the links between animal and man, should not project such a system. Unlike such jungle peoples, we were ill-equipped to account for the existence of apes when, through conquest and exploration, we entered the tropical forests and came into contact with those primates that seem to link animal and man.

And so, how did we react? After sporadic contacts and several centuries of excitement over the novelty of these creatures, we decided to teach a few captive specimens to speak as we do. These attempts, however, were not supposed to succeed, because to succeed would be to undermine that attitude toward nature—that carefully constructed vision of man's glorious isolation—upon which the West was built. And yet, once exposed to the enclosed evolutionary grade that cohabits beneath the jungle canopy, it was inevitable that some Europeans would begin to see it for what it is. A century after Darwin first confronted Europe with the truths of the jungle canopy, the lessons of Darwinism began to filter through to those behavioral scientists who were attempting to teach a chimp to talk, in particular, to a husband-wife team in Reno, Nevada.

In June of 1966, R. Allen and Beatrice Gardner acquired an infant female chimpanzee and immediately set about attempting to

4

Washoe: "more"

teach her to "speak." For a medium of communication, they used American Sign Language, or Ameslan, as it is referred to by the many deaf people for whom it is a primary means of communication. Using a gestural rather than a spoken language was a stroke of brilliance that their chimp, named Washoe, acknowledged by the rapidity with which she acquired signs. In Ameslan, a word is signified by a gesture, the gesture itself being a composite of basic signal units. Washoe's first word was not "mama" or "papa" but "more," a sign made by repeated touching of the fingertips with palms toward the signer. It was an imperative she seemingly applied to her vocabulary as well as to her infant desires for more tickles, hugs, and treats, because when she left Nevada five years later she knew 160 words, which she used singly and in combinations in a variety of conversational situations. When Washoe left Nevada for the University of Oklahoma aboard a Lear Jet, she was accompanied by Dr. Roger Fouts, her closest companion and the Gardners' former chief assistant.

In 1972 I made the first of two trips to Oklahoma to meet Washoe and Dr. Fouts and to take Washoe's measure as a conversationalist. But there I met more than one "Washoe." Since her arrival, about a dozen other chimpanzees have received intensive training in Ameslan. These training programs were organized around a new generation of experiments in which chimpanzees were to be encouraged to use Ameslan as a medium of communication among themselves.

Washoe's new home, the Institute for Primate Studies, has been hewn gradually out of an old farm. The center of the institute is a large pond where three man-made islands are populated with colonies of sober-faced capuchin monkeys, high-strung gibbons, and brawny chimpanzees. Washoe spends a good deal of her time on this chimp island and, when not there, with the adult chimp colony in a complex of cages adjoining the director's pink, sprayed-concrete home. The institute is home to a variety of other animals besides chimps. Oak-shaded cages house pigtail and stump-tail macaques; herds of sheep and cattle wander the surrounding meadows. Opposite the chimp cages a large shed is inhabited by siamangs, squirrel monkeys, and other smaller primates. Around the compound roam a tribe of hypertense peacocks who look as though they might prefer to exchange their vainglorious plumage for something less likely to attract the attention of the young chimps who saunter about and occasionally harass them. Life here is punctuated with the hum of vitality and the frequent crises that come from being around relatively unrestrained chimpanzees.

Washoe was the subject of one such crisis the day I met her; her distress was the result of the rigors of confinement and not lack of restraint. She was ashore that day, in transit from the chimp island to the adult chimp quarters, and she was outraged at the holding cage that was her temporary home. Grabbing the bars, Washoe rocked back and forth. She would occasionally emit a series of hoots that eventually erupted into deafening screams. Alternating with these screams, she made gestures that were of far greater interest to her human observers than were her characteristic primate vocalizations. She would touch her thumb to her mouth or make a series of quick signals when someone she recog-

Washoe swears, signing "dirty," in calling this macaque a "dirty monkey."

nized passed by. One handler was working in the vicinity of the cage. After ignoring several of her requests for drink and escape, he noticed that before gesturing his name, Washoe was making a sign he did not recognize. She would hit the top of her palm to the underside of her chin. He asked another handler what the sign meant. It was the gesture meaning "dirty." Washoe was saying, "Dirty Jack gimme drink." She had learned the word that meant "soiled," but now she was mad enough to swear.

When Fouts joined me a little later, I told him about the incident. He remarked matter-of-factly that this was not the first time she had used "dirty" this way. He expects his pupils to do astonishing things and, during my first visit, was amused more by my reactions than by his pupils' behavior that elicited them. Fouts has grown accustomed to living in a world in which chimpanzees swear.

Because we have lived for centuries snug in the belief that such behavior is not supposed to happen, the rest of us might be forgiven amazement at Washoe's swearing. Washoe affects not only the behavioral sciences most immediately insulted by her swearing but the everyday world as well. In fact, Washoe's swearing poses problems for people who have never seen a chimpanzee.

2. Washoe

The immediate cause of Washoe's ill-humor on the day I met her was the holding cage in which she was temporarily locked. At that time, she was unaccustomed to the institute and other apes, and her foul temper was heightened by what she perceived as an un-warranted downgrading of her status from human to animal. While in Reno sycophantic assistants hung on her every gesture; now in Oklahoma she had been thrust in with some rowdy and inattentive subordinate species, whom she could not quite place, but whom she knew were definitely not people. After having raised her station by having learned a human language, Washoe was thrown back in with dumb beasts, and she wanted to know why. She was not in the most sociable mood that day I met her, and, partly because of her lung power and partly because she was a chimpanzee whom I had just seen swear, I approached our first meeting with awe. Fouts was amused. "The differences between man and chimp tend to disappear when you work with them," he told me as we walked toward her cage.

The difference between man and chimp disappeared long ago for Roger Fouts because he has spent the better part of his academic life working with Washoe.

Roger Fouts is of moderate height and build. He dresses informally and comports himself in an understated manner. Fouts's graduate education began and ended with Project Washoe at the University of Nevada. He published his first scientific paper in 1972 in the *Journal of Comparative and Physiological Psychology* on the techniques used in instructing Washoe; subsequently, he has published six more articles, presented seven papers, and has given numerous invited addresses, all of which have been concerned with different aspects of his work with Washoe and other Ameslan-using chimpanzees. Given the intimate relationship between Washoe's linguistic development and Fouts's academic professional development, it is not surprising that he should be thoroughly at home in a world where chimpanzees talk.

With our arrival, Washoe quieted. Save perhaps the Gardners, who originally trained her, she knows and trusts Fouts more than she does any other person. Still, he inherited a difficult task when he accompanied her to Oklahoma, namely, that of explaining the loss of the lavish attention and privileges that had sweetened her days in Nevada. "You can't blame her for feeling slighted," Fouts said, as he opened the door to the holding cage. Washoe could not know that the changes in her life were not gratuitous nor that they were part of a design to use her as a catalyst in an attempt to foster the use of a human language in daily communications among a colony of chimpanzees. Until she came to Oklahoma, she had not met another chimp and did not know that Ameslan was not the normal means of communication among these animals, whom she originally referred to as "black bugs."

Washoe stepped out of the cage and, in enthusiastic gratitude, gave Roger a big hug. She is a big girl, about ninety pounds; when she moves, she gives the impression of solidity and restrained power.

The chimpanzee is classified as one of the three great apes. The others are the gorilla (*Gorilla*) and orangutan (*Pongo*). The other apes include man (who is the only surviving member of the family *Hominidae*) and the lesser apes, the gibbon and the siamang. The apes together with man belong to the sub-order *Simiae* which, together with the pro-simians, comprise the primate order.

Among the apes, the chimpanzee is man's closest living relative. Although their evolutionary paths diverged some fourteen-million years ago, man is really more closely related to the chimp than the chimp is to the monkey. The chimp weighs between 100 and 200 pounds, is shorter than man and vastly stronger. Its brain is roughly the same size, about 500 cc., as that of one of man's purported ancestors, *Australopithecus*, a tool-using, semi-erect creature who disappeared about three-quarters-of-a-million years ago.

Of the three great apes, it is an open question which is the more intelligent. An infant orangutan once scored over 200 on an IQ test used for human infants, although it is difficult to tell whether that score indicated native intelligence or that the orang had better control over its movements than an infant of the same age. The orang, however, is a solitary animal, which makes him more difficult to work with than the gregarious chimpanzee or gorilla. The gorilla's size makes him also difficult to work with, so on practical grounds the chimp is the best suited for experiments such as those constructed by the Gardners. One final reason why the chimp was selected is his apparent ability to form strong attachments to human foster parents.

Wild chimps live in tribes of ten or more in the jungles and savannahs of East and West Africa. They grow to be about human weight and have a life-span of as long as fifty years. Chimp bands subsist mainly by foraging for fruit, although they sometimes scavenge and even hunt. Their society is highly organized, and chimp culture contains a number of ritualized forms for meetings between chimps within a band and for meetings between bands. For example, Jane Goodall has observed a chimp band performing what looked like a rain dance.

Among themselves, the chimps seem to communicate both by vocalizations and by gesture. The vocalizations are calls related to alarm, aggression, and sources of excitation. The nature of the wild chimp's gestural communication is still relatively unexamined. Thus, growing up as a chimpanzee involves both a good deal of learning and not a little diplomacy, and it is these social and intellectual predispositions that make the chimp an ideal student for human, as well as chimpanzee, mentors.

After hugging Roger, Washoe looked at me and asked him who I was. She did this by tracing a question mark in the air and then pointing at me. Roger simply hooked the first finger of each hand together in the gesture meaning "friend." Acting on this information, Washoe walked over and gave me a perfunctory hug; she then took our hands, and, like three boulevardiers, we ambled through the meadow. Pulling us along, Washoe led the way toward a copse of apple trees. Remembering her incarceration, she suddenly became sulky. She jerked away from us and walked deliberately up to an apple tree. When she disregarded his gestures and attention-getting calls, Roger became nervous. "When she deliberately ignores me is the only time I worry," he said. "She's challenging my dominance, and it's times like this that she might accidentally flatten me while swinging on a branch."

With this possibility in mind, we steered well clear of the tree through which Washoe was now foraging. Roger picked up an apple and offering it to Washoe, said, "What's this?"

Washoe seemed to come out of her funk and knuckled over signing, "Fruit."

"Who fruit?"

"Washoe fruit."

Lucy: "fruit"

"What Washoe fruit?"

"Please Washoe fruit."

Thus reconciled, Roger suggested that we go for a drive, a proposal that Washoe endorsed by saying, "Go car." Given the uncertainty of her mood, Fouts suggested that I drive so that he could watch Washoe. Whereupon we piled into Roger's Austin Mini, with Washoe perched between Fouts and me, her bright stare fixed on the passing countryside, while Roger and I discussed her history.

BACKGROUND

Early attempts to teach apes to talk lent credence to the argument that language was unique to man and that apes, like other animals, were prisoners of context, of stimulus and response. The chimpanzee's vocal productions seemed to be an array of hoots and cries, elicited by external stimuli—what anthropologist Gordon Hewes has called an "alarm system." Efforts to get apes to talk foundered on the animals' inability to control vocal output. In 1916 William Furness attempted to teach a young orangutan to speak. Through supreme patience Furness managed to teach the

13

ape to say "papa" and "cup." The orang used the words correctly and later, dying of influenza, is reported to have said, "Cup, cup," in asking for a drink. Furness noted that neither the orang nor the chimp seems to use lips or tongue in making his natural calls; neither of the words the orang learned required precise control over those physiological features.

The fact that the chimp was so facile and quick to learn in other respects further bolstered the idea that language accounted for the differences between ape and man. In the 1920s, Wolfgang Köhler, the father of Gestalt psychology, conducted an experiment in which he placed in a chimp's cage a banana that could be reached only by fastening two poles into one longer pole. After many hours, the chimp, named Sultan, had a flash of insight and retrieved his reward. From then on chimps were confronted with a panoply of objects to match, stack, or unlock.

In the early 1950s, illness ended another attempt to teach an ape to talk. This time the experiment was coupled with an extensive comparative study of the problem-solving abilities of a chimp, named Vicki, and several human infants. Vicki showed herself quite capable of matching the performance of her human peers in figuring out the locks of latchboxes and in being able to discriminate such conceptual differences as color, form, age, and completeness. Similarly, she was able to sort one set of pictures according to several different criteria, and, before giving up in distress, Vicki proved able to learn six different sequences in which three strings could be pulled to retrieve a ball.

Vicki's teacher, Keith Hayes, has found that Vicki's instrumentation tasks indicated the effects of experience both in developing reasoning ability and insight and in releasing the animal from stereotypy. To summarize the release from stereotypy, Hayes cites two pioneer animal psychologists, Maier and Schneirla: "Past experience ceases to furnish the patterns of response and instead furnished the data from which new patterns may be formed. This ability frees the animal from a particular bit of learning and makes possible almost unlimited patterns of response." This is precisely the type of advantage language is supposed to have over animal communication, and we would rightfully expect Vicki to demontrate linguistic skills commensurate with the level of cognition demonstrated in her problem solving. Unfortunately, Vicki painfully learned to utter reliably only four words.

There were two explanations for her failure: 1) Vicki possessed greater linguistic abilities than she demonstrated, but physiological constraints prevented those abilities from being tapped; 2) Vicki failed to learn to speak because she lacked the neural organization necessary to generate or comprehend language. Because Vicki had trouble discriminating between numbers past a certain point (five versus six and beyond) and because she eventually refused to work on string-sequence problems, Hayes was tempted to conclude that these difficulties were related to her difficulty in speaking, i.e., the ability to acquire language might be related to arithmetic and sequence-learning abilities beyond those possessed by the chimpanzee. This explanation enjoyed broad acceptance. The scientific community largely ignored Vicki's ability to express basic propositions through her hands, and instead attended to her inability to utter propositions in sentences.

Hayes made extensive films of Vicki's training, and among those scientists who viewed the films were the Gardners, behavioral psychologists at the University of Nevada at Reno. These two scientists did not see Vicki's difficulty in forming words as evidence of a cognitive deficiency; they were struck by other aspects of her performance. They noted that Vicki was intelligible without the sound-track, and that she was perfectly dextrous—fluent—in manipulating her hands. She would accompany a word with a characteristic gesture. Thus, in the early 1960s, when Vicki was being cited as conclusive proof that the chimp lacked the mental hardware necessary for language, the Gardners began to think that her deficiency was motor, not mental, and that perhaps she might be taught some language which would exploit her facility with her hands. At that time reports were beginning to circulate about a study of wild chimps that indicated that they might communicate with gestures as well as with vocal calls. Adriaan Kortlandt, a Dutch scientist, observed chimps making a submissive gesture somewhat like hat-tipping, which seemed to vary in its execution from band to band. Jane Goodall documented gestures associated with begging, anxiety, and urging an infant to mount its mother's back prior to flight. Even now little is known about the extent of the chimp's gestural vocabulary or the complexity of the communicative system in which it is used, but the suspicion is growing that the chimpanzee might employ a primitive gesture language in the wild.

Actually, pioneer primatologist Robert Yerkes had also noted the chimp's vocal difficulty; it was he who first suggested just after the turn of the century that a gestural medium might be more suitable in establishing two-way communication with the chimp. But it was not until 1966 that this suggestion was acted upon.

All the experiments previous to Washoe had assumed that language was synonymous with speech, an assumption that implicitly excluded from the temple of language a sizable number of people who do not use spoken language—the deaf. The Gardners suffered from no such confusion of language with speech and began to wonder whether some gestural language might sidestep the chimp's obvious difficulties in controlling its vocal productions. As an experimental psychologist, Allen Gardner had done a good deal of work with rats. His wife, Beatrice, is also a psychologist, as well as an ethologist; she studied under the pioneer ethologist and Nobel prize winner, Niko Tinbergen, and was known for her work studying the hunting behavior of the jumping spider. They began their work aided by grants from the National Institute of Mental Health, the National Science Foundation, and the National Geographic Society.

WASHOE

Washoe had been captured in the wild in Africa, presumably following the death or murder of her mother, and was about a year old in 1966 when acquired by the Gardners. It is not known whether Washoe retained any memories of her mother, but her mother was the last chimpanzee she was to see for six years.

LIFE IN RENO

In comparison with other captive chimpanzees, Washoe's early life was baronial. Her home was a 24-foot trailer in the Gardners' backyard in Reno. It was equipped with a stove, refrigerator, dinette area, bathtub, toilet, and bedroom. Outside was 5,000 square feet of open space to play in. Occasionally, Washoe would be treated to a trip to the University of Nevada gym where she could swing on ropes and do other chimp-like things. On one such trip, Washoe scampered through the biology department testing doors and having a grand time. One door led into the men's room. Finding it unlocked, Washoe ran in and proceeded to bound under and over the stalls. Fouts suddenly heard a man yell, "My God, it's a gorilla!" as Washoe rocketed out the door and disappeared down a stairwell. A moment later, an ashen face peered out nervously into the hallway.

Washoe was reared in an "enriched" environment. She had a constant parade of human companions and innumerable toys and games to excite her curiosity and keep her attention engaged. Training sessions were paced to her attention span, and all human conversations were conducted in sign language to minimize any distraction that might come from using one language in conversation with Washoe while they used another in conversation with themselves. Everything in Washoe's environment was designed to educe whatever cognitive abilities she had and to encourage her to use Ameslan as a means to satisfy her desires. She was, one observer noted, "a one-hundred IQ chimp in a two-hundred IQ environment." She was named for the county in Nevada where she was raised.

THE CHIMPANZEE IN THE TEMPLE OF LANGUAGE

THE LANGUAGE

The Gardners chose Ameslan from among several possibilities. They could have invented a language to teach to their chimp, or they could have chosen from among several sign languages used throughout the world today. They quickly discarded as too difficult the idea of inventing a language. Among the sign languages, the deaf in the United States use two principal means of communication, Ameslan and finger spelling. Finger spelling is not a language but rather a means of transposing any alphabetized language such as English into a gestural mode. Ameslan is a language, and it is the primary means of communication for deaf people in North America. Although Ameslan is more efficient, the deaf who know how to read and write seem to prefer finger spelling—it has more cachet.

Each gesture in Ameslan is made up of cheremes or basic signal units. In all, Ameslan has fifty-five cheremes. Nineteen identify the configuration of the hand or hands making the sign; twelve, the place where the sign is made; and twenty-four, the action of the hand or hands. Although these signs are for the most part arbitrary (not direct pictures of their meaning), some show vestiges of what might at one time have been a mythology of the body, which gave the meaning to the sign according to the body location where it was made. For instance, the sign for "monkey" is made with a gesture in which the fingers of the two hands are drawn back across the rib cage in imitation of an archetypal scratching motion. Curiously, the sign for "chimpanzee" (a relatively recent sign) is made the same way, but higher on the chest —appropriately more toward the "people" area. Thus we might imagine a time when a sign's meaning was constructed as a composite from a vocabulary of readily recognizable sub-units. Now, for the most part, a chereme no longer conveys a particular meaning than do the basic sounds, or phonemes, that are the construction blocks of English words.

Just as cheremes are similar to phonemes, so does Ameslan have a grammar that organizes gestures into sentences, although that grammar is significantly different from English grammar. The cheremes and the grammar of Ameslan were to become important for Roger Fouts's experiment in Oklahoma. In selecting a language for Washoe, Ameslan was well-suited to the Gardners' purposes but it was chosen for different reasons: Ameslan is accepted as a bona fide language; more important, it has been studied, and its acquisition by the deaf has been studied as well. Thus, by using Ameslan with Washoe, the Gardners could compare the development of the chimpanzee's abilities with that of deaf children and the development of either with that of normal English-speaking children. Such comparisons would have been impossible had they chosen a synthetic language.

The Gardners' intent in teaching Washoe Ameslan was to determine at what point in the acquisition of language the child outpaced the chimpanzee and, in so doing, to isolate the particular linguistic abilities the child has that the chimp does not. They theorized that Washoe would demonstrate certain abilities humans associate with language, but that eventually the chimp would prove incapable of understanding a question or the negative or word order. In that way, they hoped to define more precisely what is unique about human language.

Things did not work out this way; indeed, the Gardners did not expect them to.

TEACHING THE LANGUAGE

The Gardners developed a program of instruction for Washoe that drew heavily on methods contributed by behaviorism, a field of experimental psychology concerned with the relationship between environmental influences (stimuli) and an organism's response. In beginning to teach Washoe, the Gardners tried everything. After applying a host of different methods that fall within the stimulus-response (S-R) model of learning theory, they eventually settled on the one method that proved most successful. But without precedents to guide them, they had to begin on a trial-and-error basis. For instance, they first explored what is known as the babbling hypothesis. Briefly, this theory on the development of language holds that the infant generates a random mix of phonemes (or, in the case of manual "babbling," cheremes) from which he pieces together sounds into words under the encouragement of his parents. The babbling theory has been discredited because neurologists now believe that the human infant lacks the necessary neural connections to learn spoken language during much of the time it babbles; thus, exposure to correct sounds is irrelevant at that stage. Nevertheless, the Gardners tried it out. They applied it by selectively encouraging proper cheremic responses among Washoe's gestural repertoire in hopes of her ultimately piecing together signs appropriate to the situations in which the gestures were made. Washoe was at least a year old when the experiment began and, thus, nearly past babbling age. In any case, the only sign the Gardners could attribute to this method of instruction was "funny."

With the beginning of her language training and the learning of her first sign, Washoe became acutely aware of her hands. She discovered she had fingers that were manipulable, and this focusing of her attention on her hands facilitated her acquisition of signs. Signing seemed to replace babbling for Washoe.

After their attempts to exploit babbling proved unproductive, the Gardners (and subsequent instructors of chimps in Ameslan) found that their greatest success lay within a framework of instruction called GUIDANCE. Guidance includes a number of different teaching models. One method attempts to get the chimp to imitate a gesture attached to a particular reward, such as a raisin. In effect, Washoe had to ask for a raisin in order to get one. But soon the Gardners abandoned attempts to entice Washoe to imitate a gesture when they found that they could teach her a sign more

Lucy: "hat"

quickly by simply taking her hands and MOLDING them into a proper configuration. The discovery occurred when they taught Washoe "tickle" by taking her left forefinger and drawing it across the back of her right hand. They also found that after a point rewards were not necessary to teach Washoe new signs.

The overall procedure involved in teaching Washoe a sign by molding is simple. For instance to teach her "hat," the instructor would show Washoe a hat, then take her hand and put it in the correct postion for "hat." In this case, the instructor would take the chimp's hand and make the animal pat the top of its head. If a

21

reward was being used, Washoe would then be given a raisin. This procedure would be repeated until Washoe began to make the sign without the instructor's aid, at which point he would gradually loosen his hold on the chimp until Washoe was making the sign by herself. This loosening technique is called FADING. It is similar to the technique used in teaching autistic children to produce consonant sounds. Both molding and imitation fall within the realm of guidance, which is one method used in the stimulus-response model.

Simply stated, the S-R approach proposes that an organism will associate a stimulus with a response if the two are contiguous in time. This idea has been interpreted in a variety of different ways. But the behavioral theory that most influenced the Gardners was the one proposed by William Edwin Guthrie, who died in 1950. Guthrie's work was primarily theoretical; he performed only one real experiment in his entire scientific career, but the result of that was a law of behavior. Guthrie's Law is nearly a restatement of this principle of contiguity: "A combination of stimuli that has accompanied a movement will on its recurrence tend to be followed by that movement." It is a pure behaviorist's statement. There is no mention of drives, reward or punishments, or repetitions' deepening neural connections; contiguity and only contiguity is the essence of learning. Molding most dramatically embodies this idea of contiguity. At first the Gardners were hesitant to employ guidance. They converted because it worked, and worked better than any other method of teaching.

In addition to learning through molding, Washoe picked up a number of signs through other means. One stemmed from her observation of Ameslan conversations around her. In these situations there was no attempt to encourage Washoe to learn the signs being used. Instead Washoe would spontaneously begin using a sign she had seen others use. She learned "toothbrush" this way, as well as "smoke." Another source of learning proved to be a number of gestures natural to the wild chimp, and the Gardners exploited the similarity between these natural gestures and Ameslan signs. For instance, wild chimps use a begging gesture much like the Ameslan sign for "come" or "gimme." Similarly, agitated chimps often shake their hands to signal urgency, and this gesture is very similar to the Ameslan sign meaning "hurry." Washoe quickly picked up these signs.

A final method of instruction the Gardners employed is called SHAPING, which derives from techniques B. F. Skinner employed to influence the behavior of rats. It involves the rewarding of "successive approximations" of desired behaviors. For instance, if Washoe wanted to go outside, initially she would bang on the door of her trailer. The Gardners took advantage of her desire by requiring that she make the open sign before they would let her out. At first she would make the sign on the door or object she wished opened until she gradually learned to make the sign without being in contact with a door or container.

WASHOE TAKES OVER

In these ways the Gardners channeled Washoe's attention toward her hands and their utility not just as a tool to manipulate her environment but as a means to manipulate words. The lessons of her enriched environment were not lost on Washoe; by the time she knew eight signs she began using them spontaneously in combinations. Early in training she demonstrated that she knew the signs did not just refer to the particular object used during instruction but to other objects that shared its characteristics. She correctly identified babies of different species, a picture of a dog as well as a real dog, and so on. She called a wristwatch a "listen," but she also knew "listen" to refer to the act, as evidenced the time she called attention to a barking dog by saying "listen dog."

The Gardners could teach Washoe words, but it was up to her to appropriate them and to demonstrate that she understood their meaning and their utility. The evidence of the ways in which she subjectivized her use of Ameslan and made it a part of her life testifies most persuasively to her abilities with language. The Gardners perceived that they might tap Washoe's abilities through a gestural medium; once tapped, the evidence flowed far faster than the pace of the Gardners' attempts to elicit it. Most of Washoe's output and innovations were spontaneous, which strengthened the impression that the Gardners were releasing abilities hitherto dammed up rather than painfully dragging Washoe beyond her intellectual depth.

Some innovations indicated Washoe possessed unexpected abilities that the Gardners were not prepared then to evaluate. They referred to these unexpected bonuses as "lagniappe," a Creole expression that refers to an extra measure of goods a shopkeeper gives to a customer. Examples of lagniappe occurred when Washoe would invent signs. On occasion the Gardners themselves were forced to adapt Ameslan signs for objects for which they did not know the proper gesture. "Bib" was one of these objects, for which the Gardners used the Ameslan sign "wiper," made by touching the mouth with five fingers in a wiping motion. One day Washoe was asked to identify her bib and, unable to remember the "wiper" gesture, drew the outline of a bib on her chest. The Gardners acknowledged that Washoe's sign was just as good as theirs, but they noted that the purpose of the project was not to learn a language devised by an infant chimpanzee but to teach Washoe a human language, and they insisted that she use the "wiper" gesture. Later they discovered that Washoe's "bib" sign was, after all, the correct gesture in Ameslan.

During these first few months Washoe also invented a sign as a variant for "hide" (subsequently, she has invented other signs as well). Hide-and-seek was one of her favorite games; it also allowed for spontaneous free-form expression of her Ameslan abilities. To initiate the game, Washoe's companions would make the Ameslan sign for *hide* which consisted of taking one hand balled into a fist with thumb extended, touching the thumb to the lips and then placing the extended thumb hand underneath the other hand which was held fingers together palm down. The game started when everybody covered their eyes with their hands, and it was this gesture of covering the eyes that Washoe felt better expressed what the game was. When she wanted to play, she would not say "hide" but "peekaboo" (as her variant was called) or "We peekaboo hurry." However, because it was not a valid sign in Ameslan, the Gardners did not include it in their lists of Washoe's vocabulary. Washoe used Ameslan in other unorthodox ways as well.

During our drive, Roger recounted an episode in which Washoe used the language as an instrument through which she might revenge an insult. As he described this incident, which had occurred a few years ago, Washoe continued her dispassionate survey of the countryside. There was no way of knowing whether she savored the retelling of this early piece of cunning. Male and female chimpanzees behave quite differently when angry. A male usually works himself up into a rage and in so doing gives everybody around fair warning that he is angry, whereas a female often expresses her anger through what is termed "treacherous attack"—lashing out and biting without warning. One day in Nevada, after some minor squabble Roger found himself facing Washoe across a table. Washoe gave every evidence of having forgotten whatever it was that earlier had made her angry. Seductively she signed, "Come Roger." Fouts edged around the table. As soon as he was within striking distance, Washoe dropped her pretense and lunged at him.

GATHERING DATA

Almost everything Washoe said during the five years she was in Reno was logged in an early diary or recorded through other means. The Gardners graded the reliability of her utterances by whether she said them spontaneously or according to the amount of prompting a given sign required. To be considered reliable, a word had to be used appropriately and spontaneously at least once a day for a period of fifteen consecutive days. By the end of the third year, Washoe reliably knew eighty-five signs and was regularly using three or more of them in combinations.

Apart from logging the daily flow of verbiage, observers with tape recorders would murmur a constant record of Washoe's signing at specific occasions, such as during play or meals. Washoe naturally increased her use of food signs during meals, and her use of such signs as "tickle," "go," and "peekaboo" during play. She used such pronouns as "you" and "me" far more frequently during play than at meals. Children know the importance of establishing who is doing what to whom during play. Evidently Washoe did too.

The method of recording and testing that seemed to have been most interesting to Washoe was the series of double-blind procedures used in her formal vocabulary testing. During the first of these tests, she would find herself seated in front of a box that from time to time would be opened by a human companion who would ask Washoe what was there. Washoe, although perhaps bewildered as to why the human obsrever could not look into the box and see for himself, would accommodatingly reply, and the observer would write down the first sign she made. The point of this procedure was to prevent the recorder from giving Washoe any cues as to the nature of the object, which would be placed in the box by another experimenter who neither Washoe nor the observer could see. Washoe did not seem to mind so much identifying the obvious to her slow-witted companions as she did the long waits while the exemplars were changed. Furthermore, if the exemplar was a Coke, she would, on occasion, abruptly terminate the game by grabbing it and running up a tree.

The Gardners answered Washoe's first objection by setting up a procedure that was paced to her desires to see what was in the box rather than the program of the experimenter; they then solved the problem of Washoe's larcenous intentions by using slides rather than the objects themselves. Ultimately, Washoe found herself facing a slide show in a 38″ × 21″ × 26″ box. One observer crouched beside the box and recorded her answers while another stationed outside the testing area observed the proceedings through a one-way mirror. Washoe would commence any "trial" by opening the door to the box, and when at the end she let the door close, the slide would change. In this way the Gardners ensured that during formal testing any sign that Washoe made was elicited by the exemplar presented and not by cues from an observer or (because of random order of presentation) through some memory of the order of the test.

Although Washoe made some errors during these early testings, she nonetheless performed remarkably well. The Gardners discovered that even when she made a mistake the errors occurred for the most part within the correct conceptual category. For instance, she would sometimes mix up objects like a brush or a comb, but the error would still be within the category of grooming articles. Similarly, she would occasionally mix up animals; once she identified a cat as Roger.

On the other hand, Washoe would identify correctly objects that the literal circumstances of the testing situation might have caused her to misconstrue. For instance, she distinguished between baby and adult animals and people even though the exemplar for each was miniaturized by the model or slide. Her performance continued to improve throughout her training.

COMBINATIONS

Washoe uttered her first combination of words in April 1967, ten months after the start of her language training. She said, "gimme sweet" and later, "come open." She was then between eighteen and twenty-four months old, which is about the age that human infants begin to form two-word combinations.

As Washoe began to combine signs in series such as "you tickle

Lucy: "key"

me," the Gardners set about to explore how these two-, three-, four-, and five-word phrases compared with the early utterances of children.

One question was whether or not these combinations were words randomly strung together, or whether they reflected some sense of grammatical order. Most of the doors, closets, and cupboards in the trailer were kept padlocked, which meant that if Washoe wanted to eat or inspect the contents of any of these areas she had to request that they be opened. Fouts and the Gardners noted that she used consistent word order in requesting access to these places. She would say, "open key food" to get in the refrigerator, or "open key clean" to get at the soap or "open key blanket" in asking to be given a blanket. In requesting people to do things like let her out or hug her, Washoe placed the pronoun

28

"you" before "me" 90 per cent of the time. During this test period, however, 60 per cent of the time she would also place both "you" and "me" before the action verb in phrases such as "you me out"; while 40 per cent of the time "me" would follow the verb, as in, for instance, "You tickle me." What this division represented, says Fouts, was a shift in Washoe's word order that occurred during the testing period, because after this testing period she consistently separated the "you" and the "me" with the action verb. She was shifting toward English grammar in her multiple-sign constructions, a word order preference shared by other chimps presently at the institute in Oklahoma.

On the way back toward the institute from our drive, we had stopped for a drink at a market. I fetched the treats from a small market, while Roger humored Washoe in the car. Except for Roger's narrative recounting Washoe's past, the trip was remarkably uneventful. Washoe seemed happy to be back with her old friend. We had just begun to discuss the details of the Gardners' comparison of Washoe's performance with that of children when the institute hove into view, and Washoe began to realize that the interlude was nearly over. Although she was clearly distressed over the idea of returning to her cage, Washoe made no complaint as we completed one final walking tour of the grounds and then reinstalled her in her temporary quarters. After Roger closed the door, she sat looking at him, with sad eyes, perplexed at the situation in which she found herself. This was far more difficult for Roger to tolerate than any open rebellion: "She really is a *good* girl," he said as we walked away.

3. A Tentative Comparison of Child and Chimpanzee

The Gardners' work in Reno centered on the data collected on Washoe's language abilities compared with that available for children. Whatever heated feelings the Gardners' work aroused derived not from the idea that they were attempting to teach a chimpanzee a language, but from the fact that they succeeded and were planning to compare their chimp with human children. Instead of being excited that now Western man might converse with another animal, people, especially other scientists, seemed offended that human and animal language abilities might be compared at all. When the Gardners set about to compare child and chimp, they stepped on a lot of eminent toes.

The Gardners' comparison of child and chimp, and the nature

of the responses to that comparison, first established the problems and the stakes of determining how far Washoe had impinged on what had hitherto been considered a uniquely human psychic territory. Washoe was tested, and the initial reaction set the tone for how seriously her language abilities would be taken. There was considerable motivation to write off her signing abilities as a trick of some sort—as a mechanical, yet unillumined aping of a human ability—still Washoe survived such criticism. Indeed, in surviving she spoke harshly to both the critical and empirical methods of her critics. The problems the Gardners encountered in attempting to compare their data with the data on children exposed gaps and presumptions in the study of human communication, as well as in the methods formerly used to compare animal and human communication. Washoe, it seemed, not only literally spoke to the world at large, but she spoke reflexively about the nature of the behavioral sciences that produced her tutors.

In any comparison of child and chimp, the question for both scientist and layman is: What level of "human" ability is the chimpanzee capable of attaining in language? At first, it would seem that the answer should lie in a simple comparison of the data on each as different abilities become manifest. But, unfortunately, as the Gardners discovered, any comparison is complicated by factors pertaining to the collection and assessment of the data itself.

In the first place, the Gardners were extremely conservative in their assessments of Washoe's performance. If something Washoe did produced alternative explanations, they chose the more economical. If they could explain patterns of multiple word combinations as a form of imitation rather than as a reflection of innovative linguistic ability, they did so. If they credited Washoe with any linguistic abilities at all, it was only because the data and a thorough researching of other explanations left them no alternative. The Gardners' published accounts of Washoe's performance leave the impression that they bent over backwards to explain what some would consider the miraculous in terms of the ordinary. Many scientists felt that the Gardners could have made far greater claims for Washoe; the Gardners themselves, however, were more concerned with making their data unassailable. That data would tell the story, and they knew that other experiments with other chimps would answer the vast array of questions that Washoe's demonstrated abilities posed.

The second problem in assessing Washoe's performance was that there is little agreement about what language is. The Gardners point out that some definitions of language would permit them to claim that Washoe had language after the first year of the experiment, while others could be devised that Washoe might never satisfy. But no matter what the definition, inevitably the question of whether Washoe had language arose to bedevil the Gardners.

If there exists a plethora of definitions of language, there is also a plethora of theories about its development in the child. The Gardners note that when a child can be said to have language remains an open question. Children are not born with language—that much is kown—and there is evidence that until some months after birth, a infant's brain has not sufficiently matured to the degree that will permit the child to generate and comprehend the language. Even this evidence is scanty, and only recently has it been used to inter one theory, in particular—the babbling theory. It is also known that a child first says individual words, then two-word phrases, and then multiple-word combinations that seem to gradually sort themselves according to the syntactic models offered by their parents. But when can a child be said to have language? When it says "cow home" at eighteen months? When it says "The cow went home" at three years? Or, when it says "The cow that Jack owned went home" even later? The Gardners feel that until linguists can say with certainty when a child has language, it is unfair to place the burden of proof on Washoe. This uncertainty brings us to the final problem in assessing

Washoe's performance—the comparative data on children that the Gardners had to use.

Surprisingly, attempts to gather data on language acquisition in the child antedates attempts to gather the same kind of data in the chimpanzee by only a few years; until recently linguistics was more scholastic than empirical. Researchers studying children's acquisition of language start from the natural assumption that a child eventually learns it, and this has lead to a tendency toward what might be called "empirical softness" in collecting and categorizing data on children. The Gardners often found that psycholinguists accepted as meaningful phrases in children which, if they had been "spoken" by Washoe, would have been dismissed as meaningless. Knowing that the child eventually generates syntactical sentences ("The cow went home."), psycholinguists also tended to see the germs of this syntax in early utterances of children, whereas, the Gardners were again left wondering whether or not the child at that point was behaving syntactically. In all, the Gardners claimed very little for Washoe; they eschewed all considerations of the question "did Washoe have language," and where they did claim some linguistic ability for her, they made sure that it was because the data itself forced them to. This first comparison of child and chimp would by no means settle the question about the level of human ability in language acquisition the chimp could attain.

THE QUESTION OF LANGUAGE DEVELOPMENT IN THE CHILD

Just as it is known that the human child is not born with language, it has also been established that if the human infant is not exposed during childhood to adults or other children who have language, he will not acquire language even if he is later brought into a speaking community. If, for instance, William Butler Yeats had been raised by a tribe of chimpanzees, he would never have spoken a word much less written a line of poetry. With any exposure to language, however, the infant acquires it quite readily, which suggests that during infancy the child is predisposed to learn language and that these predispositions must be fulfilled culturally. If they are not, the "doors" in the brain that open sometime during infancy to permit the learning of language forever close. The discipline most interested in the opening and closing of those doors is psycholinguistics.

Actually, psycholinguistics is a hybrid discipline that dates from 1952 when a group of linguists and psychologists got together at the behest of the Social Science Research Council. Dr. Roger Brown was one of those psychologists; he has since done pioneering work at Harvard in the gathering and categorizing of data on the child's acquisition of language. In this merging of psychology and linguistics, Brown says that it was linguistics which was imported as a whole into psychology, rather than vice versa. This was because psychologists outnumbered linguists six to one, and, at that time, linguists appeared to be essentially united in a consensus about problems, methods, and answers. Since 1952 that consensus has been sundered twice, once by what is called "the Chomsky revolution," which began with publication of Noam Chomsky's *Aspects of a Theory of Syntax*. In it Chomsky spelled out his theory of the "deep structure" of syntax common to all languages and the transformational rules by which that "deep structure" selects and translates lexical items into idiomatic spoken language. Then, more recently, Chomsky's revolutionary thesis was threatened by an academic type of palace coup in which his own pupils revolted against the Chomskyan primacy of syntax (the grammar of language) over semantics (the meanings of the message). The current crop of linguists feel that in constructing his theory of syntax, Chomsky lost sight of language's primary function, that of communication. They feel that Chomsky's model implies that language is a purely structural exercise and does not account for the function or evolutionary necessity of speech.

COMPARISON OF CHILD AND CHIMPANZEE

These convulsions among those working in linguistics are important because in studying the child's acquisition of speech, Brown and his colleagues drew heavily on tools contributed by Chomsky. And it should be noted that these same tools contain tentative assumptions about the nature of language, assumptions that are not universally accepted even within the scientific community that produced them. Consequently, the Gardners did not have bedrock data against which they might compare their own data on Washoe. Despite the controversies, Brown and his colleagues have discovered several consistencies surrounding the development of language in the infant.

ROGER BROWN'S DESCRIPTION OF LANGUAGE AND ITS DEVELOPMENT IN THE INFANT

We use language to describe how our animal ancestors became men. Because of language, Brown argues, wisdom can accrue within and over generations, reason can pry humanity loose from nature, and cultural evolution can eventually usurp biological evolution as the shaper of behavior. It is language, says Brown, that makes life experiences accumulative. Brown has identified three key properties of language through which man encodes and accumulates the lessons abstracted from his experience: 1) semanticity, the ability to symbolize an object or attribute of experience; 2) productivity, the ability to organize creatively and lawfully these symbols into an infinite number of messages; and 3) displacement, the capacity to retrieve these lessons of experience at a later time.

Brown feels that these three key properties are not manifest in children until sometime after a child begins to talk. The differences between a child's first sentences and adult communication are vast. "What goes before language," Brown writes in *A First Language*, "is only linguistic by courtesy of its continuity with a system which, in fully elaborated form, is indeed language."

THE CHIMPANZEE IN THE TEMPLE OF LANGUAGE

Beginning in 1962, Brown and two other psycholinguists, Ursula Bellugi (now Bellugi-Klima) and Colin Fraser, began to gather data on two children whom they called, appropriately, Adam and Eve. Brown and his colleagues traced and recorded the children's progress from the time they began uttering phrases of more than one word until they were between three and four years of age. Children generally say their first word sometime after they are six months old; at around eighteen months, they begin regularly to utter two-word combinations, and from then on longer utterances unfold rapidly. Brown and his colleagues arbitrarily divided this continuous development toward longer phrases into five stages or levels and sought to ascertain what rules the children were following at each level. The first level seemed similar for children learning all languages, while after Level I, cultural influences increasingly left their stamp. One characteristic of Level I performance excited Brown's particular interest:

At Level I, when the child is between one-and-a-half to two years old, he utters about 1.75 morphemes. The researchers discovered that when the child speaks in a two-word phrase, his mother almost automatically expands and repeats it in proper grammatical form. For example, when Eve said, "Mommy lunch," the mother would say, "That's right, Mommy is having her lunch." On the surface it would seem that the baby was striving for the mother's well-formed sentence, but Brown came to believe otherwise.

During speech development, the child seems to classify words with increasing sophistication: At first the baby might utter just a noun and a modifier, lumping all modifiers together regardless of their appropriateness to the particular noun, "an fat house," for example. A little later, it will begin to segregate articles from the other modifiers and so on. Similarly, he gradually relaxes the constraints concerning the number of words he can digest or generate. But at Level I, he will reduce long sentences to what Brown calls their "telegraphic" essentials, as in the case of "mommy lunch," and will lop syllables from long words as well. The question is:

36

What does the child intend by these initial telegraphic utterances? That is, does he intend to express the mother's fully grammatical expansion, or can his message be explained by some less sophisticated plan? Or does *he* understand the mother's statement according to some less sophisticated plan? The question is important both because its answer would tell us whether or not the child at that age is capable of syntactic behavior, and because Brown used his understanding of the answer in his critical comparison of Washoe's first "sentences." *

Brown found his answer in the work of two psycholinguists, I. M. Schlesinger of Hebrew University in Jerusalem and Lois Bloom of Columbia University, whose research was independent from his own. In assessing the child's telegraphic two-word utterances, Schlesinger and Bloom felt that the infant is not attempting to express well-formed sentences. Instead, he is seeking to convey certain basic linguistic relationships such as agent-action, agent-object, action-object, or possessor-possessed. The child is factoring his environment, not through the fine mesh of adult grammar, but through a broader texture of these basic relationships. At Level I, then, the child literally thinks differently from the adult. The baby is not striving for a fully elaborated sentence in telegraphic utterances like "mommy lunch," but for words that express various stages of his gradually developing ability to analyze the world. To better describe this different thought process, Brown referred to the work of Jean Piaget.

---

* Brown first reviewed Washoe's performance in 1970 and, subsequently, he modified his views in the light of "new evidence" on child and chimpanzee. It was this earlier model of language development with which the Gardners had to work. In 1970, Brown was confident enough of his assumptions about early language to write that Washoe had not reached Level I in language development. His subsequent views about both early language and Washoe will be discussed in the next chapter.

THE CHIMPANZEE IN THE TEMPLE OF LANGUAGE

SENSORY-MOTOR INTELLIGENCE

Between the ages of one-and-a-half and two years, the child's reasoning process is described by Piaget as "sensory-motor" intelligence, one which is acted out rather than thought. Its aim, paraphrased Brown, is practical success and not truth. At this stage, the child does not yet see objects or space as subject to his purposeful manipulation. In 1970, Brown felt that the child's first utterances are part of this "sensory-motor" intelligence and surmised that their characteristics are universal in mankind. But Brown then extended his own discussion of "sensory-motor" intelligence by saying that it is probably not limited to mankind alone, a suggestion with implications for Washoe.

Such guesses about the evolutionary stages of human mental development can be inferred by using Ernst Haeckel's dictum formulated in 1866. All college biology students are familiar with the phrase *ontogeny recapitulates phylogeny*—the history of the individual recapitulates the history of the species. Haeckel was saying that in developing from zygote to adult, an organism retraces its evolutionary history—for instance, the human embryo has gills and flippers before it develops limbs. While this dictum has not proved ironclad in its applications, it provides the framework within which a scientist can guess the evolutionary history of a species. Without this we could not construct an animal's phylogenetic tree. Brown's statement that "sensory-motor" intelligence is probably not limited to mankind implies that the infant at that stage is not yet human—that, in accordance with Haeckel's dictum, it is passing through some recent evolutionary step which preceded the full flowering of human cognitive abilities. The suggestion is entirely possible; the brain does not take final shape until some weeks after birth.

But to resolve the inconsistency of a non-human creature (the child at the sensory-motor stage) generating sentences, Brown made a second qualification, namely, he wrote that the infant's first sentences pre-suppose these "sensory-motor constructions, but that they also go beyond them." He suggests that the next stage in mental development, which includes the ability to "create propositions that can be expressed in sentences, must mature near the end of the sensory-motor period." It is the first blush of propositional intelligence that supplies the *human* element in the infant's two-word sentences at Level I.

Brown felt there was something more than "sensory-motor" intelligence reflected in these sentences because he believed they contain the seeds of linguistic abilities *innate* in man. From the very beginning, Brown stated, a sense of word order (syntax) appears to be present in the child's two-word utterances, i.e., he is speaking in rudimentary sentences and is not just using random combinations of words. Brown also theorized that this sense of word order probably undergoes no development even as the child fills out his repertoire of language skills. In demonstrating word order, the child intends to describe certain relationships, even if the utterance has only two words and when its meaning must be inferred from context. Oddly enough, however, Brown proposed an innate sense of word order even though he admitted word order is not essential in some languages. Parents tend to hear children's phrases in correct order regardless of how they are arranged, and, Brown says, word order is not necessary at Level I for the child to make its needs known.

By using non-linguistic tests, Brown had satisfied himself that a sense of word order is present in children from the beginning. Word order is Brown's evidence that the child's Level I sentences go beyond sensory-motor intelligence—and beyond Washoe. Armed with this theory of language development, Brown first tackled the question of Washoe's language abilities in 1970.

Brown's remarks on Washoe appeared in a paper entitled "The First Sentences of Child and Chimpanzee." This volume formed the basis for the Gardners' comparison of infant and chimp in which they included their own summary of the first thirty-six months of

Washoe's language training. In this article, the Gardners did not answer Brown's criticisms of Washoe. They sought merely to see how Washoe's utterances fit within the semantic categories Brown described for children.

WASHOE vs. BROWN'S SCHEME

In assessing their sample of Washoe's utterances, the Gardners first sought to classify Washoe's two-word combinations according to the broadest possible pattern. They began by dividing Washoe's vocabulary into two classes: PIVOTS, a term used to describe a small number of words used most frequently in her two-word combinations; and a larger class of words with which these pivots were combined. After establishing words like "come-gimme," "please," "you," and "go" as pivots, the Gardners then sought to categorize Washoe's vocabulary in order to see whether there might be some logic to the "special privileges" of certain signs. These categories were set up (see table I) in such a way that they might be compared with Brown's scheme for children. One class of signs—appeals—had no immediate equivalent in Brown's scheme and so were classified separately.

Before devising a scheme by which to compare Washoe and child, the Gardners sought to determine how Washoe's favorite signs in her two-word combinations were distributed throughout the six categories. With the exception of "me" and "you," most of Washoe's most readily combined signs were among the appeals, locations, and actions categories. They note that this predilection might be accounted for because a word like "gimme" is relevant to more situations than a word like "banana" and thus would more readily combine with words from other categories. Beyond being relevant to the same context, however, the two words might still express some special relationship where one word could not. This suggests, said the Gardners, that these signs might serve certain "constructive" functions. When a word or sign functions as a

CONSTRUCTION in a two-word combination, the combination conveys not just the meanings of the two words, but some general relationship between them. For example, "dog bite" is a construction because the positions of "dog" and "bite" establish a special relationship between the words. The use of constructions demonstrates that the child or chimp is not just mirroring his experience but classifying it—is thinking.

For Brown, the difference between construction and sequence is the difference between animal and human.

In developing their case for Washoe's use of constructions, the Gardners first presented a series of conversations that Washoe had with her human companions. For instance:

WASHOE: Please
PERSON: What you want? (Ameslan omits the copula)
WASHOE: Out

WASHOE: Come
PERSON: What you want?
WASHOE: Open

WASHOE: More
PERSON: More what?
WASHOE: Tickle

WASHOE: You
PERSON: I what?
WASHOE: You more drink

The Gardners note that by omitting the Person in these dialogues and combining Washoe's utterances, they could discern such two-word combinations as "more tickle" or "please out." Washoe would say something that would prompt her companion to ask a leading question, to which Washoe would reply and complete her initial utterance and, in completing it, indicate under the prodding

41

TABLE I. PARALLEL DESCRIPTIVE SCHEMES FOR THE EARLIEST COMBINATIONS OF CHILDREN AND WASHOE

BROWN'S (1970) SCHEME FOR CHILDREN		THE GARDNERS' SCHEME FOR WASHOE	
TYPES	EXAMPLES	TYPES	EXAMPLES
Attributive: Ad + N	big train, red book	Object-attribute[a] Agent-attribute	drink red, comb black Washoe sorry, Naomi good
Possessive: N + N	Adam checker, mommy lunch	Agent-object Object-attribute[a]	clotbes Mrs. G., you bat baby mine, clothes yours
Locative { N + V { N + N	walk street, go store sweater chair, book table	Action-location Action-object[b] Object-location	go in, look out go flower, pants tickle[c] baby down, in bat[d]
(not applicable, see text)		(not applicable, see text)	
Agent-action: N + V	Adam put, Eve read	Agent-action	Roger tickle, you drink
Action-object: V + N	put book, bit ball	Action-object[b]	tickle Washoe, open blanket
Agent-object: N + N	mommy sock, mommy lunch	(not applicable, see text)	
(not applicable, see text)		Appeal-action	please tickle, bug burry
		Appeal-object	gimme flower, more fruit

[a], [b] Indicate types classified two ways in Brown's scheme and only one way in our scheme. [c] Answer to question, "Where tickle?" [d] Answer to question, "Where brush?"
Reprinted from R. Allen and Beatrice Gardner, "Two-Way Communication with an Infant Chimpanzee," in *Behavior of Nonhuman Primates*, eds. A. Schrier et al. (New York: Academic Press, 1971). Copyright © 1971 by Academic Press. All rights reserved.

of her companions a particular relationship between her initial utterance and her reply. The problem for the Gardners was to prove whether or not this special two-word relationship exists.

The problem is especially difficult with both children and chimpanzees because the liguist cannot ask the speaker what he meant by what was said. With children and chimps it is the investigator who categorizes and interprets messages. The Gardners felt that any inferences drawn from this method were weak, but they felt compelled to use it because this same method had been used for children. Accordingly, they drew up a scheme of constructions that they believed might apply to Washoe's two-word combinations and then compared this scheme with the structural relationships Brown felt might characterize the child's early sentences (see table I).* The point of Brown's scheme is that the relation-

* Here follows the Gardners' discussion of this comparison:

Brown's attributive type includes all combinations of an adjective and a noun. Our agent-object distinction in Table III permits us to split Brown's attributive into two types, object-attribute and agent-attribute. For Brown's possessive type there is a close parallel in our agent-object type. Washoe also used the possessive pronouns *mine* and *yours*, which we grouped with attributes in Table III. As indicated in Table IV, if we were to distinguish *mine* and *yours* from the other attribute-sign, we could form a second possessive type for Washoe, object-attribute.

For Brown's Locative (N + V) [N = noun; V = verb; Ad = adjective] there is a close parallel in our action-object type. In his discussion of children's locative constructions, Brown indicates that locative prepositions, such as *in*, *out*, *up*, and *down*, were rare in the samples that he used to derive his scheme. Because Washoe did use location-signs, we can form two additional locative types, action-location, and object-location. Brown's second Locative (N + N) is formed by the conjunction of two nouns. Very few of Washoe's combinations of two noun-signs could be read as locative constructions—perhaps because she could use locative signs for this purpose. Also, combinations that were formed by the conjunction of two noun-signs could express many different relations depending upon the context. Consequently, we decided to omit all object-object and agent-agent combinations from the scheme of well-formed types which we have presented in Table IV.

Brown's agent-action and action-object types have close parallels in our scheme; his agent-object type does not. The reason for this apparent omission is best understood by considering the two ways in which *mommy lunch*

ships specified are somewhat independent of the specific words that make up the phrase, which, to reiterate, in turn implies that children's sentences are characterized by structure even at this early stage. Brown found that he could fit about 75 per cent of the child's combinations at Level I into this scheme. The Gardners, in turn, found that they could fit 78 per cent of Washoe's 294 two-sign combinations into Brown's scheme. In 1970, they believed that Washoe had at least demonstrated Level I abilities. However, they regard it as an open question whether or not such structures represent emergence of syntax, as Brown believed, or whether it in fact indicates a semantic structure that precedes syntactical construction. They believe this question pertains to both chimpanzees and children. Possibly these categories devised by Roger Brown and the Gardners map an infant's "sensory-motor" understanding of its surroundings and nothing more, and perhaps the infant's and chimp's propositional abilities appear later as the infant matures and both sensory-motor intelligence and their attendant semantic categories prove inadequate to the exigencies of communication and learning.

---

is glossed in the two places in which this combination enters Brown's scheme. As a possessive construction, it was glossed *mommy* ('s) *lunch*, and as an agent-object construction, it was glossed *mommy* (is having) *lunch*. In our scheme, expanded glosses of this kind were avoided by classifying signs analogous to lunch (e.g., *drink*, *food*) both as objects and as actions. Hence, Brown's agent-object type would be redundant with his agent-action type so far as our scheme is concerned. It should also be noted that the rules for inclusion in the sample of Washoe's 294 two-sign combinations did not permit the same two-sign combination to be classified twice, as was *mommy lunch* by Brown (1970). This is because each combination in our sample was counted only once, no matter how many times it was observed, and only the first observation was classified.

Finally, Brown was uncertain about the place for combinations with appeal-terms within his scheme. While it might be possible to absorb them into the other types of his scheme by reclassifying the appeal-signs, it seemed to us that combinations of the appeal-action type and the appeal-object type express particular structural relationships by the conjunction of categories in the same sense as do other types in this scheme. Consequently, they are included in our scheme as well-formed types.

COMPARISON OF CHILD AND CHIMPANZEE

Like the child, Washoe soon moved from making combinations of two words to longer combinations. Between April 1967 and June 1969, the Gardners recorded 245 different combinations involving three or more signs. About half of these longer combinations consisted of adding an appeal sign such as "please" to a two-word combination such as "Roger tickle," but that the additional signs in the remaining combinations conveyed additional information. Sometimes the additional sign specified an additional agent, as in "you me go out"; in other cases, name-pronoun redundancy ("you tickle me Washoe"); extensions of two-word constructions ("you me out look"), apologies ("hug me good"), which contained action, agent, and attribute; and, finally, phrases that specified both subject and object, such as "you tickle me."

"YOU TICKLE ME"

Brown believes that the child's innate predisposition toward syntactical utterances begins to become dramatically evident in three-word utterances, such as "you tickle me." In short, he says that the child must know the rudiments of syntax if he wants to convey who did what to whom outside the context in which an event occurred.

In 1971, the Gardners were not yet ready to credit Washoe with such a rudimentary syntax, principally because at that time they could still offer other explanations for consistencies in her three-word combinations. First of all, they noted that the young chimp's statements were brief, relatively simple, and homogeneous in content and that, this being the case, Washoe might be able to make the distinction between "me tickle you" and "you tickle me" through semantic rules of order. In other words, Washoe might differentiate the two phrases through an understanding that they were appropriate to different situations without understanding the syntactic rules that made them so. Washoe enjoyed tickling her friends and would sometimes sign "me tickle" before tickling someone, but for the most part she was on the receiving end of tickles. Her companions would tend to tickle her no matter how she organized the constituents of her request, which caused the Gardners to wonder why she included subject and object if almost any use of the word "tickle" resulted in gratification. An emerging syntax would require that subject and object be specified whether or not such specification was semantically necessary, but Washoe might also be imitating or trying to please her human companions.

Finally, Brown contended that the *child's* preference for certain word orders is indeed evidence of an emerging syntax. During the collection of data on her, Washoe shifted from putting both the subject and object in front of the verb, in such phrases as "you me out," to putting the verb between the subject and object, as in "you tickle me." The shift was toward normal English word order, but it occurred during data collection and consequently left the impression that she was stringing together words at random. Yet in almost 90 per cent of these long combinations, Washoe put the subject before the verb, a behavior that is clearly non-random. Still, the Gardners were reluctant to explain this tendency as the emergence of syntax. They felt that this preference might again merely be astute imitation of her human counterparts or that the consistency might be explained by some non-syntactic similarity between the phrases involving subject, action, and object, which Washoe regularly used.

Perhaps the Gardners were being too conservative. Had they then had access to data that has since accrued on other Ameslan-using chimps at the Institute for Primate Studies, they might have felt compelled to claim some syntactic abilities for Washoe, but in publishing their report on Washoe's first three years of language training, the Gardners in no way felt that they had exhausted the possibilities of teaching language to a chimp.

Washoe was only four years old at the end of this study. In the wild, a chimp may not even be weaned at this age; she would not reach sexual maturity until after age seven and might continue growing until age sixteen. The Gardners say that there was no reason to suppose that she would not continue to mature intellectually as well. Toward the end of the initial experiment Washoe acquired new signs quite readily, which might indicate that she was "learning to learn." Shortly after these thirty-six months, Washoe moved to Oklahoma, and so it is impossible to know what might have occurred had she matured within the continuous encouragements offered in Reno. Enriched as this environment was it was still impoverished compared with the milieu of the average middle-class child and positively barren compared to Adam and Eve's hyper-stimulated environment. Furthermore, Washoe was already a year old when the experiment commenced and none of her companions were fluent in Ameslan. It was as if a person were trying to teach a deaf mute child recently rescued from slavery to lip read a foreign language in which the teacher was not fluent. Still, Washoe proved a marvelous pupil and held her own with children of comparable age. The Gardners are confident that subsequent chimps will do much more.

The Gardners made little attempt to rebut Roger Brown's critical comparison of child and chimpanzee. Instead they concluded by speaking about the general problems of comparing communication across species, the comparative psychology of two-way communication. The most pressing problem, according to the Gardners, has been that the data collected on animal communication and the data collected on human communication have for the most part been incompatible. Animal sound is viewed as a message, while human messages are viewed as a composite of discrete meaningful sounds. The point is that data thus produced is thoroughly confounded with the assumption that man has language while animals do not, and therefore, one cannot evaluate that assumption with that data. Data collected on children reflects an entire mythology of language. In the opinion of the Gardners, what is needed, they claim, is an operational definition of two-way communication that would yield data comparable across the imagined animal-human abyss. For useful comparative work to be accomplished in communication, the definition of language will have to be demythologized. Consequently, they see the biggest hurdle as the notion of intention or purposefulness, which is used to characterize human language as opposed to animal communication. With Washoe the Gardners took an early step toward an operational definition of language. Having geared their double-blind testing to information with no concern for Washoe's intentions, they felt their method could be applied to many different species. To this end they attempted to record and report their data in such a way that its usefulness would be independent of the goals set for this project.

If the Gardners' work were assessed solely on the basis of what they claimed in their published reports, the furor in the behavioral sciences caused by comparing Washoe and child would seem quite out of proportion to the event. But even though the Gardners were not willing to claim for Washoe anything more than certain semantic abilities, their critics seemed to sense that Washoe was "saying" more than the Gardners were reporting in 1971.

4. The Scientific World Reacts

"As posture is focal for consideration of man's anatomical nature and tools are for the consideration of his material culture, so is language focal for his mental nature and his non-material culture. Language is also the most diagnostic single trait of man: all normal men have language; no other now living organisms do." So says evolutionary scholar George Gaylord Simpson. Washoe directly challenges this notion.

Although people have not been quick to accept Washoe as a language-using primate, the chimpanzee has had little hesitation in lumping itself with humanity. Vicki, who was the subject of an earlier attempt to teach a chimp to talk, thought of herself as human. Once when she was put to the task of sorting photographs into categories of animal and human, she came upon a picture of herself and confidently placed it on the people pile atop Eleanor Roosevelt; however, when given a photograph of her hairy and unclad father she uncharitably tossed him in with the elephants and horses. Washoe, too, thought of herself as human and, as previously reported, thought of other chimps as "black bugs."

To a distinguished array of scientists such as geneticist Theodosius Dobzhansky, psycholinguists Eric Lennenberg, Ursula Bellugi, biologist Jacob Bronowski, anthropologist S. L. Washburn, and Roger Brown, Washoe was a "black bug" as well; all of these scientists committed their doubts about Washoe's language abilities to print.

The argument against Washoe has been built largely on the criticisms of Brown and Ursula Bellugi and Jacob Bronowski. Dobzhansky, for instance, writing on the evolutionary uniqueness of man, refers to arguments against Washoe's language abilities which were advanced by Bellugi and Bronowski. Because Brown, Bellugi, and Bronowski referred to the Gardners' work with Washoe in the greatest detail, this chapter will concentrate on their criticisms, with secondary mention of the arguments against Washoe advanced by the other critics. The purpose will be to isolate the principal point of contention surrounding Washoe's use of Ameslan, to see where, in the light of Washoe, a new defensive perimeter is established to keep Washoe out of the temple of language and thus preserve our notions about the distinctions between animal and human behavior. Following this we will again look at Washoe and at that point of contention through more friendly eyes—namely those of anthropologist Gordon Hewes, who far from being threatened by her language abilities feels that Washoe tells us something about the origins of human language. Finally I will try to summarize this discussion of Washoe to see what light if any this first confrontation between Washoe and the behavioral sciences throws on the question of human origins and human nature.

In 1970, after examining the Gardners' diaries of the first thirty-six months of Washoe's language training, Roger Brown found something missing from Washoe's "sentences" that was present in the first multiple word combinations of the child—a sense of word order.

As has been noted, Brown's scheme for the development of language in the child holds that the child's first combinations serve to establish certain relationships such as possessor-possessed that characterize the occurrences in its life. He believed that these combinations reflected more a "sensory-motor" than propositional intelligence, but that these sentences still contained the seeds of the infant's propositional abilities. Even in the infant's earliest utterances, Brown detected a word order that was generally "appropriate to the structural meaning suggested by the non-linguistic situation." Brown believed that this indicated the child's intention to convey the relationship suggested by the non-linguistic situation. For instance, if a child between two and three were shown a picture of a dog biting a cat, he might say "bite cat" or "dog cat," but he will not say "bite dog" or "cat dog"; the position of the words, said Brown, would be appropriate to the subject and object position of the dog and cat (see figure 1). This is not true of Washoe, says Brown; she might be likely to say any combination of words involving "dog," "bite," or "cat."

Brown likened his characterization of Washoe's combinations to Richard Wagner's use of *leitmotiven*. What she is doing, he says, is notifying us of the recurrence of identifying circumstances and aspects of a situation, but the different motifs she recalls bear no relationship to one another save in time. He conveys the impression that Washoe's vocabulary swirls around in her mind without any order other than specific referents to the outside world. Brown noted that the Gardners had not then made any effort to

Figure 1. Pictures illustrating agent-object relations

determine whether Washoe in fact preferred to use certain combinations to describe certain situations, but Brown dismissed this with the observation that a *preference* for a certain order is not the point. Rather Brown claimed that children "practically never" mix up the word order in describing a particular situation. (The Gardners feel that it has *not* been established that children *never* reverse order.)

Brown carefully qualified his criticisms of Washoe. While he does not believe she intends the structural meanings that he feels characterize the early sentences of children, he admits that it has not been demonstrated that she lacks those meanings. Washoe might still intend to establish certain relationships in her combinations even if her word order were scrambled because, says Brown, at Level I, word order is not essential to the child's communication to convey what the child means. Moreover, the two-word sentence is very simple and even if the parent were not privy to the context to which the sentence referred, he could probably figure out the meaning of the sentence. There is, says Brown, no "communication pressure" on either the child or the chimp to use the correct word order at this level. This pressure begins to build when the child starts to use three-word combinations that specify subject and object relationships. If the child wants to report to its father that a "car hit truck," he must use word order or some other "structural signal" to convey which word is in which semantic role.

When the child begins to report on the day's events, such as "car hit truck," he is also beginning to demonstrate what is perhaps the most critical property of language, DISPLACEMENT—the ability to report on events not concurrent with the act of communication. Displacement is universal in human language. It allows us to make experience cumulative and to retrieve the lessons learned from earlier experience. When we retrieve or utter a message that is disengaged in time from its context, we must somehow reconstruct those structural elements and relationships—were the message not displaced—that would be immediately apprehensible to the listener. Brown views "need" for displacement as the selective pressure in the evolution of language that spurred the development of attributives, possessors, locatives, agents, objects, and the other complexities of sentence structure. What we call grammar arose as a superstructure to support and organize thought processes as man gradually freed himself from the awful weight of immediacy.

Brown feels that a child's two-word combinations are not displaced at Level I. They refer to, and are explicable by, the immediate context. As the child matures and begins to use more varied and lengthy sentences, he also begins to refer to events displaced in time from the act of communication and correlatively begins to sort and combine his words according to the hierarchical plan of the sentence.

The importance of displacement to notions of language and word order might best be understood in contrast to traditional views of animal behavior and language. Until now it has been thought that animals are prisoners of the moment, their communications being responses to immediate stimuli understood in terms of the basic urges of nature. Ethologist Oskar Heinroth was fond of describing animals as "very emotional people with little ability to reason."

How does Washoe stand on this balance beam of emotions and reason? Washoe on occasion says "no" when asked if she wants to do something. In fact, this is how she learned the word "no." One day after several failed attempts to teach her "no," the Gardners

53

told Washoe that there was a big dog outside that wanted to eat her. A little later they asked her if she wanted to go out. Washoe said "no." The stimulus that caused Washoe to say "no" was only her memory that earlier she had been told that there was a big dog out there—an event not concurrent with the act of communication. Being freer from the moment that we have been taught to expect, does Washoe have the concomitant grammatical superstructures which this freedom makes necessary? In 1970 Brown did not think so, and cited the absence of word order as his argument. In 1970 Brown believed that Washoe had not even attained Level I.

Still, Brown left open the question regarding whether or not Washoe understood the hierarchical nature of the sentence. He knew that she was still young and that the Gardners had not examined Washoe's longer utterances to see whether word order was appropriate to context. Significantly, in *A First Language*, Brown's most recent book, he welcomes Washoe to Level I, and abandons his previous argument that word order is as innate in man as "nut-gathering" is in the squirrel. He reached this conclusion because, since he first wrote about Washoe, a good deal of data has been collected on the Level I performance of children speaking a number of different languages, such as Finnish, in which word order has less sequential importance than in English. Brown believes that Level I language abilities are quite similar across cultural boundaries. Although Level I abilities would support a considerable degree of cultural evolution, it is at Level II that the syntactic devices associated with displacement begin to emerge. Brown now believes that this will prove to be the barrier for the Ameslan-using chimpanzee.

Brown is a distinguished psychologist. The Gardners regard him as a friend among psycholinguists, and indeed his reputation serves to illustrate the pitfalls of the study of the development of language. Because we know that word order is eventually critical to the generation and comprehension of adult English we tend to see it as "innate" in the child's first utterances, even when it is not necessary for the infant to make its meanings known. On the other hand, not expecting to find language in the chimp, in 1970 Brown tended to make a harsh assessment of Washoe's word order even when her word order had not been thoroughly analyzed. Scientific approach was thus, in the Gardners' words, thoroughly "confounded" with Brown's opposite expectations for child and chimpanzee.

In that 1970 article, Brown did express his belief that there would continue to be "no evidence" of these abilities in the chimp, and this further focuses attention on the opposite expectations generally held for child and chimp, and on the motivations conditioning criticism of Washoe's early sentences. "No evidence" is not a proof; one cannot prove a null set. However, if one does not *believe* that Washoe has a sense of word order, then lack of evidence of word order seems a more meaningful indication that she does not have it.

In summary, Brown pictured language development in the child as a process whereby communication gradually displaces itself from immediate context and becomes richer as the child develops hierarchical sentence structures. These reconstruct the context from which communication is disengaging. The differences between two-word telegraphic sentences and longer "car hit truck"-type sentences were critical for Brown. In these more complex sentences, structure becomes important for the generation and comprehension of message. Brown contrasts the gradient of the child's gradually unfolding structure—the gradual disengagement of language as a system separate from thought processes tied to the moment—with data on Washoe to suggest that she never gets past Level I. This argument against Washoe was picked up and embellished by a colleague of Roger Brown, Ursula Bellugi. She also focused on Washoe's word order and has also subsequently modified her views.

LANGUAGE, NAME, AND CONCEPT

In 1970 Ursula Bellugi co-authored with philosopher-mathematician Jacob Bronowski an article criticizing Washoe's abilities in *Science*. Bellugi was one of Roger Brown's co-investigators of the development of speech in the Adam and Eve study, and this article drew heavily from these experiments. The article, together with Brown's, almost tipped the balance against serious consideration of Washoe's abilities in Ameslan, and, even as late as August 1973, long after the article has been recanted by one of its authors, arguments against Washoe based on it still cropped up at the International Ethological Conference during conversations among scientists hostile to the Gardners' work.

Bellugi and Bronowski delved into the meaning of word order and its relationship to the intrinsic humanness of language and to the workings of the human mind. To emphasize the importance of word order, the authors describe five important steps by which language might have evolved in man. The first four steps express "displacement," and they are as follows:

1. A delay between the arrival of the stimulus and the utterance of the message that it has provoked or between the receipt of the incoming signal and the sending out of a signal;
2. the separation of affect or emotional charge from the content or instruction that a message carries;
3. the prolongation of reference, namely, the ability to refer backward and forward in time and to exchange messages that propose action in the future;
4. the internalization of language so that it ceases to be only a means of social communication and becomes also an instrument of reflection and exploration with which the speaker constructs hypothetical messages before he chooses one to utter.

These four steps allow man to give information about the environment that is not an instruction to act. Communication, therefore, can be less emotional and less bound to an immediate context. In keeping with Brown's earlier characterization, these four steps would necessarily require the concurrent evolution of some grammatical structures to fill in for the missing contextual references. Thus, the fifth step is the emergence of the structural ability made necessary by the first four. While the first four characteristics are described by the authors as behavioral, they describe the fifth as logical:

> 5. the structural activity of reconstitution, which consists of two linked procedures—namely, a procedure of analysis, by which messages are not treated as inviolate wholes but are broken down into smaller parts, and a procedure of synthesis by which these parts are rearranged to form other messages.

RECONSTITUTION is the means by which the mind replicates nature. It allows man to construct events far displaced in time and is the superstructure of abstract thought.

Bellugi and Bronowski grudgingly admit that Washoe is capable of demonstrating to some degree the behaviors described by the first four characteristics, although they claim that at age three the child is better at each. Where the authors feel that Washoe's presumptions to humanness are exposed is on the question of reconstitution, the fifth, logical characteristic of language. They claim that reconstitution is a process "different in kind" from the other four, and most of their article is an attempt to explain this faculty and its development in the child.

First, they recount the steps by which the child acquires language, comparing this with the Gardners' (at that time incomplete) report on Washoe. Essentially they recount Roger Brown's scheme; however, they do call attention to details Brown omitted. For instance, they contrast the three-year-old's supposedly well-organized utterances with Washoe's purported randomly organized combinations, but then they also fault Washoe for not asking questions and for not negating. They say: "Despite the ample opportunity to learn about questions (and certainly some opportunity to learn negative sentences as well), there is no evidence in the diary summaries that Washoe either asks such questions or negates." This they infer to mean that Washoe, unlike the child, has no familiarity with the rudiments of basic sentence types. One drawback of the "no evidence" approach is that any argument based upon this tactic deflates as evidence begins to surface. As previously noted, Washoe did learn to negate, and she also asked and asks questions; these behaviors simply were not reported in the diaries Bellugi and Bronowski examined. But these are just superficial details. Bellugi and Bronowski are right when they state the real genius of humanity is dramatically demonstrated in the way man reconstructs for himself the underlying rules of grammatical structure.

To the authors, as the child gradually sifts language through increasingly more precise categories and distinctions, he demonstrates, the "logic that binds the development of language to the evolution of the human faculties as a whole." The infant does not just learn names for the various objects in its environment, which then swish around in its head until someone teaches it grammar to put the words together; rather, the child plugs the words its parents use into a set of rules and relationships already unfolding in his brain. "We see," say Bellugi and Bronowski, "that small children whose cognitive powers are limited in many respects show a remarkable ability to reconstruct the language they hear, just as they reconstruct [give structure to] their experience of their physical environment; the process and the capacity are not specifically linguistic, but are expressions of a general human ability to construct general rules by induction. What is involved is not just the capacity to learn names as they are specifically taught. Far more basic and important is the child's ability to analyze out regularities in the language, to segment novel utterances into component parts as they relate to the world, and to understand these parts again in new combinations." This is reconstitution.

In elaborating on their discussion of this ability, Bellugi and

Bronowski attempt to cast reconstitution in a philosophical and evolutionary light. First, they show how this act of analysis and synthesis is necessary for the child to understand even the simple sentence "The chair broke." To understand this sentence, the child must know what a chair is, and this requires that he gradually tease from his specific knowledge of the word as it is assigned to a particular chair the phenomenological attributes that establish "chairness" if he is to understand the synthesis in a new sentence. This in turn requires that he ignore the differences of chairs and attend to the similarities—an act of analysis that, therefore, must precede his understanding the word's synthesis in a new sentence. Similarly, he must analyze "broke" by searching for some correlative situation in which the word occurred and then determine what meaning of "broke" the situation suggests that might pertain to the chair. The words do not exist, say the authors, save in the relationships in which they are understood.* The child's understanding of the sentence requires an inductive analysis as lofty and intense as any performed by an adult. This model of language, say Bellugi and Bronowski, "expresses in miniature a deeper human capacity for analyzing and manipulating the environment in the mind by subdividing it into units that persist when they are moved from one mental context to another."

This human capacity to reconstitute the environment symbolically through language—and, in fact, through technology—rests on another ability, to reify experience: "an analysis into parts of the objects, properties, and actions of life which, as concepts, can

---

* Bellugi and Bronowski's position that there is no pre-existant vocabulary outside of the relationships in which the words are used places them in one camp of a debate about the nature of language that antedates Descartes. Descartes articulated a position (later modified by Locke and Wittgenstein, among others) that words variously interpret unchanging phenomena— there is a fixed, perceptible world variously translated by language. Recently, a number of psychologists have challenged this view in light of experiments on Gestalt perception. They believe that the process of perception modifies the perceived, i.e., that there is no absolute phenomenon.

be manipulated as if they were objects." REIFICATION began when man was forced by the rigors of survival to stand back from the moment and adapt his behavior to the traumatic changes that first spurred such events as the evolution of tools.

In order to abstract himself from the ongoing flux of experience and purposefully manipulate his behavior, man needed a model of reality to work with. Reification describes the process by which he constructed that model; it allows the reconstruction of reality in symbolic terms. It was that which enabled man to gain power over nature, whereupon he supposedly parted company with the rest of the animal kingdom. "We may even speculate," say Bellugi and Bronowski, in support of this view, "that the human mind began to reify objects by their function when man began to make tools as functional artifacts for future use."

The reified object (the symbol) and the act of analysis through which it is manipulated, form an "interlocking whole." One cannot exist without the other. From this perspective, the mere *knowing of the name* for an object is meaningless since the name only has meaning in the relationships described by sentences and the deeper cognitive processes these sentences express. Bellugi and Bronowski are so persuasive in establishing the interrelatedness of semanticity and syntax that it seems to undermine their criticism of Washoe: Since they admit Washoe understands semanticity, how can she have one without the other? One is in fact tempted to forgive them their criticisms of Washoe for the sake of their lucidity in characterizing the relationship of language to thought and technology.

LANGUAGE AND TECHNOLOGY

What Bellugi and Bronowski attempted was to transform Washoe from evidence that the abilities necessary to acquire language are *not* unique to man into evidence that they are. To this end, they first pinpointed what they considered Washoe's failure to demonstrate a sense of word order; they then elevated word order into a manifestation of not only a nuclear linguistic ability but also into a manifestation of the core inductive thought processes of the mind. The article seems, in essence, to be an essay on the relationship of language and thought. Then, as a secondary effort, Bellugi and Bronowski examine word order in the development of language in children and in Washoe to isolate and ground in fact that particular relationship. What they evidently did not realize was that they could have supported their arguments on reconstitution more effectively by allowing Washoe's *success* in understanding the significance of word order, rather than by presuming her failure.

The authors use reconstitution to describe a link between the separate manifestations of man's genius in technology and in language. In the making of both tools and symbols man reconstitutes his world, a world that is first reified into a suitable symbolic surrogate in order that abstract thought processes can be applied. Bellugi and Bronowski postulate this relationship between language and technology, but it is fully developed by an anthropologist with an entirely different attitude toward Washoe.

AN EVOLUTIONARY PERSPECTIVE ON DISPLACEMENT AND RECONSTITUTION

The relationship between language and technology has often been alluded to but has proved mercurial when people have attempted to make it specific. Washoe offers an opportunity to do just that; anthropologist Gordon Hewes has attempted to exploit this opportunity and, in so doing, support his particular bias about the origins of language. He did so in an article entitled "An Explicit Formulation of the Relationship Between Tool-Using, Tool-Making, and the Emergence of Language."

Gordon Hewes has devoted a good part of his professional life to studying the origins of language. Among other achievements, he has assembled a definitive bibliography on the literature of language origins. He has followed Washoe's development closely because he regards her performance with Ameslan as evidence to help support his particular theory of language development in man. Before man developed a spoken language, Hewes believes, he made use of one using gestures—hence, Hewes's interest in Washoe—and this language probably evolved in concert with tool-using and tool-making in man's prehistory.* Until recently, people were content to establish the relationship between tool-using and language only on a metaphorical intuitive level; relatively little effort was expended to make this relationship explicit. At first, the relationship of language and tools may seem obvious, but we begin to falter when asked to say how. It is only when this relationship *is* made explicit that the importance of establishing such a connection begins to become evident.

While it is impossible to reconstruct the cultural prehistory of man with any certainty, the relationship between tool-making and language can be approached, on the one hand, through the study

---

* It should be noted that there are eleven other theories of language origins, each of which has adherents who feel that they have evidence supporting the primacy of their favorite hypothesis and the inadequacy of the others. Here is Hewes's summary of the different language origin theories: "Language origin theories fall into the following categories: (a) interjection, or *pooh-pooh* [the idea of giving these theories trivial names began with Max Muller]; (b) imitative, onomatopoetic, or *bow-wow;* (c) imitative of sounds produced when objects are struck, or *ding-dong;* (d) work-chant, or *yo-he-ho;* (e) mouth-gesture, or *ta-ta,* in which mouth parts imitate the movements of hands, arms, or other parts; (f) babbleluck, based on acquisition of associations between spontaneous infant babbling sounds and features in the external environment; (g) instinctivist, in which language appears at a certain level of human cognitive evolution, and is inborn thereafter; (h) conventionalist, in which individuals deliberately agree to create language in order to improve their social life; (i) contact, in which language is the natural outcome of man's social, communicative needs; (j) divine or miraculous, in which language is a gift of the Creator; (k) chance mutation, in which language is the outcome of a random biological event; (l) gestural sign, in which propositional communication was initially by hand and arm movements, with vocal language appearing later.

of aberrant behavior as the result of brain damage, and, on the other, through the search for comparative behavior in other higher mammals. And, of course, we can use Haeckel's dictum as a rough guide to check guesses about evolutionary priorities.

In his study of human behavior, Hewes points out one arresting piece of evidence that holds implications for the relationship of language and technology: similar damage to certain parts of the brain can upset a person's ability to put together both actions in a series and words in sentences. He writes:

> Neither tool-using actions nor words, whether gestural or vocal, normally appear as isolated bits of behavior. Instead they are components of more complex programs of action. Such programs can be disorganized or destroyed in cases of damage to the brain, and the disturbances of language are remarkably similar to those in motor skills. Some forms of aphasia are syntactical—the patient can still produce words, or recognize them, but cannot combine them into meaningful sentences, just as some forms of apraxia exhibit a deficit in programming sequences of meaningful action, rather than in isolated motor acts such as reaching or holding. The condition known as ideomotor apraxia . . . suggests a disturbance in an underlying deep structure very similar to that which makes propositional language possible. Both motor-skill sequences and sentence constructions are adversely affected by the same lesion in many instances. *It could be that this fundamental capacity to acquire and utilize complex patterned sequences, expressible in tool-manipulation, in gesture-language, and later in speech, is the "deep structure" Chomsky really should have been writing about, and that in the long course of hominization, it is the evolutionary growth of this kind of syntactic capacity that has been so important, and not its separate manifestations in technology and language.* [Emphasis added]*

This suggests explicit evidence of the relationship between language and technology. Indeed, when one moves beyond the divergent paths of modern speech and technology to think in terms of the close association of organizing movements both in

* Gordon Hewes, "Primate Communication and the Gestural Origin of Language," *Current Anthropology*, vol. 14, nos. 1–2 (1973). Reprinted by permission of University of Chicago Press.

sign language and in tool-use, it becomes more plausible that the *grammar* to both should be handled by the same part of the brain. If man once communicated by a gestural language, then it is clear that the same logic might have governed both the manipulation of tools and of words.

Hewes's remarks suggest not only a model for the relatedness of language and technology but also a scenario for language origins that might explain the evolutionary grounding of grammar. As Bellugi and Bronowski point out, grammar allows for the lawful manipulation of symbols and, by extension, the lawful manipulation of the environment. Through language and other symbolic systems, grammar's reconstitutive properties allow humans to examine the worth of various behaviors as prototypes or propositions, but without the prohibitive expenditure and risk that would be necessary if all such prototypes had to be tested in the world. It should be apparent that what is lawful in symbolic manipulations must, to be of value, follow the laws man extracted from experience at the dawn of human evolution. If this were not the case, these symbolic manipulations would have little survival value. In essence, Roger Brown says as much when he discusses the nature of displacement (implying that grammar evolved to supply a superstructure to thought processes as man's communication became more displaced), although he does not tie his mention of displacement to any program of selective pressures that might have spurred the displacement in the first place. Hewes's work also helps to reconstruct such a program and in so doing to give more dramatic meaning to both reconstitution and displacement.

Briefly, the interrelatedness of these properties might be summarized as follows: displacement is the time frame that allows man to step out of context and, thus, to reconstitute his environment symbolically and technologically. This act of reconstitution requires a vocabulary of symbolic surrogates to represent the actions and attributes of the environment from which thought processes become displaced. Reification describes the process by which that surrogate world is created. If we go back and speculate on the events that led to the development of this surrogate, displaced world, the reasons for the interrelatedness become clear—as do Washoe's achievements.

EARLY MAN

Displacement perhaps originated when man began to do things like fashion twigs to conform to stalks he had previously found stripped and ideally suited for enterprises like fishing for termites. Wild chimps today fashion sticks for probing termite mounds, and it is entirely possible that the termite fishing twig might have been one of our first tools as well. The first termite fishing twig was probably discovered serendipitously. Then instead of relying on nature to supply him with stalks suitable for getting at termites, ancestral man began to take matters into his hands, that is, to make things like stripped stalks *happen*. We can only speculate what extraordinary changes in his life created the selective pressures to impel and reinforce the decision to begin to usurp nature's authority over his movements. Apparently, the selective pressures that impelled that act of usurpation persisted, and perhaps even intensified, because, reinforced over hundreds of thousands of years, man gradually increased his ability to manipulate his hands and, through them, his environment. Just as these acts of toolmaking became more complex, so too selective pressures encouraged man to abstract himself from the tyrannies of his emotions and the moment. As abstraction increased, so did the logic of man's successes in controlling his movements and the abstract properties of the objects so manipulated begin to surface as distinct from the ordinary sense data processed by the brain. And similarly so did we gradually establish the elements of an organic system of symbols and logic, which reinforced by and reinforcing man's displacement from immediate time and space, gradually increased our ability to work our will on that immediate environment.

The key to the acquisition of this ability to state a proposition through movements is displacement, which gave man the ability to detach himself from the exigencies, outrages, and joys of the moment—to be a little less emotional. Only when freed momentarily from the pressing obligations of appetite and fear could man contrive his gestural propositions. In the beginning the same series of movements might have served both tool-making and communicative functions; thus the same grammar might relate the individual movements of a series in both "technological" and "linguistic" propositions. Similarly, at first the requirements of displacement would have been minimal, but as man gradually moved from termite sticks to more sophisticated weapons and tools, the demands to displace increased. Eventually, the necessity for cultural transmission of tool use created pressures for elaborating a system specialized for this type of communication.

To propose that man learned to make tools because he first had language is implausible; rather, it would appear that language evolved to exploit and enhance the adaptive value of tools. It is also reasonable to surmise that just as the size of man's first tool kits was limited, so too was his early vocabulary limited. Hewes notes that six words or six tools have far more than six applications; perhaps, then, very early tools, like very early words, reflected some intermediate step in the evolution of human cognitive faculties, something like the "sensory-motor" intelligence with which the infant rough-hews the world at Brown's Level I. Just as early man gradually extracted the tool-like and then the abstract properties of objects found in nature, so can we imagine him gradually abstracting, reifying, and refining the words or gestures he used to refer to those objects.

We would properly expect the name for a tool to reflect the level of analytical sophistication that originally produced the tool, when events conspired to make it necessary for early man to refer to it by name. For instance, if a sponge were only used as a device to retrieve spilled blood, we would expect its name to reflect this particular function, not its general properties of absorbency; however, should a culture eventually note its general properties of absorbency, we would expect it to possess a language capable of reflecting that analysis. Similarly, we would expect the modern infant's maturing propositional abilities to recapitulate such intermediate steps, and the notion that the infant's first sentences reflect a "sensory-motor" rather than a propositional intelligence suggests just that.

Finally, it should be noted that man's acquisition of the ability to make tools, to use what we call language, and to analyze reality did not occur in a few short generations, but developed gradually, although probably on an accelerating curve. The earliest stone tools date from 2.6 million years ago. Hewes pointed out that if by 100,000 B.C. language had developed to the point where man used a vocabulary of a thousand words, on a growth curve, this would still only imply the initial acquisition of one word every 10,000 years, not, he says, a "dizzy increment."

From a perspective that views the interrelatedness of language and technology, "displacement" and "reconstitution" can be understood in terms of their physical rather than their abstract properties. Reconstitution describes the act of manipulation of the environment; displacement, the detachment from nature's clock of stimulus and response that would permit such manipulations. (Bellugi and Bronowski properly described "displacement" as a behavior, but felt that "reconstitution" was a logical process. Looking at early tool-making man, we can see that reconstitution might be considered a behavior as well.) Given this perspective which views the logic of both language and technology as rooted in an ordinal ability to program motor actions, Washoe's achievements do not seem freakish at all.

Chimps in the wild have been observed both using found objects as tools and fashioning rudimentary instruments. Jane Goodall notes that chimps at the Gombi Stream Reserve strip stalks which they insert into termite mounds. She has also observed them using leaves as sponges. On one occasion a chimp used such a sponge to wipe brain matter from the inside of the skull of an infant baboon that the chimp tribe had caught and killed in a cooperative hunt. In captivity, training programs have been able to educe far greater cognitive and manipulative abilities than those recorded from limited observations in the wild. Vicki demonstrated this, even though she failed to learn to speak.

Vicki, the chimp who categorized herself as human and her father as animal, made that particular distinction as part of a general exploration of her cognitive abilities. While Keith Hayes and Catherine Nissan only managed to teach Vicki laboriously to produce seven words, she showed herself to be quite capable of matching the performance of her infant human peers in figuring out the locks of latchboxes and in being able to discriminate such "conceptual" differences as color, form, age, and completeness. Similarly, she was able to sort one set of pictures according to several different criteria, and, before abandoning in distress a series of puzzles, showed herself capable of learning a series of six sequences in which three strings could be pulled to retrieve a ball. As early as the 1920s, other captive chimps had been observed stacking boxes or using poles to get at hard-to-reach fruits, picking locks, and so forth.

Instrumentation tasks, say Hayes and Nissan, show the effects of experience in developing reasoning ability and insight as well as in releasing the animal from "stereotypy." They summarize this ability by quoting two pioneer animal psychologists, Maier and Schneirla: "Past experience ceases to furnish the patterns of response, and instead furnishes the data from which new patterns may be formed. This ability frees the animal from a particular bit of learning and makes possible almost unlimited patterns of response."

It should be clear by now that an animal's relationship to past experience depends on the property of displacement, because only if it can displace itself from immediate patterns of response can it purposefully alter its behavior. Second, when the animal draws on past experience to furnish data on which to impose new patterns, it is demonstrating reconstitution. Schneirla's and Maier's summary presumes that the animal has factored past experience into units similar to data and understands experience as separate and distinct from himself and capable of being manipulated.

Vicki did have some trouble discriminating between numbers past a certain point (five, six, and beyond) and after her initial successes, she eventually refused to work on string sequence problems. Because she also had great difficulty learning to speak, Hayes and Nissan were tempted to conclude that both numbers and sequences were difficult for Vicki because they involved or were built on abilities central to the acquisition of language. Washoe's example must disprove this, but, more to the point, in light of Washoe and the foregoing critical discussion of those abilities common to tool use and language, one would expect Hayes and Nissan to wonder why an animal such as Vicki, so adept at organizing the movements of her hands, should not have been able to learn at least the rudiments of language.

Perhaps this might have more readily occurred to the two psychologists were it not for the apparent estrangement of speech from any of the tasks Vicki was asked to perform. If Hayes and Nissan had been making their explorations in a deaf culture that used Ameslan, they might naturally have attempted to teach Vicki sign language with the result that they might have found no gap between her facility for language and her facility with abstract problems. Nor in such a case would they expect a gap. While spoken language may appear to be separate from higher mental functions, the interrelatedness of hand manipulations in tool use and hand manipulations of gestural language is virtually inescapable.

In attempting to teach the chimp sign language, the Gardners were exploiting a particular facility of the chimp that had been recognized and exploited for other purposes for decades. If there is a relationship between language and propositional thought, as Bellugi, Bronowski, Brown, and others forcefully argue, it is then illogical to applaud the ape for its puzzle-solving and conceptual abilities but to condemn it for lacking the linguistic manifestations of these abilities. This is especially valid in the case of a gestural language that relies on an ability to hierarchically organize hand movements, which people acknowledge the chimp possesses in non-linguistic areas.

A SHORT EVOLUTIONARY LOOK AT GESTURAL LANGUAGE

It is largely the relationship between gesture language movements and tool-making and tool-using movements that led Gordon Hewes and others to believe that before the development of speech, man made use of a gestural language. As Hewes puts it, "The visual, kinesthetic, and cognitive pathways employed in tool-making and tool-using coincide with those which would have been required for a gestural language system. Speech, on the other hand, utilizing the vocal-auditory channel, implied the surmounting of a neurological barrier . . . [namely, associating visual stimuli with sounds]." In other words, once man was impelled to manipulate his hands propositionally in order to make tools and when pressures for propositional communication mounted, it was natural that he would exploit this same ability to program motor actions.

While it was well suited for silent communication across long distances in hunting, gestural language did have its limitations. Communication at night was severely limited, the language monopolized the use of the hands, and, as Hewes points out, most manual sign lexicons are limited to between 1,500 and 2,000 items —far smaller than the lexicons in spoken language. To acquire even this number of signs is a formidable task unless the sign language is "alphabetized" so that words can be constructed from a limited number of characters or "cheremes." Under severe selection pressures from our expanding and diversifying culture, human language could well have shifted from a visual-gestural to a vocal-auditory system.

Although communication probably shifted from gestures to speech, Hewes claims that certain aspects of the visual-gestural channel continued to be used. By the Lower Paleolithic period, man had exhausted the early advantages of gestural language and pushed its development to its limits; nevertheless, as spoken language flowered, certain aesthetic and technological advantages of the old visual-gestural channels were retained. Hewes refers to Upper Paleolithic art as "frozen-gesture" and notes that ancient Egyptian and Chinese hieroglyphics had numerous representations of arm gestures. Thus, before spoken words would be encoded in scripts, man overcame the evanescence of language by representing it in gesture.

As speech branched further from its technological and gestural roots, says Hewes, the visual-gestural and vocal-auditory channels underwent a division of labor. Hewes writes: "The old visual-gestural channel became the preferred mode for advanced propositional communication in higher mathematics, physics, chemistry, biology, and other sciences and technology in the familiar forms of algebraic signs, molecular structure diagrams, flow-charts, maps, symbolic logic, wiring on circuit diagrams, and all the other ways in which we represent complex variables, far beyond the capacity of the linear bursts of speech sounds. The vocal-auditory channel continues to serve the needs of close, interpersonal, fact-to-face communication, in song, poetry, drama, religious ritual, or persuasive political discourse." In short, the visual-auditory remained the preferred mode in those areas where language and technology merged.

There is evidence to support Hewes's belief that speech was preceded by a gestural language. Reconstructions of the supra-laryngeal tracts (the vocal area necessary for the generation of consonants and vowels) in cranial casts of Neanderthal made by Phillip Lieberman and Edmund Crelin led them to believe that Neanderthal, a recent ancestor, could not generate the full range of sounds available to modern man. They speculate that this limitation might have led to Neanderthal's disappearance through a competitive disadvantage to his more articulate Cro-Magnon neighbors. They also note that at birth the infant's supralaryngeal tract more closely resembles Neanderthal's than it does modern man's, which might be further evidence of the recent evolutionary development of speech. Both deaf infants and chimps learn their first sign long before normal infants say their first word, which supports the notion that ontogenetically and phylogenetically we are equipped for gestural language before we are equipped for speech.

There has been little study of the natural sign languages used by the Plains Indians, Australian aborigines, and a few other peoples; however, anthropologist Glenn McBride reports that La Mont West believed they all shared the same syntactic form. If true, McBride feels that it is a "reasonable evolutionary hypothesis that the deep structure of modern language is closely related to that of natural sign languages." This idea meshes nicely with Hewes's belief that "deep structure" is the grammar that originally permitted us to organize motor actions. Again within this scheme, Chomsky's "transformational grammar" might actually reflect a retracing of the evolutionary path from a gestural to a vocal mode of language.

Washoe also supports Hewes's theory. Although tongue-tied, she can run on at length in sign language. Washoe and other chimps have about the same brain capacity of australopithecines, our earliest hominid ancestor. While attempted reconstructions of australopithecine supralaryngeal tracts indicate that he could not speak, in the light of Washoe, there is no reason not to suppose that, like Washoe, he possessed the capability to acquire the rudiments of a gestural language. Hewes notes that the australopithecine was far ahead of the chimpanzee in (natural) tool-making, making it even more likely that he could have used a propositional language of some sort. And, if he lacked the phonological apparatus and control necessary for speech, Hewes feels, it is likely that his medium of communication was that part of his body which he manipulated propositionally in tool-making—his hands.

For Hewes, Washoe was clearly not a threat to man but an opportunity to learn about him—an opportunity to fill out his own scenario for the evolutionary development of human language. If in parsimonious fashion nature first exploited man's hands in enabling his first propositional movements in both technology and language and only later, as use of the hands became overburdened, shifted communication to a vocal-audio tract, then Washoe might be seen as reflecting some commensurate level of pre-speech, propositional abilities. She makes sense in terms of Hewes's scenario, although she does not make much sense within the awkward framework used by Bellugi, Bronowski, and Brown to keep her apart from any behavior considered exclusively human. Their framework leaves too many questions unanswered: How could Washoe understand words as symbols without understanding the principles that relate one symbol to another? How could the chimpanzee demonstrate a high order of intelligence in handling abstract problems and yet not possess a commensurate ability to put words together in rudimentary constructions? Within their framework, Washoe casts more shadow than light. Just the opposite is true from Hewes's perspective.

I have tried to summarize the views of Washoe's most persuasive critics and, in so doing, to focus on what is perceived to be the essential linguistic trait that differentiates language and other forms of animal communication. For Bellugi, Bronowski, and Brown, the tower of human nature is built on the ability to reconstitute symbols displaced in time and place from their environmental referents, and the linguistic manifestation of that ability is understood to be word order. Other critics, such as Theodosius Dobzhansky have referred to this criticism based on word order in forming their own negative assessments of Washoe. And yet, the cursory profile of gestural language presented here shows that while it is a language, there are significant differences between sign language and spoken language. One is not a mere translation of the other; they have different adaptive functions, and they impose different constraints on communication—gestural language is more telegraphic, less redundant—and, most important, they have different grammars. All of which means that word order in English may not have the same significance as word order in Ameslan. Bellugi and Bronowski did not know this when they wrote their article for *Science*, because at that time, as Bellugi has subsequently admitted, they had little knowledge of Ameslan. In correspondence to Fouts, Bellugi wrote, "In the end, to say the least, all of us who have written about word order and its implications for structure should be forced to eat all those words."

This admission focuses attention on Brown's question about why anyone cares whether a chimp has language, specifically why two scientists would care so much that the chimp not be credited with language that they would publicly make assertions about the grammatical structure of a language with which neither was familiar. Clearly Washoe's threat to learn language was not diminished by the sallies of Bellugi, Brown, and Bronowski. Indeed, it is not Washoe's ability that begins to look insubstantial after these criticisms but the temple of language itself. Washoe is a profound anomaly to the ancient model defining animal and human behavior. So far, the energy spent attempting to assimilate Washoe within that model has backfired and is sending reflexive quakes to the center of the notion of language itself.

Roger Fouts divides the arguments for the uniqueness of language to man into two principal groups: the check list approach and the structural-physiological approach. Critics using the check list (such as Bellugi and Bronowski) say that the chimp does not use language because, while it is capable of demonstrating such characteristics as semanticity, it lacks others such as reconstitution. The structural-physiological approach (Eric Lennenberg and Noam Chomsky, for instance) says that only man has language because only man has the neural apparatus necessary for its comprehension and generation. Fouts likes to explain these approaches by using them to decide whether a Cadillac and a Volkswagen are both cars. In comparing a Cadillac and a Volkswagen, the structural-physiologist might say that the Volkswagen is not a car because it lacks a radiator. The check-lister would agree with this conclusion, but his rationale would be that the Volkswagen lacked four doors, power steering, and power adjustable front seats. Both approaches look for differences, not similarities, and neither really looks under the hood. Both base their arguments for the intrinsic uniqueness of Cadillacs (or the intrinsic uniqueness of language) on the empirically inadmissible principle that there is no evidence to the contrary. What the Gardners and Fouts are doing is gathering this evidence. It has always been there; they are simply the first researchers really to look for it. People have said that the chimp lacks the neuronic organization necessary for language, but nobody has really searched for such areas in the chimp brain.

Fouts and the Gardners cannot determine whether the chimp brain contains language areas similar to man; that is an undertaking for a neurologist, and Dr. Norman Geshwind intends to do just that. But Fouts can test the chimp's abilities against some generally accepted check list for language. This is what he intends to do in the next generation of experiments.

The Gardners' original work with Washoe was pioneering. They established a means by which man might enjoy two-way communication with another species; however, their brilliance was in seeing beyond prejudices that confuse language and speech, which was essentially common sense rather than genius. Conceiving of a way to speak to the chimp was the product of expecting that it could be done and being willing to maneuver around that practical problem that had frustrated previous attempts to teach a chimp to talk. One has to wonder why this didn't occur earlier.

One reason was brought out by the approaches of the various critics: for the most part researchers have been more interested in proving that other animals couldn't have language than in trying to demonstrate that they could, and when the evidence on Washoe first began to be disseminated, she was perceived not as an opportunity but a threat. Indeed, if Washoe were the only chimp capable of using Ameslan she would have been explained away as a freak; however, once one chimp entered the temple of language others soon followed and it became increasingly difficult to get them out.

The Institute for Primate Studies now has about a dozen chimps with varying degrees of skill in using Ameslan. Fouts has now begun to extend and fill out the original work done with Washoe. One would like to think that criticisms of Washoe would provide some points of departure for his work, that the critics would have used Washoe to focus attention on some kernal linguistic ability that Fouts might then seek to explore. Unfortunately, the critics have focused their attention on the deep anxieties summoned by the idea that a chimpanzee might be capable of language. And so, essentially, Fouts has had to start afresh, using Washoe as the bedrock on which to construct a new view of language, rather than using her to modify old views.

5. The Institute for Primate Studies

High in the branches of a cottonwood tree on a lushly forested island sit three gibbons. These graceful blond acrobats daily come whistling through the leaves to this spot, assembling like a tribunal of elders to witness and judge the arguments that erupt in a colony of raucous, young chimpanzees on a neighboring island far below. While the gibbon island is verdant with cottonwoods and willows, the neighboring island has only sparse groundcover. A brown African hut used as a communal lodging dominates the center of the chimp island. A fence gives it the air of an abandoned compound. Instead of cottonwoods, there are tall poles where the chimps occasionally perch to spend long periods sitting motionless like figurines. Their gibbon jury, though practiced in observ-

The "rundevaal" on the chimp island at the Institute for Primate Studies.

ing the unfolding life of the forest, must be confused to see the strange behavior that occurs intermittently between two chimps. One chimpanzee will gesture intricately toward another, perhaps touching his chest and then drawing a finger across the top of his hand. This act would then cause the chimp to which he was gesturing to come forward to tussle and tickle. A keenly observant gibbon might notice that the largest of the young chimpanzees most often resorts to this strange method of communication and that this chimp seems to be a protector of the younger and smaller chimps on the island. This chimp is Washoe. The gestures, of course, are in Ameslan.

Plucked from the wilds as an infant, Washoe was raised by humans. Then, alienated by her upbringing from her fellow chimps, she had been thrown back into their company. Although Washoe eventually adjusted to her own kind, this was not through any understanding of the design that brought her from Nevada to Oklahoma. The mini-conversation recounted above was one of the first fruits of that design. Washoe is to be an emissary from humanity, a Prometheus to chimpanzees, who, it is hoped, will encourage a select group of chimpanzees to use Ameslan not only in communicating with people, but also in daily communications among themselves. Just as evolution produced language in man, so now would we vastly intensify selective pressures and attempt to foster the use of language in a community of our closest relatives.

In the midst of a world where animals don't talk, the chimp island is the seed of a world in which they do.

The setting for these experiments is called the Institute for Primate Studies. It is a curious place. Although now loosely affiliated with the University of Oklahoma in Norman, the institute more directly reflects the efforts and ambitions of Dr. William Lemmon, the big, bearded clinical psychologist who built it, populated it, and now runs it. The grounds of the institute are part of Lemmon's farm, which he has been gradually converting into an ever more suitable environment for studying and breeding various primates. The institute has two principal objectives: 1) to study the social development of the chimpanzee in various rearing conditions in order to gain a better understanding of the chimpanzee, and so, perhaps, to better understand human maternal behavior; and 2) through breeding, to ensure the survival of the chimpanzee at a time when it is gravely threatened in the wild. From the standpoint of posterity, this second objective alone would justify the institute and it has had manifest success in encouraging births. The chimp rarely breeds in captivity, which indicates that the chimps view the institute as hospitable. These surroundings vary according to a chimp's age and the studies of which it is a part.

The adult colony is housed in a forty-square-foot concrete structure. Inside there are seven interconnected rooms which can at any time be sealed by sliding doors. One series of rooms connects to outdoor cages and another to a large wire cage on the roof. A visitor can walk between and above the cages by means of walkways, an initiation a secret society might envy for its terrors.

Roger Fouts took me for a tour of this complex of cages shortly after I arrived in Oklahoma. I was wearing army fatigues and a T-shirt in anticipation of an adult chimp amusement, namely, to throw excrement at newcomers. They do this as the culmination of a threat display. The threat display is intimidating in and of itself; however, because the wire separating chimp from newcomer takes any real threat out of these displays, the chimps in frustration and adaptation throw fecal matter to get across their message.

Roger and I discussed this innovation as we entered the brownish-pink building, casually chatting in an effort to convey the fiction that I was not a newcomer at all but a long-time habitué of the institute. The ruse worked for about twenty seconds while Sebastian and Burris, two adolescents, looked up curiously to see who had entered.

THE CHIMPANZEE IN THE TEMPLE OF LANGUAGE

Sebastian, Burris, and the rest of the adult colony have not been subjected to any formal language training, although the dominant male, Pan, has picked up a few signs informally through contact with Ameslan-speaking people, while Manny, another adult male, has acquired some signs through contacts with Washoe. Melvin rounds out the adult male population. The females are Wendy, Mona, Caroline, and Pampy. Pampy gave birth in 1968 to the first infant born at the institute. Since then all the females have given birth to offspring.

It was Sebastian, recovering from his shock over the audacity of my intrusion, who first saw through my treacherous deception. He stood up in the back of his ground-floor wire mesh and, holding the wire behind him, worked himself into a series of deafening screams. Finally, he loosened his grip on the wire and charged toward us, banging his fists on the side of the cage as he ran. He also scooped something up.

"Duck!" screamed Roger.

I hit the floor.

Floop! Something smacked into the wall where my head had been an instant earlier. Either Sebastian or Burris, I couldn't tell who, scored a clean hit on my left shoulder as I was recovering. As I brushed myself off, Roger remarked that they rarely miss twice. Sebastian had galvanized the rest of the adult community, and Roger and I had to pick our way through a withering bombardment as we finished our tour of the building. I didn't mind; now baptized, I was more interested in the chimps and their displays than in whatever dividends might accrue to me as their stimulus.

The common image of the chimp has been created largely by the appealing infants who regularly appear in nightclub acts and circuses. Consequently, people tend to think of chimps as affectionate, miniaturized caricatures of humanity. This fiction is rudely shattered when one comes into contact with an adult male; one then begins to understand why performers prefer to work with infants.

In the wild, an adult male can weigh as much as 150 pounds; in captivity they are even heavier. Pan, for instance, weighs close to 200 pounds. That is big, but size does not begin to convey the chimp's strength. There is not a human alive who can match a full grown adult male chimpanzee for power. Fouts says that on a body weight basis, the chimp is between three to five times as strong as a man, while if the comparison were based solely on the strength of arms, the chimp would be about eight times as strong.

The adult chimp is very affectionate, but he is also easily aroused, and this is where problems begin for his handlers. Chimp society is characterized by highly ritualized social interactions involving, among other behaviors, threats and submissive postures. There is a lot of Sturm und Drang, but in a chimp community, energy outflow results in little violence or damage, because the interactions are ritualized, and because each chimp is as tough and resilient as his neighbor. People, however, are not so tough or resilient, and they risk injury in the presence of an aroused male. Furthermore, normal postures, through which a person might feel he is expressing friendliness, are to a chimp expressions of aggression. Standing erect is an aggressive posture; grinning expresses fear. To a chimp, a door-to-door salesman would seem a bizarre combination of aggression and insecurity—a good candidate for a threat if not a clout.

The people at the institute are aware of these clues as well as of the chimp's strength, and so one day when Pan, finding his cage unlocked, sauntered out into the sunlight, Sue Savage, an assistant, who was outside at that time, immediately crouched in a submissive posture and approached Pan begging his indulgence. Pan, the benign ruler, gave Sue a reassuring pat and continued his stroll. A year earlier Sue had lost the end of one finger through carelessness around chimps; this time, through quick thinking, she saved herself from the possibility of more serious injury.

Still, for all their strength, the chimps accept Roger and Dr. Lemmon as dominant. Washoe, for instance, is far stronger than Roger, and yet she not only accepts his authority but reacts in genuine fear when he is angry. This is not through any misapprehension about his strength, because Roger has noticed that she is much more gentle in tussling with him than she is with other chimpanzees. Rather, her discretion seems to be related to the respect and affection any social animal has for the older member of the community that reared and cared for it.

Until recently, Fouts lived next door to Wayne Wells, the 1972 Olympic free-style wrestling gold medalist. At 163 pounds, Wells is as fit and strong and competent as any human could possibly be in the type of combat that would be effective against a chimp. For a while Roger toyed wtih the idea of inviting Wells out to the institute to play with the chimps to see how Wells, more a peer to the chimps in strength, would be received. Fouts and Wells once discussed the idea and Wells declined. He felt that a chimp, not knowing what wrestling was, might react uncontrollably and hurt either itself or Wells. Viewed from the perspective of a champion wrestler's caution in dealing with a captive chimp, the bravery of people like Jane Goodall, who lived with wild chimps, becomes more evident.

Bespattered, Fouts and I left the adult cage complex. Dr. Lemmon's amorphous, brownish-pink, sprayed concrete home adjoins the chimp building on one end. The other entrance opens onto the main yard of the farm, which is surrounded by a cluster of sheds and cages.

Besides chimps, the institute houses a variety of other animals. Just beyond the yard, in a meadow, there is a complex of oak-shaded open-air cages that houses pigtail and stumptail macaques. Among the storage sheds and barns that border the yard stands a long metal shed. One side contains indoor/outdoor cages that shelter three siamangs, a female mandrill, and about ten squirrel monkeys. The siamang is a small, soft-furred primate, which in some ways is similar to both a monkey and an ape, and is classified as a lesser ape.

We walked over to the cages and visited with the little apes. Seeing us approach, one of the siamangs pushed his back against the wires of his cage in a request to be groomed. I accommodated him as best I could, whereupon the siamang, by way of thanks, began searching through the thin hair on my arm with his small perfect hands. Although it serves the manifest biological function of keeping a primate colony free of parasites, grooming seems to also serve such important socializing functions as keeping the colony together reassured of one another's help and company. Deprived of a partner for grooming, the little siamang felt lonely and insecure.

This creature's lonely plight suggests one of the *non*-linguistic problems Washoe poses. For instance, consider our attitudes toward social mechanisms and the feelings of mutual interdependence that reinforce them. At the lower end of the scale of social organizations is the white ant colony, which depends for its survival on the faithful execution of specific tasks by different member ants. The ants are not "educated" to perform their specific functions, but, instead, do so according to genetic instructions. Any one ant is an incomplete part of a whole, which is the colony. After studying such ant colonies, a pioneering ethologist, Eugene Marais, concluded that the soul or mind of the white ant lay not in the individual ant but in the colony as a whole. The individual ant was a "cell," while the colony was the organism; and it was the colony that had to adapt to the exigencies of natural selection. Thus, the pressures on the colony organized the genetic histories of its constituents.

While the white ant appears to have strong genetic predispositions to proper behavior toward his fellow ants and his community, these predispositions seem less rigidly enforced as organisms become more complex. A human being has more flexibility in choosing his posture toward his fellow humans than does a white ant, and, because of this, he relies on learning concepts such as the golden rule to reinforce proper behavior toward conspecifics.

Other mammals share this flexibility to varying degrees, and the question naturally arises about whether or not they also share feelings of responsibility or altruism toward their fellow creatures. Before Washoe, the answer to this question would probably have been no, since notions of responsibility have been traditionally bound up with notions about reason and language. These, in turn, have been traditionally thought to be exclusively human virtues. Washoe and her fellow chimps force us to re-examine notions of responsibility, of the social mechanisms common to both animals and men, and of the influences that condition these behaviors.

If we are to credit the chimpanzee with certain abilities necessary to the acquisition of language, do we then have to credit it with all the concomitants of language with which we have credited ourselves? If the chimpanzee can, through symbols, distance itself from its experience, can it also distance itself from its fellow chimps and see its fate in their plight?

I asked Fouts if he had ever noticed anything that might be similar to altruism in the primates at the institute. He mentioned one incident that had occurred within the shed we were then touring. An overhead pipe had sprung a leak and was spraying water on a baboon in a cage. The position of the cage prevented the baboon from reaching out and stopping or deflecting the water; however, a baboon in the neighboring cage could reach the pipe, and when Fouts arrived to inspect the leak, the good neighbor had his hand around the leak so it could not soak his friend. The baboon might simply have been intrigued by the spray with no altruistic intent at all, or he might have been trying to help the other baboon. A reading of such incidents, I was to discover, depends heavily upon the perspective from which the incident is viewed.

The metal shed that houses the siamangs, squirrel monkeys, and mandrill also houses the training area for the instruction and testing of Ameslan. It contains a raised platform from which observers can record the chimps' signing behavior. In more natural situations, like the chimp island, Fouts uses videotape as well as observers to record the chimps' behavior.

About 100 yards east of the main yard is the small lake that contains the three man-made islands. On these islands roam three colonies of primates restrained only by the water isolating the little tracts of land, which more naturally serves the function of iron bars. One island is grassy and surmounted by two tall poles connected by a rope, which is there for the benefit of a small colony of new world or capuchin monkeys. Next in this archipelago is another islet of about a half acre. In contrast, it is densely foliated with cottonwoods and willows, which provide an arborial habitat for the gibbons. Of all primates, the gibbon is perhaps the most perfectly adapted to life in the trees. It can flash through thick branches faster than a man can run and has the equilibrium, timing, and confidence that would shame any mortal high-wire performer.

As noted, the gibbons' entertainment is provided by the colony of juvenile chimpanzees who inhabit the third island, on which, instead of trees, there are tall poles. For shelter there is a brown, African hut, a "rundevaal," which is heated in the winter and is equipped for videotape observations of its occupants. The chimps on the island are all juveniles, and all have had training in Ameslan. Thelma, Booee, Bruno, and Washoe spend most of their time here, either sporting about the hut or sitting contemplatively atop the poles.

Visitors come and go by means of a rowboat. The first day of my tour a young assistant, Steve Temerlin, rowed out to the island with Kiko, the newly acquired two-year-old chimp who was to be introduced to the permanent residents. As he disembarked, Steve was greeted by Washoe. She ignored Kiko and gave Steve a big hug. From the effusiveness of her greeting, I half expected Washoe to put a lei around his neck. As we watched this, Jane Temerlin, Steve's mother and foster mother of Lucy, a seven-year-old chimp skilled in Ameslan, told me about some of the cultural exchanges that have occurred between the islands. On one occasion, when the rowboat was carelessly moored near the chimp island, Thelma jumped into it and, paddling with her hands, rowed over to the gibbon island where she received a hostile reception. A few days later, a male gibbon leapt from an overhanging branch into the rowboat and paddled over to visit Thelma, indicating perhaps some interspecific primate protocol. Most chimp communication, however, occurs among themselves or is directed from them to humans standing on the mainland. Most shore-directed communication is in Ameslan, and, far more significant, Ameslan is increasingly being used by the chimps on the island to communicate with one another.

The remaining fauna at the institute are non-primates. Herds of sheep (which will figure in future experiments Dr. Lemmon has planned) and cattle graze in the meadows. Then there is the tribe of nervous peacocks. Finally, tethered to a tree is a large, supposedly ferocious, dog. A recent acquisition, the dog was intended to bolster the authority of the handlers in dealing with Washoe.

A dog was chosen because Washoe had on earlier occasions indicated a dislike and fear of dogs. Recall that in her training in order to teach her the word "no," the exasperated Gardners told her that outside was a big dog who wanted to eat her. At that age dogs inspired sufficient fear in Washoe that she inaugurated her use of the word "no" so that she might not have to face one. This year during a car ride, a large dog began to chase the car Washoe and Roger were riding in. Washoe frantically signed "dog go" and pointed in the opposite direction from the one in which they were traveling. With this background, it seemed that a big, mean dog might be the suitable enforcer when Washoe was reluctant to obey her handlers. The test came one day while Washoe was out walking with Roger. The dog was tethered to a tree and upon seeing Washoe started to bark and growl furiously. Washoe whirled and, seeing the cause of the commotion, swaggered aggressively toward the mastiff who promptly put its tail between its legs and hid behind the tree. Washoe took a casual swipe at the dog and then strolled back over to Roger who reports that, in regarding her bravery, she seemed the most astonished of all.

There is one last environment where one of the institute's chimpanzees might find itself. Just as the institute depends on satellite facilities for such services as food preparation and computer services, it also depends on certain outsiders to provide foster homes for chimps to be raised as members of human families and in isolation from their own species. The foster homes are made up of carefully screened families, such as the Temerlins, in the Norman area. The program was started by Dr. Lemmon in order to assist his study of the chimps' social development, and it dovetails perfectly with Fouts's studies of the chimps' acquisition of Ameslan. Indeed, the chimps raised in human families learn Ameslan far faster than chimpanzees in whom human language has to compete with their predispositions toward the normal calls and gestures of their species. Each of these living situations is organized to suit both the original intentions of the institute and its more recent purpose of exploring the chimps' new-found language abilities.

That evening when I left the institute, Washoe was atop one of the tall poles, a lonely and contemplative figure framed against the evening sky. She was a dramatic sight, not for her vigil atop the pole, but more for the drama invested in her as the link between the world of animals and the world of men. Washoe is a living contradiction—an animal that has language—and in life, as in myth, the embodiment of a contradiction is a potent cynosure.

6. The Chimp Colony: Lucy

Lucy is the oldest of the institute's chimps currently being raised in species isolation. Her foster parents are Maury and Jane Temerlin. Maury is a psychologist who teaches at the University of Oklahoma; Jane is Dr. Lemmon's assistant. Lucy was born on January 18, 1966, and removed from her mother four days later; she has been with the Temerlins ever since. Like an institute in miniature, their house is a modern rambling structure of glass and plaster. The east window of the living room looks out on several large wire mesh cages that house a garrulous and excitable crew of blue and white macaws; the south window looks out on a patio and two ponds. When the Temerlins are out, Lucy lives in a spacious indoor-outdoor, wire-enclosed duplex. When they are at home, she lives and sleeps with them as she has done since infancy.

During my two trips to the institute in the summers of 1972 and 1973, I met Lucy on several occasions and attended a few of Roger Fouts's sessions with her. Fouts and a number of his assistants visit with Lucy one after another for an hour or two each, five days a week. During some sessions, she would be taught new words, during others tested on vocabulary or some aspect of her word usage, while during still others, Lucy and her companion would just talk and review the signs that she knows. Each assistant kept a record of her utterances on a work sheet (see table II) and described any novel circumstances, difficulties, or errors that occurred during her signing. Imagine how Lucy must feel. There she is, happy just to have a visitor, and the visitor insists on asking her the names of objects that both of them already know. Then when she tries to start a conversation, all the visitor does is sit there and write.

The aim of these worksheets was to build a statistical profile of selected aspects of Lucy's word use, and in this way Fouts has elicited and documented some extraordinary behavior. Lucy's vocabulary is about eighty words. It could be much larger, but the investigators are more interested in the way she uses her vocabulary than in its size; they cannot examine all aspects of language at once. A study of any behavior must exclude what might be called "static" data in favor of whatever is sought within the experimental design. When the behavior investigated is language, however, this aspect of scientific inquiry begins to work against the ultimate object of the inquiry.

In focusing on one aspect of language, the investigator must be inattentive to other uses of language that lie outside the thrust of a particular experiment. While the investigator is looking for one aspect of language, Lucy may be gaily demonstrating another. Unlike the investigator, the outsider naturally attends to evidence that the chimp is exploiting the *communicative* aspects of language and is not merely solving problems. And so, as I was introduced to Lucy and the chimps at the institute, I paid particular attention to

TABLE II

LUCY'S VOCABULARY AT THE START OF TESTING

baby doll	cold	hug	mirror	smell
ball	comb	hurry	more	smile
banana	come-gimme	hurt	no	smoke
barrette	cry	in	nut	spoon
berry	cup	Jack	oil	sorry
blanket	dirty	Janet	open	Steve
blow	dog	key	out	string
book	drink	kiss	pants	Sue S.
bowl	eat	least	pen-write	swallow
brush	enough	lipstick	pock-groom	telephone
candy	flower	listen	pipe	this-that
car	fork	look	please	there
cat	fruit	Lucy	purse	tickle
catch	go	Maury	Roger	want
clean	handkerchief	me	run	what
coat	hat	mine	shoe	yes
				you
				yours

the flavor of their use of Ameslan, and to those aspects of "speech" that might be obscured by a data table. I found that I reacted to different things than Fouts did. Indeed, the contrasts between Fouts's and my perspectives on Lucy brought out this important characteristic of the investigation of the chimps' use of Ameslan—that the examination of behavior can at times obscure the behavior itself.

This became clear when I met Lucy the next day. I arranged to show up at the Temerlins a little while after Roger began his morning session. Accordingly, at about 9:30 A.M. I walked around to the patio and peered through the living room window. I could see Roger and Lucy gesturing and cavorting on the couch. Fouts disengaged himself and got up to let me in.

I settled unobtrusively onto a couch to observe and to take

notes. Lucy promptly abandoned Roger, hopped onto my lap, and, after some unselfconscious staring, commenced a minute inspection of my face and clothing. She looked at my eyes, peered up my nostrils, and then briefly groomed my hair, presumably looking for lice. I had a scab on my knee, visible because I was wearing tennis shorts, and when Lucy had finally worked down to it, she looked over to Roger and touched the tips of two index fingers together. "She's saying you're hurt," said Roger.

I thanked Lucy, who, chuckling and grimacing, ran back over to Fouts. He showed her a picture of a cat and asked her what it was. "Cat," Lucy replied. For a moment Lucy continued to identify the pictures Roger showed her, but as soon as I picked up my pen to take notes she was dying to see what I was up to, and she raced back over and again hopped onto my lap. As I tried to note this, she grabbed the pen and began to scrawl furiously. Roger pointed out that she was using her right hand (I am left-handed so she was not imitating me) and that she was also holding the pen in a manner similar to a precision grip. Roger also said that Lucy seems to consistently hold objects in her left hand in the power grip. Psychologist Jerome Bruner has observed that in children the dominant hand develops a variety of precision grips while the other plays the role of the steadier, and, to stress the parallel between tool manipulation and language, that the dominant hand plays the role of the predicate to the subordinate hand's subject.

What is significant about Lucy's proclivities in drawing is that right-handedness and left-handedness in humans are related to what is called lateral dominance—the organization and division of labors between the two different hemispheres of the brain. The extraordinary selective pressures that produced language in man required the rapid development of certain parts of the brain, and as a result, rather than both developing equally, the left hemisphere was pushed out of shape to accommodate the renovations necessary to equip man for language. It is possible that the chimp brain is in the first stages of being lopsided that way as well.

After Lucy grew tired of drawing ferocious circles, she looked at me and noticed that the white shirt I was wearing had an alligator insignia on it. Lucy pointed to it several times and tracing a question mark in the air asked me what it was. I looked plaintively over to Roger, who suggested that I put my palms together as in prayer and then make the snapping motion of an alligator's jaws. With this advice I laboriously told Lucy that the insignia was an alligator. The chimpanzee cannot flex its hands backwards from the wrist as easily as a person can, and so, when we asked Lucy to identify the insignia, she, after some fumbling, made the sign with the snapping motion originating from the tips of her fingers. It is a testimony to the accuracy that Roger demands of his chimps that he thought Lucy was just babbling and making a confused version of "book," a sign made by unfolding the closed palms in imitation of an opening book. Only after she persisted in her variation did Roger accept that she was attempting to make the snapping sign. This incident made it clear that Fouts was not reading anything into Lucy's signing. It also gave me the feeling that published accounts gave a very conservative and formalistic picture of what the chimps were doing. While humans were peering at the chimps through the lens of experimental design, the chimps themselves were indeed exploiting Ameslan as a means of communication.

This feeling was further reinforced the next day when I arrived to observe another session. This time I was wearing a blue shirt, but again it had an alligator insignia. Roger asked Lucy who I was. After jumping onto my lap and pointing excitedly at my green insignia, Lucy said, logically enough, that I was an alligator. "Errors" like this did not fit within the scheme of the day's investigation. But was she in error, or was Lucy extracting some characteristic commonly associated with me and using that as the name for me—the very meta-linguistic process that recapitulates the way man came to name his tools and environment?

When conversing with Roger in Ameslan, Lucy would look at him with intense concentration; however, her movements in making signs were not intense, but leisurely, as though communicating by using Ameslan was the most natural thing in the world for a chimp to do. She seemed to understand spoken English. It was eerie to be talking with Roger about Lucy's mirror or doll and then have her run over and pick it up. Roger noted that earlier that week he had lost Lucy's doll. He glossed his error by replacing the doll with a slightly different one, which he handed Lucy the next day. Lucy was very suspicious of this new doll, and the day after this surreptitious exchange she went over to her

Washoe: "book"

Washoe: "baby"

toy chest and signed to Roger "out baby." She wanted to see where this strange doll had come from.

During that second session, Lucy was in a manic mood. Again she broke away from Roger when I began taking notes. She grabbed my note pad and pen and scrawled feverishly, as if she were short for time during a final exam. Besides the question of hemispheric dominance, there was another interesting aspect to Lucy's scrawling. It exemplified the chimp's interest in imitating what it sees others doing.

Critics have suggested that any preferences for word order shown by the chimpanzee result from imitation of human models without any understanding of the significance of word order. Many people are tempted to write off all evidence of simian cognitive ability as dumb mimicry; however, the job Lucy did in transcribing my notes (even though my handwriting might leave some wondering whether my scratchings showed any evidence of higher cognitive abilities) would not have caused me to hire her either as mimic or stenographer, and would leave me to doubt that Lucy could precisely imitate behavior if she did not know what she was doing. Moreover, Fouts has demonstrated that imitation is the least effective method of instruction. My suspicions received support a moment later.

After abandoning the note pad, Lucy settled down to improve on the knot with which I had tied my sneakers. Although the determination was inspiring, she would only work herself into a frustrated fury. To get her attention, Roger called her back for tussles and little games. One of these was the swallow game.

Here, Roger will take a pair of sunglasses and pretend to swallow them by turning his head in profile to Lucy and sliding the glasses past his open mouth on the side of his face that Lucy cannot see. Lucy thinks this is hysterically funny, and she will with unflagging interest and excitement sit inches away from Roger while he performs this bit of legerdemain. Promptly after Roger finished today's performance, Lucy grabbed the glasses, and taking her indestructible mirror hopped across the living room to another couch. Holding the mirror with her feet, Lucy, to her own vast amusement, performed the swallow trick, passing the glasses along the obscured side of her face exactly as Roger had done. Then she signed "look, swallow." After her third performance of the swallow trick, Lucy drooled on the mirror, and, while she looked at her distorted image with a bemused expression, spread the saliva around with her finger.

Lucy has her own games to play with Roger. Sometimes she will grab his watch or some other possession, which she won't return until Roger identifies it with the proper sign. Washoe, Fouts noted, has a raunchier sense of humor. One day while riding on Roger's shoulders, Washoe pissed on him and then signed "funny" in a self-congratulatory way.

When Lucy grabs Roger's watch and demands that he identify it to get it back or when she takes the mirror and plays the swallow game by herself, she is obviously imitating her mentors,

Lucy playing the "swallow" game.

but such mimicry is no less fraught with meaning than the solitary play of children when they name and talk to their toys. Like the child, Lucy talks to herself, plays with words, and uses these periods of self-absorption to explore her developing language skills. In any event, we should not downgrade imitation in either ape or man. It is the evolutionary device that permits the learning of new behaviors. It permits flexibility.

Dutch psychologist Adriaan Kortlandt, who has visited both Fouts and the Gardners and has observed chimps in the wild as well, feels that the significance of this type of play has not been sufficiently emphasized by the Gardners themselves. He also feels that self-imposed experimental blinders prevented the people working with Ameslan-using chimps from seeing a lot of what is going on. He once watched Washoe "read" an illustrated magazine. As she did, she signed "cat" when she came upon a picture of a tiger, and "drink" upon seeing a vermouth advertisement. He refers to this as "thinking aloud," and he noted that when Washoe was not rewarded, she tended more to think aloud rather than talk to the Gardners. He feels this indicates that the "apes have a lot more to think about than to say."

To the outsider, such thinking aloud is far more persuasive than a data summary of the degree to which the chimp has integrated language into its life. It shows that the infant chimp is not merely pleasing its masters for rewards or solving puzzles, but is rather turning around and examining its new tool. We would expect behavior like this from a child, and we would be suspicious if a chimpanzee purported to have language did not use language in these peripheral ways.

During that second day, I also watched Lucy refute the idea that the chimp's choice of word order is determined solely by mimicry rather than by a sense of structure. Roger had noted that Lucy consistently used the correct order in such three-word combinations as "Roger tickle Lucy." After watching Lucy request several such tickles, I began to wonder what would happen if Roger said "Lucy tickle Roger." I asked Roger if he had ever done this.

He said no, and then after thinking a moment about the possibility of unfortunate consequences from saying such a thing, he turned to Lucy and said, "Lucy tickle Roger." Lucy was sitting beside Roger on the living room couch. She sat back for an instant confused. Almost testingly she said, "No, Roger tickle Lucy." Roger again said, "No, Lucy tickle Roger." This time I could see comprehension brighten Lucy's eyes. Excited she jumped onto his lap and began tickling him while he rocked backwards uttering little grunts in imitation of chimp laughter. For the next few minutes, Roger and Lucy politely requested and exchanged tickles. Fouts has since filmed these exchanges with Lucy.

There are other possible explanations for this incident than the

A CONVERSATION WITH A CHIMP, TESTING WORD ORDER:

Roger Fouts signs "Roger" in saying, "Lucy tickle Roger."

Lucy signs "Roger . . ."

"...*tickle*..."

"...*Lucy*," *confused that her
name is not used as the
recipient of tickling.*

Roger signs "no" and repeats: "Lucy tickle Roger."

Suddenly comprehending, Lucy leaps to tickle Roger.

reflection of a rudimentary sense of syntax. For one thing Ameslan syntax is not a simple mapping of English. Then, too, because a sentence such as "Lucy tickle Roger" is short, it is possible that Lucy understood it according to some semantic rather than syntactic scheme. Rather than noting that "Lucy," and not "Roger," was in the subject position, she might have been noting that Fouts was uttering this set of words traditionally associated with tickling.

However, Fouts taught Lucy to say "Roger tickle Lucy" and still says it himself sometimes when he is going to tickle her. Thus, even though the words associated with tickling are said by Roger, ·Lucy expects to be tickled when Fouts says "Roger tickle Lucy." It must have been something about the words, rather than the speaker, that triggered her tickling. Fouts has since noted that Lucy correctly interprets the difference between such variations as "Roger tickle Lucy, we tickle you," and "you tickle me, tickle Roger." Up to the moment I observed, Lucy had never heard "Lucy tickle Roger," and so she could not merely have been associating a set of words with an appropriate situation.

This brings us back to a syntactic explanation: in all probability, after her initial hesitation Lucy was cueing to the position of the words in the sentence. Similarly, although Ameslan has a grammar different from English, at the institute Ameslan signs are combined according to English grammar. Like Lucy, Washoe eventually adopted what appeared to be grammatical word order, but it was her transition toward its use that confused efforts to quantify her word order preferences in three-word combinations. At the beginning of the test period, Washoe put subject before object, although she put both before the verb; at the end she was using traditional subject-verb-object word order.

Fouts is not surprised that Lucy would have a sense of word order. Psychologist Jean Piaget has said that teaching language to an animal consists largely of mapping the animal's already-existing knowledge. The chimp's capacities for tool-making and tool manipulation show that the chimp has the "already-existing ability" to purposively organize its movements in a non-random way. Why then should its hand movements suddenly be random because it is working with *symbols* for objects and not with objects themselves? Moreover, the chimp lives in intricately organized and highly gregarious bands, a fact that demands his understanding structure of a high order. Thus, it would indeed be odd for a language map to be random in a creature as highly organized as the chimp. So much for word order; let us now turn to the word itself.

Man has traditionally associated words with power and manipulation in magic and religion. In magic, to know the *name* of a force is to be able to invoke it; rituals of white magic are littered with *words of power* that summon or dispel various natural and supernatural forces. Similarly, the ancient Hebrews concealed the name of the deity from all save the highest priests. He might only be referred to indirectly; by being unnamed, this god was beyond man's power and manipulation. In mythology, those who cannot name are impotent, while that which cannot *be* named is threatening. Man can control only what he can name, which summarizes concisely man's intuitive understanding of the relationship between language and thought. As it is for man, so it is for the chimpanzee.

How Lucy understands the *word* has been Fouts's principal concern. Bellugi and Bronowski forcefully argue that words and the laws that govern their manipulation form an organic whole—i.e., the process of distillation through which man abstracted the symbolic nature of the objects around him was impelled by demands for those objects' manipulation. Within this interlocking whole of word and grammar, we might not expect to find differing levels of analysis; but we would expect some relationship between the sophistication of an animal's ability to symbolize and the sophistication of its ability to combine those symbols in sentences. We would not expect to see an animal prove capable of mastering appropriate Latin case endings for nouns, yet prove incapable of combining those words in meaningful combinations, simply because the level of analysis necessary to use Latin case endings appropriately would presume the ability to analyze and understand Latin grammar. More to the point, if the chimp understood signs in Ameslan to be surrogates for particular objects, we might expect chimps to demonstrate little ability in combining such tokens; yet if the chimp demonstrated that it understood the general properties of particular words and the utility of words in analyzing particular situations, we might expect a commensurate level of abstraction in the grammar with which the chimp organizes those words. Understanding the attributes and combinatory functions of a word like "sweet," for example, is not understanding the word's meaning, but is an analysis of those situations in which what is represented by "sweet" is appropriate. An analysis of "sweetness" represents the type of factoring of the environment Bellugi and Bronowski referred to in their discussion of reconstitution, and the general application of "sweetness" reflects the synthesis that was the second part of that process. Simply stated, to understand a symbol, one must understand its applications; thus, in light of this, it seems illogical to state that an animal can understand the symbolic nature of a word while having no understanding of the rules which integrate that word into sentences.

Lucy gave me a taste of her conception of the symbol when she linked me with my alligator emblem and gave me the sign for alligator as a name. Between my first and second visits to the institute, Fouts made a formal study of Lucy's conceptual abilities by investigating how she used her vocabulary. We discussed the results when I returned to the institute and met Lucy again in the summer of 1973.

The experiment revolved around Lucy's classification of twenty-four different fruits and vegetables (see table III). At the time, the words in Lucy's vocabulary that related to food were "food," "fruit," "drink," "candy," and "banana." She used "food," "fruit," and "drink" in a generic manner to refer to those three classes of items while she knew that "banana" was specific for bananas. Fouts says that the most interesting results of the experiment were the "serendipitous findings concerning her responses to particular items." For instance, she consistently referred to the citrus fruits (four out of the twenty-four fruits and vegetables) as "smell fruits," linking them with their singular, tangy odor. This was the kind of response Fouts had been hoping for, because it indicated that Lucy was rummaging through her vocabulary for words to *describe* the characteristics of objects for which she had no sign. Lucy had no sign, beyond the generic term "fruit" to describe particular classes of fruit, and so she resorted to segregating them by their attributes. The investigators found that Lucy, in classifying these items, seemed to fix upon the same criteria that a naïve person might select. For instance, her broadest division seemed to segregate the fruits from the vegetables. She preferred the word "fruit" for fruits, while she consistently termed vegetables "food." As noted, she classified the citrus items as "smell fruit," but it was radishes and watermelons that truly summoned her descriptive powers. For the first few days of the experiment Lucy referred to radishes as "food." Then she tasted one. Promptly spitting out the mouthful, she called it a "cry hurt food." Throughout the remainder of the experiment she used "hurt" or "cry" to refer to radishes.

Fouts also found that once Lucy learned the specific name within a general category, she resisted applying that name to any other item. For instance, they taught her "berry" for cherry, which she previously knew only as a "fruit." They found that once it was established that a cherry was "berry" she resisted applying "berry" to other items. Thus she seemed to understand the difference between general terms and specific items.

Lucy liked watermelon, and she three times referred to it as a "candy drink" thereby plumbing the fruit for a third of its attributes—sweetness.

TABLE III

LUCY'S RESPONSES TO THE VARIOUS FOODS OVER THE FIRST FOUR
DAYS OF TESTING

STIMULUS OBJECT	1	2	3	4
apple	fruit	fruit	fruit	fruit
orange	fruit	fruit	that Lucy smell	fruit
peach	fruit	fruit	fruit	fruit
plum	food	fruit	fruit	fruit
nectarine	that food	fruit	fruit	food fruit
grapefruit	that fruit	smell	fruit	smell
¼ watermelon	drink	drink	that drink	drink fruit
lemon	smell	smell	smell	food
lime	smell	fruit	smell	smell
banana	banana	banana	banana	banana
cherry	fruit	food fruit Roger	food fruit	fruit
raisin	food fruit	fruit	smell food	food fruit
Thompson seed-less grapes	that drink	fruit	food fruit	fruit
frozen strawberry	food	fruit	cold fruit	drink fruit

TABLE III (*continued*)

LUCY'S RESPONSES TO THE VARIOUS FOODS OVER THE FIRST FOUR
DAYS OF TESTING

STIMULUS OBJECT	1	2	3	4
frozen blackberry	fruit food	fruit Lucy	fruit	food
radish	that Lucy fruit	drink food	Lucy Lucy food	cry hurt food
stalk celery	smell pipe food	food pipe	smell pipe Roger	fruit food
cherry tomato	fruit	fruit	Lucy smell drink food	food
tomato	that fruit	food	food Lucy	food
sweet pickle small	food	pipe candy	pipe smell	food Lucy
sweet pickle large	food	food	flower fruit	fruit fruit
peas	food	food	food that Lucy	food
corn	food Lucy	food	flower food	food

Lucy principally used "drink" to refer to watermelon, an attribute of the fruit we recognize in our own appellation for it. On occasion she came even closer to the English word by calling it a "drinkfruit." "Drink fruit" is about as close to watermelon as any analyst might be expected to get, if the analyst's most specific term for fluids was "drink" and its most specific term for melons was "fruit." Given the vocabulary she had to work with, Lucy came treacherously close to the creative symbolization that produced the English word "watermelon," and we might suppose that she came upon "drinkfruit" by an analysis of its attributes similar to that which produced our own word. These examples indicate that Lucy was making productive use of her vocabulary. By generating an infinite number of new and different sentences from a finite vocabulary, Lucy was demonstrating productivity.

Just as it is thought that most animal communication is closely tied to basic urges and is not displaced in time and space from the stimuli that initiate the message, so it is also thought that each signal an animal sends is an autonomous and specific message, which, if it can be combined with other signals at all, can only be combined in strictly limited ways. For man, each word is perceived to be a building block that he can organize through grammar with other building blocks into an infinite number of messages, but the animal is supposedly limited to sending and receiving messages that are prefabricated and, so to speak, handed to it whole. According to this logic, Lucy should not have been able to apply "candy" to watermelon and other sweets, because to do so requires that she look past the prefabricated surface of the signal to the building blocks—candiness, for instance—that make up the message. To do this Lucy had to summon her powers of reconstitution.

When Lucy invented a sign for "leash" she demonstrated her understanding of the word's utility. She hates the leash, but because of a nearby highway, it is a necessary accouterment if she is to venture out. Fouts referred to the leash as a "string," a sign made by pulling the little finger. Lucy, however, refers to the leash by making a motion of putting it on. As in her invention of my alligator sobriquet, Lucy here abstracted and reified the properties of the leash into a symbolic representation and, in so doing, was demonstrating how she analyzed the world.

LUCY INVENTS HER OWN WORD FOR "WATERMELON":

"sweet/candy"

"drink"

Lucy: "string"

Washoe has displayed productivity as well, say Fouts. Once riding in a rowboat with Roger at the institute, she referred to two swans as "water birds."

Lucy has recently begun using Ameslan to express her emotional states. The most poignant example of this occurred one day when Jane Temerlin, Lucy's foster mother, left the house during one of Roger's training sessions. Lucy ran over to the side window to watch Jane drive off, and as she did, Lucy signed to herself "cry me, me cry." It was the first time Fouts had seen a chimp describe an emotion rather than revert to normal chimp expressions of distress.

On another occasion, Fouts exploited Freud's hypothesis that verbal behavior tends to reduce physical activity in order to save himself from some roughhousing at Lucy's hands. Lucy has gotten very big and very strong in the past year. One day Lucy was keyed up and she came charging toward Fouts from across the Temerlin's living room. As she was charging, Roger (in Ameslan)

Washoe signs "bird" in calling a swan a "water bird."

said "sign!" (the imperative for her to tell him what she wants).

Lucy halted briefly, said "tickle," and then resumed her charge.

"Who?" said Roger.

"Tickle Lucy."

"Ask politely!"

"Please tickle Lucy," said the chimp as she reached Roger. By now Lucy was thoroughly calmed down.

Upon my return visit to the Temerlin's, I was surprised at how big Lucy had become. She is now approaching sexual maturity and occasionally interrupts training sessions with immodest passes at her male mentors. In order to satisfy Lucy's developing maternal instinct, Dr. Lemmon gave her a kitten to raise. Lucy immediately proved herself to be an over-protective mother. She would carry the kitten everywhere, calling it "my baby." The problem was that the cat, being a cat, did not want to be carried everywhere. Although Lucy carried it properly, she was quite insensitive to the cat's wishes, and as a result, the cat hurt its pads grabbing onto the wire cage in futile resistance whenever its demonically smothering foster mother tramped by and scooped it up. As soon as the Temerlins noticed the cat's sore pads, it was promptly taken away from Lucy. Lucy was stricken with grief. Sue Savage, one of Lucy's trainers, explained to Lucy that she had hurt the cat's paws (feet). Lucy seemed properly chastened. When the cat was eventually returned to her, she immediately cradled it and pointed to its feet, signing "hurt, hurt."

Lucy has met other cats that she has not liked so much, which brings us to a final indication that this particular chimpanzee has stamped her imprimatur on language. Like Washoe, Lucy has taken to swearing. She demonstrates that her invention of the word "leash" did not occur out of fondness for the object, inasmuch as she refers to it as a "dirty leash." On another occasion, after an argument with a local tomcat, she referred to the animal as a "dirty cat." Lucy, like the other chimps, seems to take her relations with other animals very seriously.

THE CHIMPANZEE IN THE TEMPLE OF LANGUAGE

If there is one use of language which, for the outsider, demonstrates that an animal understands and exploits the creative aspects of language, that aspect might be swearing. Lucy's use of "dirty" exploited a purely descriptive term for pejorative associations. These pejorative associations were the product of her own deduction and not the product of instruction. By putting her feelings into words, Lucy was also bending words to suit her feelings. More to the point, she was telling us what she thought of that cat, and that is what language is all about. If Lucy's use of Ameslan was mere "aping" of her mentors, we should not expect her to swear.

When Lucy reaches maturity, she will be reintroduced to her own kind. Hopefully she will have an infant of her own, and—this is Fouts's fondest wish—will teach it to communicate using Ameslan.

Based on the differences between my perceptions of Lucy on my first and second visits to Oklahoma, she seemed to be rapidly approaching the age where not only would she need other chimps to fulfill her social and sexual needs but might be maturing to the point where her superior strength would make it difficult for human companions to deal with her. Raised as the Temerlin's infant, she is mindful of their wishes and accepts their dominance; however, as people are perceived to be more and more peripheral to the institute and family, so does their authority with Lucy diminish. When I first met her, she was about six and I was still stronger than she. Sessions of tickling and playing with her were just plain fun. She was then, and still is, quite affectionate and liked nothing better than leaping from couch to couch and roughhousing. During my second visit, I again looked forward to these little tussles; but this year during tickling sessions, I found myself tensed and wary. It was not that I was afraid she might strike out; rather she seemed more deliberate, controlled, and she emanated vibrations of contained power. There was no longer a question of who was stronger, and on the whole I thought it was very nice of Lucy to want still to play with me. There were other differences between the visits as well. Last year Fouts and I would occasionally take a break to have coffee; this year when we had coffee, Lucy had a cup as well. As she has matured, Lucy has also become more generous; often as she requests food for herself, she gives food to Roger and tells him to eat.

CHILDHOOD'S END

To take the proper measure of the chimps' language abilities, it is important to follow them through maturity. Studying only the infant chimp might leave an observer with a false impression of what the Ameslan-using adult is like. The infant prodigy in Ameslan is thoroughly impressive, but it is very dependent on the humans around it and this tends to dampen evidence of the animal's individuality and make it merely cute. Exposure to the infant also heightens the impression that the chimp would like to be human if only it could. During their maturing, it becomes clear that rather than being failed human beings, they are very successful at being chimps. Rather than smugly reassuring an adorable, dependent infant chimp, the human begins to feel threatened by the vigor, power, and personality of the adult. Since the chimp is a serious animal, we cannot help but be impressed with the seriousness of the idea that these animals can communicate with us in one of our own languages. It is not very threatening when an adorable, dependent infant begins to sign; it is another matter when a self-possessed and somewhat intimidating adult demonstrates its facility with language. Man may need to feel that language is exclusively his if only to compensate for his manifest physical inferiority.

This becomes all the more clear when one is exposed to a chimp not caged in a zoo or being put through a comical routine in a circus. Putting any animal behind bars will transform it from a source of fear into an object of pity, and in doing so will pervert the observer's perceptions of the animal, and in most cases make the animal neurotic, which seems to confirm the original judgment imposed by the cage. We put animals in cages or turn them into performers in part to disarm ancient memories that it was, after all, we who were cast from Eden. Lucy, however, does not live in a cage, she is a member of a family, and my picture of the chimp was commensurately less confused by the symbolic baggage of the zoo, although Lucy was still vastly displaced from a milieu where she would really flourish—a chimp community.

During my second visit with Lucy, I was reminded of Arthur C. Clark's *Childhood's End*, in which man, under the supervision of a race of sterile, rational overlords, becomes the vehicle for the birth of his own successor. In schooling a colony of chimps in Ameslan, we are giving our most cherished tool to an animal already well-equipped by nature to survive in a world without men. We do not know yet how this tool will be used.

7. The Chimp Colony: Ally

Like Lucy, Ally is being raised in species isolation, and like Lucy he was born at the institute. His father is Pan, the institute's dominant male, and his mother is Caroline. Unlike Lucy, who was nearing four when the Ameslan program began at the institute, Ally has been exposed to Ameslan almost from the day he was born. His foster mother is Sheri Roush, a social worker, and his home is a ranch house, which, like the Temerlin's, is fitted with a spacious wire mesh enclosure for those periods when Ally must be left home unattended. Perhaps it's the growing Ameslan facility of his mentors, perhaps it's the fact that he has received instruction right from birth, or perhaps it's because Ally is a very bright young chimp, but Ally has a vocabulary of ninety words, although he is only three. He picks up new signs daily, and his gestures have almost textbook clarity.

One circumstance that hampered the interpretive efforts of both Washoe's friends and foes was the absence of comparative data on other chimps. Without this data, it was impossible to determine whether Washoe's proclivities and difficulties with certain words or combinations had to do with general properties of the chimp mind, with the method of instruction, or with Washoe's own idiosyncrasies. For instance, Bellugi and Bronowski thought it significant that in the first months of training Washoe had not yet negated or asked questions. Washoe subsequently did both, but Lucy and Ally have demonstrated that whatever tardiness Washoe displayed in demonstrating these behaviors did not result from any conceptual difficulty in the chimp. Both learned "no" and "not" as a matter of course, and both regularly ask questions when they want to find out about something. Different chimps do have vastly different personalities, and this alone makes it perilous for the critic to treat them as faceless, interchangeable representatives of the chimp mind. Similarly, Fouts feels that on the basis of their experience so far, saying one chimp is better than another in using Ameslan is like saying that a good engineer is brighter than a good doctor. He has detected differences in the performances of various chimps, but he has yet to detect extremes. Still, without denigrating the other chimps, it can be said that Ally is a remarkable student.

Ally introduced himself to me as I settled into a coffee alcove off the living room in yet another attempt to observe unobtrusively Fouts and his pupils. Ally walked over to the alcove, sized me up, and then with clipped precision pointed at me, drew his left finger across the back of his right palm, and signed his name. Evidently he found me worthy of giving him a tickle, and we roughhoused a little. Being a male, Ally indulged more fully than infant females in foot slapping, charging, and other aggressive postures. Chimps also grin in what is called a playface when they get excited and, in the ecstasy of tickling, like to bite on something. In the excitement of a tussle, this play biting can become more aggressive. As I swung him around, Ally became excited and started slapping the floor and grinning. Then, as though he realized he was getting overheated, he abruptly sucked his lips over his teeth to prevent himself from grinning.

Besides his nascent aggressive postures, Ally, who has never seen another chimp, occasionally does other chimp-like things. Once he made a nest for himself out of objects lying around his room; however, unlike the wild chimp, Ally signed the name for each object as he put it in place.

Ally now abandoned momentarily his vague attempts to intimidate me and noticed that my trousers were fastened with buttons and not a zipper.

"What that?" he signed.

"Button," replied Roger.

"What that?" Roger then asked, pointing to the button.

"Button," replied Ally who then leapt up on my shoulders.

Unlike Lucy, who is either a smothering mother or hostile, Ally gets along well with cats. This is because he grew up among them and quickly learned to respect the local residents' tempers. After about ten minutes, one wandered into the room, and Ally jumped down from my shoulders to greet it. The cat licked Ally's face. Ally made a sudden gesture, and the cat rocketed out of the room. Ally rocketed after it, and Sheri Roush swiftly followed screaming, "Don't you bother that cat."

Ally halted. He understood Sheri perfectly, even though she was not speaking Ameslan. English is Ally's second language.

The chimps at the institute are exposed to a good deal more English than Fouts would like to permit. Unlike Washoe's trailer in Reno where a great deal of effort ensured that Ameslan was the only language used in Washoe's presence, some of the chimps at the institute, like Ally and Lucy, are being raised in normal households where English is used by the families among themselves and, often, in conversing with the chimps. Beyond this, the chimps' mentors sometimes accompany gestures in Ameslan with their spoken translation. "Hey, what's this?" an instructor will sometimes say when gesturing to keep the chimp's attention. (Formal testing, however, is conducted in silence.) Both drawbacks and dividends result from this confusion of communication channels. One may reasonably assume that chimps would find a deaf household a more fertile milieu in which to acquire Ameslan, because they would not be distracted by seeing their mentors communicate in two media, one of which was inaccessible to them. Furthermore, the chimps' foster parents are amateurs in Ameslan and are not nearly as comfortable or fluent with the language as a deaf person. These circumstances might place a greater limitation on the Ameslan performance of the chimp than any lack of native ability, and back in Reno, the Gardners are cur-

Ally offers a bite of his meal to one of the institute's cats.

rently testing this assumption by having two new chimps tutored by deaf instructors. Nevertheless, there are also positive opportunities presented by these bilingual households, opportunities that Fouts is now attempting to exploit.

As I have noted, Lucy seemed to keep an ear turned toward my conversations with Fouts while she was engaged in play. Last winter Fouts and two assistants, Bill Chown and Larry Goodin, made an explicit effort to teach Ally ten words in both English and Ameslan. First, they used English to test Ally's understanding of the ten spoken words. A trainer would say, "Bring me the spoon," and when Ally correctly selected the spoon five consecutive times from among a variety of objects, it was assumed he reliably knew the word. When Ally knew all ten words in English, the list was divided into two sections and training began. One of the three investigators would teach Ally the Ameslan equivalent of each of five spoken words. For instance, he would say "spoon" and make the appropriate gesture. When this training session was finished, the first investigator would leave and another would come in. The person who followed did not know which of five signs his predecessor had taught Ally or which of them Ally had acquired. He would simply test Ally in Ameslan in all five of the items by picking one up and gesturing "what that?" As in the double-blind procedure used in formal testing, this method prevented the investigator from cueing Ally to the correct answer. Ally eventually demonstrated that he knew all the objects' signs in Ameslan.

While it had been known previously that Ally could acquire signs in Ameslan, in this case Ally learned the appropriate Ameslan word for a variety of objects solely on the basis of his previously knowing the English word. There was no spoon around when he was taught its Ameslan sign; the only stimulus was the instructor's word, "spoon," associated with the molding of Ally's hands into a particular gesture. When he was asked "what that?" and shown a spoon, Ally had to connect the object with its English word before he could make the appropriate gesture.

Among the things Ally had to do to make this appropriate response was to link a gesture, learned from hearing the word, with a stimulus that was visual. The ability to transfer stimuli from a visual to an auditory mode is called CROSS-MODAL TRANSFER. This ability is considered to be central to the acquisition of language, and even now, some behavioral scientists do not believe the chimp can make such associations.

Here Ally may be demonstrating that the block preventing the chimp from speaking is not neurological (although we would never expect the chimp to speak with the facility of a person, who has been equipped for that task over several million years) but phonological—that is, the chimp lacks the necessary mechanisms for generating and controlling particular sounds.

In demonstrating this cross-modal transfer, Ally is also demonstrating a degree of displacement. When he received his instruction in Ameslan, the English word for the object of which he was learning the name served as the stimulus. No object was present, and, to understand what the English word referred to, Ally had to retrieve a memory displaced in time and place from the act of communication. Displacement, reconstitution, reification, and cross-modal transfer are intertwined. It would be unlikely that Ally could have cross-modal transfer without displacement or be able to reify his environment symbolically without cross-modal transfer, nor could he demonstrate reconstitution without all of the above.

As Roger and I discussed his studies, Ally continued to demand tickles with increasing self-confidence and belligerence. "He wants to see how dominant you are," said Sheri.

"I'm dominant as hell," I told Ally as I tossed him in the air. By this time, he was poking me in the chest like a drill sergeant when he said "you" as part of "you tickle me." Fouts assured me that I was not the first visitor to be besieged with insatiable demands for

Roger in conversation with Bruno and Booee.

tickling. Shortly before this visit, Bill Chown was similarly pestered by Ally for tickles during a regular afternoon session.

"You tickle Ally," said Ally poking Chown in the chest. Chown ignored him.

"You, you, you," said Ally growing more insistent. Chown still ignored him.

Finally Ally, by now exasperated, said, "You tickle Ally, you nut!" (Ally is often called a nut, and he also knows the word to refer to the fruit.)

Each afternoon Bill Chown and Larry Goodin have regular signing sessions with Ally. The three of them will sit in a circle and, as items are brought out of the omnipresent item bag, they perform an Alphonse-Gaston routine. A brush will be brought out and Bill will say, "Larry brush Ally"; then a ball will be brought out, and Larry will say, "Ally give ball to Bill"; or something else will be brought out and Ally will say, "Give pen to Ally." The purpose is to test Ally's understanding of subject-verb-object word order in a fast-paced situation where the objects and agents are constantly changing. I asked whether Ally had ever said something like "Bill brush Larry." Fouts said that he doubted that Ally had said anything like that, and if he did, it was probably a mistake. Ally, after all, is still an infant.

Although the engineer-doctor analogy was fresh in my mind, I could not help thinking that Ally was an extraordinary chimp and that he would make his mark on the world. Consider the reception of his first efforts with oil paints on canvas. One of the assistants collected several of his canvasses and showed them to an art historian, not telling him that the works had been executed by a chimpanzee. The critic was beside himself with enthusiasm. "I knew Pollack was coming back!" he told the beaming graduate assistant.

8. The Chimp Colony: Bruno and Booee

Ally, Lucy, and two other chimps named Salome and Tanya will shortly be re-introduced to their own kind. They will not be thrown in with the adult colony at the institute, but instead will meet Washoe and four other chimps named Bruno, Booee, Cindy, and Thelma. Together they will form the nucleus of a language-using chimp society.

Bruno, Booee, Cindy, and Thelma have spent most of their time since 1971 together on the chimp island at the institute. Occasionally one of them is taken ashore for training or because of misbehavior, and on occasion all are brought ashore for testing, but for the most part they have been together. It was with data collected on these chimps that Roger first attempted to compare and analyze the differences in acquiring Ameslan signs among chimpanzees.

The four chimps involved in this study were first taught ten signs: "hat," "show," "fruit," "drink," "more," "look," "key," "listen," "string," and "food." When he was with the Gardners, Fouts had tried different methods of teaching Washoe, but here he was interested not in determining the most effective method of instruction, but in the discrepancies that accrued when four chimps were taught Ameslan under a controlled learning situation and method of instruction. Consequently, for all the chimps, Fouts used molding and fading, which he had found with Washoe to be the most productive teaching method, and tested them in the double-blind box. Fouts compared the chimps' performance by counting the number of minutes it took before each chimp could identify an object, without prompting, on five consecutive occasions. He discovered that a chimp's performance in a testing situation sometimes more accurately reflects the chimp's reaction to the testing situation than it does his competence with the language. He also discovered that variations in acquiring signs had a great deal to do with the personality of the chimp and that it would be hazardous to pass judgment on the chimp's cognitive abilities based on one chimp's acquisition of particular signs. Finally, he noted consistencies among the chimps' experience in learning the ten signs that might tell something about the way a chimp thinks.

Bruno was born at the institute in February 1968. His father is the ubiquitous Pan and his mother is Pampy. He is a young tough and tests exceptionally well in Ameslan. His sign means "proud." At first, he had little interest in mimicking these strange movements he was asked to perform. Fouts says that when he first started to teach him "hat," a sign made by patting the top of the head, Bruno would look at him with mild curiosity as if to say, "I'd really like to help you, but I can't for the life of me understand what it is that you want me to do." After a while Fouts got exasperated and threatened Bruno. Bruno immediately started signing "hat, hat, hat."

Booee is genial and perhaps a little insecure. His parents are unknown, but it is known before he came to the institute that his brain was split in a laboratory. Splitting the brain by severing the corpus callosum is an operation performed on humans in severe cases of epilepsy and on chimps in experiments to determine the properties of the right and left hemispheres of the brain. The operation took place when Booee was quite young, and so far there has been little manifest evidence of its effect on his behavior except in his paintings, which invariably consist of two distinct scribblings in opposite corners of the canvas. Booee seems to inspire great affection among the assistants and trainers around the institute. He is a willing learner, in part because of his great love of the raisins that are occasionally used as a reward, but he tests poorly, partly because of the absence of said rewards in testing situations.

Both Cindy and Thelma were born in the wild sometime in mid-1967. Both had had some home rearing before they came to the institute, and neither has the powerful personality of a Washoe or Lucy. Cindy performed well during acquisition because of her almost desperate desire to please her instructors. An instructor would place his hand on top of her head in molding "hat" and Cindy would leave it there as if to say, "If that is what you want me to do, fine." Thelma is a little flakey. Roger describes her as a dreamer who could be thoroughly distracted by a fly in the training cage. Neither Cindy, because of the absence of reinforcement from the instructor, nor Thelma, because of her lack of concentration, performed well during testing. All of the chimps were over two; Cindy was nearly five when training began, and none profited from the enriched environment in which Washoe, Lucy, and Ally were reared.

Some of the consistencies that characterized the performance of the four chimps were perplexing. For all the chimps, "hat" was difficult, "shoe" was easy. "Look" was difficult, "listen" was easy. "Look" is made by placing an index finger next to the eye, and

Fouts speculates that "look" might have been difficult because of a natural aversion to having an instructor place a finger near the eye. Due to his interest in raisins, Booee acquired signs roughly three times faster than Thelma and more than twice as fast as Bruno; however, in the raisinless testing situation Booee scored only 59.72 per cent, while Bruno, who learned signs when he wanted to and not because of rewards, scored 90.28 per cent.

The significant consistencies were the errors. When a food exemplar was presented, the errors predominantly were the wrong choice of signs within the category of foods. Booee erroneously called some foods and fruits "drinks." Thelma tended to mix up foods as well. Similarly, some of the errors resulted not from conceptual confusion but from the similarity of one gesture to another. "Listen" is made by placing an index finger on the ear, while in "look" the index finger is placed next to the eye. Booee tended to mix them up. Finally, many errors occurred because each of the chimps had a favorite sign. Cindy liked "string," while Thelma used signs in the food category with reckless abandon.

The comparison did establish that Washoe was no freak; but neither is her word-use archetypical of all chimps. Due to the strong personality differences among the chimps, one chimp's experience in learning a particular word could not be understood to hold meaning for all.

This experiment and the previously described explorations of word-use by Washoe, Lucy, and Ally are part of Fouts's effort to gather baseline data for the present generation of experiments in which he is exploring the chimps' use of Ameslan among themselves. But long before Fouts was ready to begin formally exploring chimp-to-chimp communication using Ameslan, his pupils spontaneously began signing to one another.

Bruno and Booee now have vocabularies of about forty words apiece, and they are inseparable pals. Bruno has lived up to his name. He initiates all sorts of games, pranks, and outrages and is constantly testing the authority and patience of his companions. He is a brat. Booee is his personable companion and audience who seems to regard Bruno's outrageous behavior with considerable admiration. My memories of my first visit to the institute are of Bruno in unceasing action and of Booee barely keeping pace.

I remember seeing the Temerlins' son Steve trying to get Bruno out of the rowboat and onto the island, while Bruno adroitly maneuvered out of his grasp. As Steve's warning became more threatening, so Bruno seemed to be enjoying himself proportionately more. Finally, Steve clouted Bruno on the back with a loud smack, and Bruno, shrewdly deciding that he had driven this particular human to the limit of his patience, jumped ashore.

Later, ashore, Bruno made a series of leaps at me from the seat of a tractor while I tried to converse with Roger. Bruno would jump on my shoulders; I would swing him to the ground. He would run back up on the tractor and jump again, this time a little more roughly. I would put him down a little more roughly. (I was not about to be bullied by a five-year-old chimp.) This continued on its inevitable escalatory course, until I too began to get exasperated. Finally, I began to get menacing, and Bruno, after contemptuously dismissing my threat, swaggered off to play in an apple tree. On the way there he leapt at one of the peacocks, who ran away shrieking hysterically.

During that first visit, Kiko, a newly acquired male infant, was also introduced to the chimp island. It was a disaster. Steve Temerlin rowed him out there and attempted to introduce him to Bruno and Booee. The two older chimps teased little Kiko unmercifully. They would chase him around the rundevaal, run up to him and give him a smack and then run away before the outraged Kiko could retaliate. It was like watching a gang of boys haze a new kid on the block. Each of these escapades would end with Kiko's running to Steve and jumping into his arms. When around Steve, Kiko became terribly brave. Once reassured he would sally forth a few feet, shake his fists at the two roughnecks, and then dive behind Steve for cover. It was clear that without Steve to stick up for him, poor Kiko would be run ragged, and so he was temporarily taken off the island. He was brought back over the ensuing weeks; however, it was only sometime later when Washoe was also on the island that Kiko had any peace of mind.

Washoe, as mentioned earlier, did not care for other chimpanzees when she first saw them, referring to them slightingly as "black bugs." Over a period of months, however, she began first to tolerate them and then genuinely to like them, although it is still an open question whether or not she categorizes them in the same class as humans. When Steve or Roger visits the island, she rushes to greet him with extravagant hugs as though she is a titled lady who has been unfairly closeted with the illiterate masses, and who at last can talk to someone of her own station. Nevertheless, there is also a bit of the Florence Nightingale in her, and Roger notes that she seems to seek out the persecuted and maladjusted chimps when she is both on the island and ashore with the adult chimp colony. On the island, Kiko, of course, naturally attracted her attention—since he was virtually unrivalled in having underdog status—and she protects him from the more flagrant torments of Bruno and Booee.

We can only speculate what questions passed through Washoe's mind when she first attempted to talk to the strange creatures on the island and in the adult colony. And their initial lack of responsiveness must have confirmed her initial judgment that any creatures as vulgar as these certainly could not speak. If she did have these thoughts, then her wonderment when Bruno or Booee first responded to her signing must have been similar to our wonderment when she first began to "talk" to us.

From her first days on the island, Washoe signed to her fellow chimps. Indeed, she signed to every person within eyeshot, mostly with instructions to take her off the island as quickly as possible. With the chimps, however, she first confined her remarks to requests for portions of whatever treats they happened to be eating. She began to get responses when she signed "come hug."

Washoe's most striking conversations take place when she is ashore with the adult colony. She is approaching sexual maturity and has begun menstruating. Ashore, she enjoys harmless copulation with an immature chimp named Manny. Manny lives in a neighboring cage; consequently, whatever assignations they have must take place through a wire mesh. When Washoe is in the mood, she signs "come hug" to Manny, who, although he has no language training, quickly deciphers this message and is only too happy to accommodate. Sometimes Washoe terminates such assignations prematurely, leaving Manny helpless and frustrated on the other side of the wire. At first when she did this, Manny would throw a tantrum, but now he has begun to sign "come hug" himself.

Bruno and Booee speak to each other quite a bit, although talk of food dominates their conversation. At the moment, their conversations are mostly one-way: Booee will ask Bruno for a raisin, and Bruno will run away to gobble it down. Representative of these importunings were Booee's requests for orange juice: "Gimme food drink . . . gimme drink . . . Bruno gimme." A typical conversation for a five-year-old.

Fouts recalls witnessing one such "conversation." Booee approached Bruno, who was eating a raisin. This time Booee said, "tickle Booee," possibly as a device to get Bruno's mind off his food. Bruno replied "Booee me food," or, as Fouts tentatively translated the phrase, "don't bother me, I'm eating."

Because of their frequent misbehavior ashore, Roger often has to tell either Bruno or Booee to go and sit in a corner of whatever cage they are in at that moment. On one occasion after being sent to the corner and fidgeting for some minutes, Bruno signed "Booee come" to his better-behaved friend. On another occasion, the situation was reversed. This time Booee signed "Bruno come."

Clearly, at this point, chimpanzee conversation falls somewhere

A CHIMP-TO-CHIMP CONVERSATION:

Booee sees Bruno eating a raisin.

3

Bruno signs "food" in saying, "Booee me food," or, translated, "don't bother me, I'm eating."

Booee signs "tickle," possibly to get Bruno's mind off his food.

short of a Restoration drawing room, but these are just the first teasing glimpses of what Fouts's next generation of experiments will be about. When these first conversations took place on the chimp island, they had just begun to talk to each other. They used the language because it had become useful to them as a means of communication. Even without reinforcements, they are increasingly using Ameslan to talk to one another. In the coming series of experiments Fouts plans to use extraordinary, well-nigh diabolical, reinforcements to encourage the chimps to talk to one another, reinforcements that capitalize on the chimps' appetites and fears, and, as we shall see, should reveal something not only about chimp-to-chimp communication using a human language, but also about chimp-to-chimp ethics when the chimps have to coordinate their efforts to get some desired reward.

It might do well now to consider briefly these language-using apes in terms of the direction in which they are being coaxed. The Gardners' work with Washoe proved that a chimpanzee can communicate with a human using a human language. They showed that Washoe understood the symbolic properties of a gestural mode of communication and that her early combinations compared favorably with the types of sentences used by infants just learning to speak. Through his initial work with Bruno, Booee, Cindy, and Thelma, Fouts confirmed that Washoe was not a freak and provided some data by which to assess the impact of the chimp's personality, the learning situation, and the testing situation on a chimp's performance with Ameslan. The work with Lucy probed the ways in which a chimp used its vocabulary to classify the world around it, while Ally's tri-lingualism was used to test the chimp's ability to transfer information from one sensory mode to another, and to plumb further the chimp's understanding of the word. Beyond this, Fouts has initiated as yet unpublished investigations of word order in the multiple word combinations used by Lucy and Ally. Finally, he has collected masses of intriguing lagniappe—swearing, the invention of signs like "leash," the reapplication of signs as the chimp matures, such as Washoe's use of "come hug," and Lucy's melancholy description of her emotional state in "me cry."

These efforts with the chimps are an empirical equivalent of exploratory surgery. Through them, Fouts hopes to develop a picture of some aspects of chimp language-use in communicating with people before launching his attempt to explore language use by chimps in communication among themselves. Fouts wants to piece together a mosaic of language abilities within a chimp colony. His design, organizing the various facets of the institute's Ameslan experiments and forming the pattern of this mosaic, stems from a list of design features for language developed by linguist Charles Hockett.

Hockett's is one of several lists specifying the design features of language (Hockett himself has more than one), and the different lists propose radically varying models of what language is. As the Gardners noted, there are ways of defining language that Washoe satisfied as early as 1966 and there are ways of defining language that Washoe could never satisfy. In fact, in response to Washoe, some definitions of language have appeared that certain humans might find claustrophobic. Fouts chose Hockett's definition because it is widely cited and because its design features propose behaviors that Fouts can attempt to elicit point by point. But should his chimp community prove capable of demonstrating these seven design features, what then? Why, then, something is wrong with the way we have been looking at language.

9. One Man's Description of Language

Charles Hockett published his thoughts about the key properties of language in his book *A Course in Modern Linguistics*. Hockett has since revised this list of design features, but Fouts elected to investigate the original list. He chose it for three reasons: it is widely known, it proposed behaviors that might be investigated, and it was meant to contrast human communication with animal communication to show what one has that the other lacks. Hockett had taken the trouble to attempt to show what properties of human speech appeared in animal communication and what others didn't. Needless to say, Hockett himself believed that only human communication manifests all seven of his design features.

Hockett's rationale for looking at language in terms of a list of characteristic behaviors is that he intends to use it to explore language's phylogeny ("We should like to know how language evolved from what was not language.") and its effect on the species in which it developed. Breaking language down into a series of behaviors allows for comparability and, hence, for conjecture about the origins of particular behaviors, such as displacement.

Hockett discusses his seven properties in terms of both human communication and the particular communication of four vastly different creatures: the bee, the stickleback fish, the herring gull, and the gibbon. He chose these animals because they demonstrate the variety of communicative systems in the animal kingdom. When a bee locates a source of pollen, it returns to the hive and, by a dance, tells the others the location and amount of the cache. (Karl Von Frisch won a Nobel prize, in part, for his explanation of the bee dance.) The male and female stickleback are cued to complete their mating cycle by changes in their color and shape. The infant herring gull spurs the parent to feed it through pecking motions made in the direction of the parent's bill. And a gibbon community has a system of calls appropriate to different defensive and social needs. In each of these types of communication, Hockett suspects that at least one of his key properties is present and, in fact, that the lowly bee dance demonstrates six.

Hockett lists these seven key properties as DUALITY, PRODUCTIVITY, ARBITRARINESS, INTERCHANGEABILITY, SPECIALIZATION, DISPLACEMENT, and CULTURAL TRANSMISSION. In comparing the five different communicative systems, he charts them as can be seen in the table on page 138.

One immediately notices that, in light of our previous discussions about language, no mention is made of the workhorse characteristics reconstitution or semanticity. There is little agreement among linguists and psycholinguists on the proper terms by which to describe language. Each has his or her favorites. Actually, Hockett's properties of duality and productivity are, from a different perspective, concerned with what have here been described

TABLE IV

	BEE DANCING	STICKLEBACK COURTSHIP	HERRING GULL CARE OF OFFSPRING	GIBBON CALLS	LANGUAGE
Duality	No(?)	No	No	No	Yes
Productivity	Yes	No	No	No	Yes
Arbitrariness	Slight	—	—	Slight	Great
Interchangeability	Yes	No	No	Yes	Yes
Specialization	Yes	Some	?	Yes	Yes
Displacement	Yes	No	No	No	Yes
Cultural Transmission	No	No	No	No(?)	Yes

as reconstitution and semanticity. For instance, reconstitution describes a cognitive process; productivity, on the other hand, describes a linguistic dividend of that process—the ability to generate and understand sentences that have never been said before.

Let us examine Hockett's seven key properties of language:

DUALITY, or duality of patterning: This means that human language has both a phonological system and a grammatical system, or, to be more scientific, a cenematic structure and a pleramatic structure. The ceneme is the single phoneme which of itself is merely a building block. A plereme is the smallest meaningful unit constructed out of these cenemes, which in speech is a morpheme. The pleramatic structure assigns meaning to messages according to semantic convention. The cenematic subsystem allows for the construction of words, the pleramatic subsystem allows the construction of sentences. Instead of a separate signal for each message, human speech uses a finite number of sounds, or phonemes, which can be arranged in a vast number of ways into morphemes. This permits that vital feature called productivity. Although pleramatic structure does not presume that the words will be combined in sentences, it does imply that the different messages follow the same logic in construction. A gibbon call, for instance, is not pleramatically structured. If the sentence is more than one plereme, it is pleramatically complex, and if such a system can demonstrate pleramatic complexity, then it can also demonstrate productivity. Thus, according to Hockett, it is possible to have duality without productivity—as in, for instance, a language that consists of a vast number of one-word sentences constructed from a small number of basic signal units.

Hockett does not rule out the possibility that some other species might communicate with duality of patterning, although he says that he has not come across one. Duality recalls our previous discussion of semanticity, and perhaps now is the time to extend on that discussion introduced with regard to Lucy's word-use.

If semanticity refers to the assignment of meaning to some abstract symbol, then it is duality that permits the construction of such symbols. If an animal lacks the capacity to understand duality, then each message it sends, perforce, must have been prefabricated during the course of phylogeny. On the other hand, duality can free the animal from dealing with such prefabricated whole messages and permit it access to building blocks from which it can construct its own messages. Without a cenematic and grammatical subsystem, an animal can only utter a limited number of messages given to it by nature. With such subsystems it can say a lot more.

This is how Hockett explains duality; however, Hockett has not said the last word on the number of messages a non-dual system —such as gibbon calls—can generate, nor, indeed, is the concept of duality versus non-duality accepted without argument.

PRODUCTIVITY: Just as there can be duality without productivity in animal communication, so can there be productivity without duality, says Hockett. Productivity means that the organism is equipped to generate and understand an infinite number of messages from a finite number of meaningful units or, as Hockett puts it, that "a speaker of a language may say something that he has never said nor heard before and be understood perfectly by his audience, without either speaker or audience being in the slightest aware of the novelty." Hockett says that the mechanism that permits this is ANALOGY. Analogy, the first part of reconstitution, describes the ability to factor out similarities in utterances, which are then reconstituted in novel utterances, so that a finite number of structural relationships are used to assimilate vast and disparate pieces of information. It is the process of analogy by which the infant reconstructs the grammar of the adult.

Without pleramatic complexity, a system of communication can demonstrate productivity if new, one-word messages are coined by a type of analogy termed BLENDING. This entails the gradual construction of new signals from parts of old signals. Without duality, a system can still demonstrate productivity as in the case of bees that report on entirely novel sources of pollen. While the bee dance demonstrates productivity, says Hockett, it lacks duality because the smallest meaningful aspects "of a given dance are not composed of arrangements of meaningless but differentiative feature of the sort that would constitute cenemes." The semantic conventions that assign meaning to particular aspects of the bee's dance are built into the insect's genes, and this brings us to Hockett's third design feature.

ARBITRARINESS: If there is no readily apparent similarity between a plereme and its meaning, the plereme's meaning is arbitrary. On the other hand, if the plereme represents its meaning, it is ICONIC. Hockett uses the analogy of a map that by definition, iconically, represents the contours of some terrain; however, in most circumstances the width of the line that represents a road or a river is not drawn to scale—it is arbitrary. The road map is much like the bee dance in that the dance is arbitrary because it does not look like the direction and distance of a source of pollen, but is iconic within the terms of that relationship—the message is conveyed by locating the pollen on an axis of distance and an axis of direction rather than through the lawful construction of arbitrary units. To have duality, a system must build its message from arbitrary sub-units and not merely depict its meaning.

An arbitrary system of signals with duality of patterning permits much wider application than an iconic system in which there must be a new word for every meaning. "Human beings can talk about anything," says Hockett, "bees can only talk about nectar."

We see in duality and arbitrariness two features necessary for reification. Arbitrariness permits the construction of what Hockett refers to as "a digital system," which in turn permits the abstract reification of the environment. What we also see is that, at least in human communication, these design features are inextricably inter-connected. One cannot have duality without arbitrariness.

INTERCHANGEABILITY: This means simply that any organism equipped to send a message must be able to receive one. Communi-cative behavior is defined by Hockett as acts by one organism that trigger another. Thus, when the female stickleback's belly dis-tends, it triggers the male's mating ritual, but the roles cannot be reversed, and so the stickleback lacks interchangeability. On the other hand bees, gibbons, and humans are all equipped to send and receive the types of messages Hockett is considering. (There is also interchangeability in the herring gull alarm calls, but in his herring gull example, Hockett is concerned only with the trigger-ing of parental behavior.)

SPECIALIZATION: Communicative behavior is specialized if the behaviors it triggers are not directly related to the physical conse-quences of the message. This means that specialization for com-munication occurs when the animal does not act out all its mes-sages. For instance, a right to the jaw is not specialized, because the behavior it triggers—whether it be collapse, flight, or a return punch—is directly related to the physical consequence of the first. On the other hand, when a threat is stated, the behavior it triggers has little relationship to the physical consequences of expelling breath, and so it is clear that whatever was communicated was transmitted through a system specialized for communication and merely for the immediate accomplishment of tasks. Hockett notes that in the stickleback the males respond directly to the physical aspects of the female's message—the distension of her abdomen and the expulsion of roe—while the female reponds to a change in the male's coloration, which for her has no direct physical consequences that are related to the message. Thus, the female's communication is not specialized, while the male's is. Specialization, says Hockett, is a matter of degree, with no species so specialized for communication as man. At the time Hockett wrote this, little study had been made of dolphins and whales, which, we now suspect, are perhaps supremely specialized for communication.

DISPLACEMENT: Hockett's definition of displacement is the same as everybody else's—that a message is displaced to the extent that "the key features in its antecedents and consequences are removed from the time and place of its transmission." Little need be added to previous discussion of this feature, except to stress the interrelatedness of the demands for displacement in cognitive and communicative functions and the reification of the environment in our dually patterned and arbitrary system of signs. Hockett notes that the bee, like man, demonstrates displacement because both the antecedents and consequences of the dance are displaced from its transmission, although he implies that, to reflect true displacement, the bees ought to be able to sit back and reminisce about the past hoards of pollen.

Finally, there is CULTURAL TRANSMISSION. It is interesting to make cultural transmission a design feature of language, since language, as Roger Brown earlier suggested, is what has made cultural evolution possible. Language makes life experience cumulative; the lessons learned in a lifetime can suffuse through a culture in a generation rather than in the millennium that nature requires to sort the fit from the unfit. We now know, too, that the wonderful adaptiveness of cultural evolution burdens both man and the earth with long-term costs, which the harsher, but more reliable, mechanism of genetic evolution anticipates. However, any cost/benefit assessment of cultural evolution aside, Hockett is undeniably correct in regarding cultural transmission as a principle feature of human communication; language, in whatever parochial expression it takes, is passed to the young of a tribe as part of its cultural heritage, even though genetic predispositions make this form of learning possible.

Hockett divides cultural transmission into two principle subsystems, namely, teaching and imitation. He describes imitation as a "type of interstimulation in which the conditioning behavior of one individual stimulates *similar* behavior from another." Hockett feels *Homo sapiens* is the animal most adept at this, but the other apes are also adapted to *ape*. Hockett does not draw any distinction between meaningful and meaningless imitation.

Hockett claims that language is the only communicative system the conventions of which are transmitted culturally and not genetically; here he is wrong. A plethora of songbirds learn their song from their elders, and, as we shall see in Part Two, their example suggests possibilities for the origins of human speech.

It is to the origins of human speech that Hockett turns after presenting his seven design features of language. Indeed, the promise of developing a scenario for the emergence of language from what was not language was Hockett's justification for developing 'his list in the first place. He notes that some of these properties are interrelated and suggests this interrelatedness implies that some design features necessarily emerged before others; the predecessor of all these features, says Hockett, was specialization. Before communication might develop along the lines that led to language, there had to be some distinction between the animal's everyday behavior and its communicative behavior.

Similarly, before man parted company with his fellow apes, Hockett feels that our ancestors—as well as those of the gorilla, the chimp, the orang, and the gibbon—had developed interchangeability, displacement, and some degree of cultural transmission. Hockett credits the other apes with at least the seeds of these design features, because they are such good imitators and because imitating a behavior that is being taught out of context requires some degree of displacement.

Productivity, arbitrariness, and duality developed in human communication over the fourteen million years following man's divergence from the genetic paths of the other apes. Nor, says Hockett, has any other ape developed those properties in the interim. He believes that the emergence of productivity was probably contemporaneous with the emergence of arbitrariness; after all, arbitrariness permits the productive use of a small group of symbols. But Hockett expresses confusion about the order in which duality and productivity emerged. Either might have preceded the other, or they might have developed at the same time.

In Hockett's scenario, productivity, duality, and arbitrariness developed by way of blending from the unproductive, non-dual, and iconic system of calls used by our ape ancestors. Hockett formulated this scenario before Hewes's gestural hypothesis had begun to come into vogue. His hypothesis seems to elaborate on one formulated long ago by Edward Lee Thordike, termed *babbleluck* —that, over a period of time, man began to associate sounds with features in the external environment and so built the basis of his vocabulary. Hockett, on the other hand, argues that at some point early man produced a new call that was constructed of parts of two old ones by blending. "We can imagine," says Hockett, "these innovations usually not being understood by the hearers, but occasionally—and increasingly often—being effective, so that the habit of building such new calls in time gained ground." The blending of parts of these calls would gradually detach them from their iconic roots, rendering them increasingly arbitrary, and would lead to the development of cenemes, from the subdivided sounds, and pleremes, from their reconstructions. Hockett does not say why the first prehominid blended two calls to make some new hybrid; since he proposes to justify his list of design features in terms of the selective pressures that caused man to develop language, both his list and his hypothesis about its origin would be more convincing if he did. Hockett's argument suffers from the very property that he lists as one of language's strengths—it is arbitrary. Without a grounding in selective pressures, all one can do is appraise Hockett's presentation of his list in terms of its internal consistency at an abstract level. And, in spite of interdependencies of many of these design features, the way Hockett presents it, the list is internally consistent. We can see how an unproductive system of calls could, through blending, gradually move from iconicity to arbitrariness. We can also see how this system of calls would, as words are pieced together, change from being a closed system to a productive one. And, further, we can see the gradual development of a *dual* system of phonemes and a grammar to govern their manipulations as calls began to take their sound according to a logic that combined their constituent sounds, rather than through the environmental stresses that produced the original vocabulary.

Actually, Hockett's scenario is not altogether incompatible with that proposed earlier by Gordon Hewes, in part because of its terseness. Had Hockett been aware that there is vocal learning in other species, he might have been able to argue for his scenario in terms of the selective pressures that would promote the development of language according to his plan.

If Hockett fails to answer why language developed, he is on firmer ground when he speaks about the effect of language on our ancestors once development began. The adaptive utility of propositional communication and thought, says Hockett, gave better-equipped genetic strains a competitive edge over their close relatives. As a result of this competitive edge, the inefficient evolutionary adaptations that occurred in response to the extraordinary selective pressures necessitating language quickly succumbed. Language was nature's response to what must have been emergency conditions in man's past, and we can imagine that language itself gradually surfaced as the best (on the short term) of a number of innovations in response to those conditions. This, says Hockett, is why we see no great variation in the language abilities of the various human races, and why we find no intermediate links between man and the chimpanzee.

This recalls our earlier reference to Lieberman and Crelin's suggestion that Neanderthal vanished because he could not compete with his more articulate contemporary, Cro-Magnon. These two scientists believe that Neanderthal's supralaryngeal tract had not developed to the point where he could generate the full range of sounds available to modern man, while they believe there is evidence to suggest that Cro-Magnon was much farther along in this regard. The implication here is that Neanderthal was some intermediate step, as yet not fully equipped for language, and that he paid the penalty close relatives sometimes pay when competing for food within the same ecological niche—extinction. Hockett, in 1958, anticipated this line of reasoning. Biogeographers assert, he wrote, "two closely related species cannot live side by side in a single ecological niche. It seems that if a set of related species or strains are in competition in a single ecological niche, the one which has made the most successful adaptation in time crowds out those most similar (and genetically closest) to it, though more distantly related other species or strains may survive because they are not so directly in competition with the first. It is a race in which the winner destroys—or interbreeds with—the runner up. This is one of the mechanisms by which strains become separate species: they destroy the intermediate types and become isolated by so doing."

It is intriguing to note that our closest surviving relative is the chimpanzee, not so different an animal from what we suppose our earliest ancestors resembled. Apparently, whatever emergency split man from the other apes, the other apes survived it without the evolutionary rescue that we call human nature.

While Hockett feels that cultural transmission preceded pleramatically complex communication, he notes that one effect language had on our predecessors was to favor the enlargement of the sphere in which behaviors were transmitted culturally rather than genetically. He reiterates the truism we noted earlier: "Learning via already understood symbols may obviate the considerable dangers involved in learning via direct participation," although he says nothng about the relationship between this type of learning and its obvious pressures for the increase in displacement.

In short, Hockett says that once communication took hold, it acquired a life of its own. Through the agency of culture, learning increasingly usurped nature as the arbiter of our movements and life style, and it left man with an additional consuming drive beyond the drives of hunger and sex—a need to communicate. We need to use our specialized system of communication, even when it is not needed, to guide such needs as mating, parental care, defense, and aggression. Lack of communication, says Hockett, will blight the human spirit, and, he claims, this is not true of any other animal. Hockett is correct that people become neurotic when they cannot communicate, but when he says this is not true of other animals, Hockett is dead wrong.

Dolphins, like people, seem to communicate for the sake of communication; chimps are in constant communication with each other. And this need for reassurance goes beyond basic drives. We would expect the same to be true for the other social apes, as well as such highly social animals as elephants and wolves.

Hockett restates this proposition to read that "much human communication is itself about communication." This is certainly true for a linguist and, we might add, for people who find themselves in situations involving marriage counselors, psychiatrists, and other shamans who try to patch up breakdowns in communication, but we wonder how true this is for the average person during an average day as opposed to the average whale during his average day. How much of the eskimo's silent communication is about communication? Surely it is true that we are more obsessed

147

with communication than any other animal, but this obsession might be looked upon as a failing in human communication rather than as an added dimension.

This is one man's description of language as part of the spectrum of communicative systems. There is certainly no consensus that it is the best description; for instance, Noam Chomsky sees such principles as "analogy" failing to account for the innovative aspects of language. (On the other hand, Hockett sees flaws throughout Chomsky's system.) Nevertheless, Hockett's list has one outstanding virtue: it permits comparison of animal and human communication feature by feature. And it was with Hockett's list in hand that Fouts set gleefully to work.

10. A Language-Using Chimp Community

DESIGN FEATURES	WASHOE, LUCY, AND ALLY
duality	yes
productivity	yes
interchangeability	yes
specialization	yes
displacement	yes
cultural transmission	yes

This is Fouts's view of his pupils in terms of Hockett's list. His informal evidence that the chimp community has the abilities described by these design features stems chiefly from the chimps' use of Ameslan in communication with people, although the chimps have begun to talk to one another.

Hockett credits apes with possessing the rudiments—or, as he puts it, "seeds"—of cultural transmission, displacement, and interchangeability, in addition to a specialized communication system. This would seem to suggest that Fouts need only focus his efforts on eliciting productivity, duality, and arbitrariness. Duality and arbitrariness are properties of the language used and not what the chimp does with it. A chimp cannot use a communicative system that is arbitrary in iconic ways and still behave appropriately to the system. Similarly, human speech manifests duality, but we do not demand that speakers explain it, and we would accept that the chimp using Ameslan demonstrates duality if the chimp uses the language appropriately and if that language is characterized by duality. Although it is a gestural rather than spoken language, Ameslan does, in fact, manifest duality of patterning. Each signal is constructed of cheremes, or basic signal units, which, like phonemes, are constructed according to semantic conventions into pleremes. This, in turn, suggests that Fouts need only demonstrate that the chimps use Ameslan productively. If this were the case, then he might use the swearing by Washoe, Lucy, and Ally, their invention of words like "fruit drink" and "water bird," and their ever-proliferating multiple-word sentences as evidence that the chimps are using the language productively, and he might end his investigation right there.

Fouts, however, does not want to present his case by patching together bits and pieces of language from two communicative systems as different as the chimps' natural vocalization and Ameslan. Rather, he wants to piece together a mosaic of abilities according to Hockett's design by seeing how the chimps use Ameslan among themselves. In this fashion, he can present a chimp community and say, "Here is a chimp community that uses a human language. This is how Charles Hockett would say people use that language, and here is how the chimps use it." The thrust will be to show how deeply the chimpanzees have integrated language into their lives. Fouts hopes to encourage his chimps to use language as a tool, the way we use it, as a device that permits us to free ourselves from the tyranny of the moment and purposefully to work our will upon the world.

To this end, Fouts has designed a program that attacks these design features one by one. Duality, arbitrariness, and specialization are not included in his program. There is no need to attack duality and arbitrariness since they are properties of the medium of communication, and specialization, that most basic design feature, was adequately demonstrated by the Gardners. This leaves productivity, interchangeability, displacement, and cultural transmission. For each of these, Fouts has specified an appropriate behavior. By using Ameslan regularly to communicate among one another, the chimp colony will demonstrate interchangeability. To demonstrate cultural transmission, Fouts will encourage the chimps to learn signs from one another. For productivity, Fouts demands that the chimps create new signs, and to demonstrate displacement they will have to use Ameslan to communicate about events not in the immediate environment. Fouts has devised situations he hopes will isolate and educe each of these behaviors.

INTERCHANGEABILITY

Fouts's approach to this design feature is simply to keep his colony of Ameslan-using chimps in close contact with one another, with hidden observers to report what they say. As noted, Booee, Bruno, and Washoe do talk to one another, and we can inspect far more word games with the introduction of the linguistically hyperstimulated Lucy and Ally.

CULTURAL TRANSMISSION

When the members of this colony seem to be on speaking terms with one another, Fouts will begin to bring a series of objects to the island for which only Washoe knows the proper sign. Then Fouts will closet himself with his charges for a series of half-hour instruction sessions. During these sessions, the only object to occupy the chimps' attention will be one of the unnamed objects. Fouts will be there only as an observer/peacemaker. If Booee or Bruno, or whoever is closeted with Washoe, does not pick up the name after ten or so sessions, the object will also be introduced to their living quarters. If and when the other chimps do start using the proper sign, it will have to be through Washoe's example or counsel.

Following work done by Japanese primatologists who observed that new behavior often is introduced to a primate colony through the young, Fouts also intends to vary the teacher with each new object and investigate who does and does not learn what from whom.

And, of course, the most dramatic evidence of cultural transmission would be provided if Washoe mothers an infant and passes Ameslan along to her child. Jane Goodall has noted that chimp infants do learn the rudiments of termite-fishing-twig-fashioning by watching their mothers. Whether this learning involves instruction remains unclear.

PRODUCTIVITY

For his investigation of productivity, Fouts will employ an experimental procedure similar to that used in isolating cultural transmission. Again the chimps will be introduced to some mysterious, unnamed cynosure; only this time not even Washoe will know the proper Ameslan sign. Again there are myriad possibilities for the chimps' response to this new object; who will invent the sign? And in what order will the other chimps begin to use a particular invention, if, in fact, any of them adopt the new word? There is also the question of whether the chimps will invent a new sign at all.

Lucy invented a sign for "leash," and Washoe invented a sign for "bib." Both were signs for objects that figured prominently in the chimps' daily routines. On the other hand, instead of inventing a new sign for "radish" (which, like "watermelon," fits within a more general conceptual category for which she had a sign—"food"), Lucy combined two signs relating to what she perceived that particular radish's attributes to be and referred to it as a "cry hurt." Similarly, the chimps occasionally refer to a new object by an existing sign, and the colony may adopt this posture toward whatever cynosure Fouts presents.

In this experiment Fouts would like to not only gather data on the chimps' productive use of Ameslan, but also use data on the different ways the chimps use Ameslan to classify new objects as a means to explore their own analyses of those objects. If the chimps create a new sign for an object, there is the possibility that the sign might bear some relationship to an existing sign for an object functionally or physically similar. For instance, Lucy might have made the "string" sign (pulling the little finger of one hand between thumb and forefinger of the other) in the vicinity of her neck to refer to a leash, linking the symbolic string aspect of leash to its direct application in leash. Or she might have combined elements of "string" and "out" and thus associated the string aspect of the leash, which she does not like, with the ultimate goal of a trip outside, which she enjoys hugely. Given an adequate cross-section, how a chimp constructs a new sign will indicate something about the way the chimp analyzes and productively exploits the cenematic and pleramatic substructures of Ameslan.

If the chimps tend to combine existing signs as wholes rather than as parts in referring to the new object, it will indicate something about the chimps' analysis of an object's features. For example, the chimps are taught "listen" to refer to the ticking sound of a wristwatch, although they quickly generalize to use the sign to refer to its accepted meaning. Fouts intends to give the chimps

Washoe: "listen"

some object combining specific features that they have learned in other contexts. For instance, if he offers them a ball with a humming electric motor inside of it, he wonders whether the chimps will invent a sign for it combining features of "listen" and "ball," or call it a "listen ball" or simply a "ball" or a "listen." Or will their response be conditioned not so much by the object's prominent features as by the chimps' assessment of its interest and utility?

There is also the intriguing question about whether or not the chimps will move from one level of analysis to another as their immersion in an Ameslan environment deepens. Will they move from combining words as wholes to fabricating new signs from what they consider to be the meaningful parts of old ones? And in so doing invent a symbolic grid upon which Ameslan gestures might be built in lapidary fashion?

At the moment, Fouts does not have enough information to determine the depth to which the chimp has analyzed Ameslan. Hopefully he will be able to amass a sufficient sample so that we can begin to determine what, if any, rules the chimp employs

Washoe: "ball"

when it invents a sign and, perhaps, glimpse the workings of another intelligence.

DISPLACEMENT

The test for displacement involves showing a selected chimp some object which the chimp colony either finds particularly desirable—such as a fruit, a toy, or the key to some tempting box—and, on other occasions, objects the group finds particularly distasteful, such as a snake. At first the nominated chimp will be brought back to the colony and then allowed to lead the other chimps either toward or away from the object. (Given the elements of greed and revenge, there is no sure way of predicting that the chimp won't lead the others away from a desired object or point them toward some nemesis.) After the chimps have become accustomed to these reconnaissance patrols, the experimenters will begin restraining the chimp selected as scout once he or she has been shown the secreted object and returned to his group; however, while this chimp is restrained, the others will be released. The earlier forays will have conditioned the other chimps to expect that the temporary disappearance of their friend means that he has been shown something, and Fouts hopes, on the one hand, that the group will be motivated to find out what their colleague has seen and, on the other, that the knowledgeable chimp will be willing to tell them. Yet, in order to tell them, the chimp must be capable of communicating about events displaced in time and space from the immediate environment. To see how long a delay between stimulus and response the group can tolerate, Fouts intends to vary the amount of time between the observation of the hidden object and the moment when the chimps are released.

Because of the nature of displacement, the answer should be most interesting. In fact, I suspect that displacement explains some of the manifest differences between man and chimp.

11. Displacement and the Evolution of the Intellect

Displacement permits our sense of time. We have a sense of time different from the undisplaced creature's. Time is a dimension for us, but it would not be for the creature that could not detach itself from the ongoing flux of experience. Such a hypothetical creature would live in instant response to internal and external stimuli, the responses resulting from natural selection. We now know that such a creature does not exist, but let us consider the implications of this once common notion of animal behavior as it serves to set in focus what is meant by displacement.

We have seen displacement described from a number of different points of view. Roger Brown suggested its evolutionary importance in general terms; Ursula Bellugi and Jacob Bronowski attempted to describe four of its behavioral characteristics as they figured in the development of language; and Charles Hockett included it in his scheme of design features that characterize speech —all of which could understandably leave the reader saying, "All right, everybody has something to say about displacement, but what the hell is it?" It is a question worth exploring, because the behavioral characteristics of displacement might be used to solve or at least to clarify some well-known philosophical problems about human nature. Displacement actually goes a long way toward explaining what, in fact, are the basic differences between man and chimpanzee.

The brains of mammals, reptiles, and fishes are similar in certain gross ways. All can be characterized as having a rear-part or hindbrain, a midbrain, and at least traces of a forebrain. As one moves "up" the evolutionary scale, the command post for control over behavior seems also to move progressively forward, and with the higher mammals seems to be centered in the forebrain. In man, the forebrain is greatly enlarged. It houses the neocortex, that new brain we are so proud of, which is the gray matter within which we perform our feats of reconstitution. In man, the structures of the midbrain and hindbrain are referred to as the "old brain" or "primitive brain." The primitive brain orchestrates responses originating from our behavioral genetic heritage, the "animal" part of our nature. Its work has to do with such things as reflexes, posture, emotions, and urges toward flight or aggression.

If the traditional model of animal behavior considers the animal a prisoner to the tyranny of the moment, then what in man we called the "old brain" is his prison guard, because within this model of behavior, every stimulus the animal encounters elicits an enthusiastic response built on the accretions of the animal's genetic behavioral heritage. In Bellugi and Bronowski's words, any information given about the animal's environment is "an instruction to act." The animal is kept pinned to the here and now; it cannot step back and assess. Displacement would then seem to mean freedom from the tyranny of these emotional responses. In their list of the five steps involved in displacement, Bellugi and Bronowski noted this aspect as "the separation of affect or emotional charge from the content or instruction which a message carries."

Recall that Ally could associate an Ameslan sign with an English word. To perform that association, he had to transfer sensory information from an audio-vocal channel to a visual-haptic (tactile) channel—i.e., demonstrate cross-modal transfer. This association was believed necessary for the comprehension and generation of language, just as it was believed that chimpanzees could not make such associations—essentially because they were felt to be too emotional.

In man, one key part of the primitive brain is called the limbic system, which involves that area of the brain called the limbic region and its various interconnections with other parts of the brain. It is located between the forebrain and the hindbrain, and is interconnected with both. It is, in the words of neuro-linguist Harry Whittaker, "quite similar in man and animals." In man, the words *limbic system* refer to the major structures having to do with emotions; the central language system involves several interconnected areas in the cortex, as well as connections to the limbic system and other subcortical structures. The direct connections between different areas in the neocortex enable man to associate information from different modalities. These associations form the basis for the symbolic units of spoken language. Until evidence such as Ally's ability to transfer from the audio-visual channel to the visual-haptic channel began to appear, it was believed that other primates lacked direct connections within the neocortex and hence could not make such associations. Instead, it was thought that in other primates these different sensory channels were tied in to the limbic system. One piece of evidence seeming to support this was the chimp's lack of control over its vocal productions.

Gordon Hewes, even while lauding Washoe's accomplishments in a gestural language, felt inclined to believe that the pongids operated under severe constraints conditioning the cross-modal transfer of sense data from the audio-vocal to the visual-haptic channels. In his article "An Explicit Formulation of the Relationship Between Tool-Using, Tool-Making, and the Emergence of Language," Hewes describes the ape's audio-vocal system as basically an "alarm system" thoroughly tied to the limbic region. He wrote, "The inability of apes to acquire even a few quasi-articulate speech sounds does suggest that their cortical auditory centers are somewhat isolated from the centers where visual inputs and voluntary, precise motor outputs are integrated with comparative ease. . . . Sound signals only seem to trigger various holistic 'emotional' responses, such as alarm, attention, fear . . . followed by more or less stereotyped behavior patterns such as flight, attack, protective mothering, submission, and the like."

The reader should here bear in mind that the neurology of language is exceedingly complex; much of what is known about it is only hypothesis, and it does not lend itself to broad reductions. However, little is known about the human brain, even less is known about the brain of the chimpanzee. The notion of the limbic region is introduced at this point only because it has figured in a commonly believed explanation of why the chimp cannot talk, and because on a metaphorical level it might help to explain the importance of displacement.

We can see that if one believed that all incoming data from the perceivable world was channelled through the limbic system and responded to in terms of the animal's behavioral genetic heritage, then such an animal would be thoroughly pinned to the immediate moment. This animal would be too emotional—too caught up in living—to do much thinking. Before it could ruminate on some incoming piece of information, an urgent message from the limbic system demanding immediate action would, in effect, short-circuit that process. Similarly, if information stored in one part of a chimp's gray matter had to pass through the tumultuous, busybody world of the limbic region before it could be associated with information in another modality from another part of the neo-cortex, it is easy to see how restricted those associations would be.

The model of nature behind this conception is somewhat wooden. It views the animal as being something like an automaton, mechanically filling out a pre-programmed role that reflects the history of its species, and we know that most mammals are much more flexible than that: species evolve and animals do learn during their lifetimes, and if an animal were utterly imprisoned in some predetermined design, how would it make the associations necessary for change? This wooden notion of animal behavior has a corollary in the notion that only man is conscious. If the animal is regarded as living only in response to internal and external drives, it is easy to look at it as not being conscious.

Now it has become clear that the problem of deciding whether other animals were conscious had more to do with definitions and their attendant symbolic luggage than with evidence. As the Gardners noted in their summary of Washoe's first thirty-six months, the problem of consciousness was "solved" when researchers decided that an animal might be said to be conscious if it remembered stimuli displaced in time and space. Thus, any animal possessed of memory is, to a degree, conscious, and, furthermore, if an animal can learn from its experience, then it must have some memory. Accordingly, within this perspective, almost any animal could be said to be conscious, because almost any animal can learn. Viewed in this light, "displacement" does not seem to have any dramatic meaning, because memory only implies *access to* events displaced in time and space from the act of remembering. A model of animal nature better suited to this perspective is implied by Oskar Heinroth's remark that animals are "very emotional people with little ability to reason."

However, I think that displacement does have a valid meaning distinct from access to memories displaced in time, and that its meaning might account for some of the manifest differences in animal and human behavior, although I also believe the distinction is still one of degree. A metal at higher temperatures becomes first a liquid and then a gas, but it is still a metal. Similarly, in man, ever increasing demands for access to data displaced in time and space led to the gradual evolution of a surrogate, displaced world of the mind—a competing brain, which first began to impinge on and then to vie with the old brain's authority over behavior. We would feel like running and the mind would tell us to play it cool. Displacement originally allowed man to update and, within limits, to adapt the action memos of his brain to the realities of his environment. In man, displacement has been so exaggerated as to create a competitor to the old brain, arrogant and foolish though that competitor may be.

Just as it seems clear that an animal is not inert in the times between action memos from its brain, it is possible to imagine that an animal can be conscious but, as Heinroth's remark suggests, too caught up in events to do something about them. To use an analogy, an executive enmeshed in the day-to-day running of a company can sit back and examine the basic premises of what he is doing only at the peril of his competitive edge over the dozens of other well-qualified people chafing to get 'his job. And in an orderly ecosystem, as within an ordinary job, the individuals that fill the slots are replaceable. With an animal, any dalliance or hesitation in response to stimuli might cost it its life—a strain of gazelles with a tendency to ponder before taking flight would not last long. Given some of the immediate costs of displacement in disrupting nature's painfully prepared plan of survival, we can assume that neither the immense exaggeration of this property in man nor the ratiocination it permitted occurred as a casual accident; rather, they were necessary for our survival in ways that outweighed their initial attendant dangers. Displacement served some vital survival function, and man was gradually equipped not merely to summon past experience, but to ignore the pressing business of living—the stream of action memos—and assess an ever-increasing mass of data before taking some action.

For man, the significance of displacement is rooted in a gradual usurpation of authority over behavior by the new brain. This usurpation permits him to pull off a remarkable trick—to be, in effect, dead while living. While the world of the old brain is the history of the species, the world of the usurper, the new brain, is a surrogate world; it is a model abstracted from the mass of sense data, and its rapid construction was permitted by a series of strategic anatomical interconnections that permit the pooling and exchange of sensory data. These are the cross-modal transfers referred to in connection with Ally. Once enabled to make such exchanges of information, the neocortex could, in effect, pool sensory information and reconstitute that information in an abstract portrait of reality. Neurologists have mapped the conduits between the different areas of the new brain, and the neural spike that gradually drove from area to area to allow cortical-cortical connections confirms that the new brain's act of usurpation was a compelling necessity. In order to survive, we must assume that man had to change his ways faster than the evolutionary process of revision in the old brain permitted; in fact, we had in certain cases to overrule these instructions, and so, gradually, we became equipped to overrule them.

In our discussion of Washoe's critics, we speculated about what events might have spurred the need for displacement. In our prehistory it was suggested that selective feedback from the first serendipitous discovery of tools, such as termite-fishing twigs, eventually encouraged man "to make such tools happen" and allowed us several million years ago to reach about the level the wild chimpanzee supposedly is now. Pressures must have persisted for more elaborate productions, and it should be clear that even the propositional demands for the simplest productions in tools or hunting strategies could be beyond the reach of a primate if it did not have the time frame, the peace of mind, and the detachment to pattern whatever motions or gestures were necessary. As more elaborate tool-making and hunting strategies demanded that man more and more abstract himself from the immediate business of living, so did the logic of man's successes in controlling his movements. Also, the virtues of the objects he manipulated began to surface as distinct from the ongoing mass of sense data processed by the brain. Displaced from the immediate environment, the mind needed a surrogate with which it could work, and so we gradually abstracted the elements of an organic system of symbols and logic, which, reinforced by and reinforcing displacement, gradually increased our ability to work our will on that immediate environment. We can see that as the weapons used became more elaborate, it became more dangerous to fashion them during the act of hunting, thus reinforcing the need that construction of such tools be displaced in time and space from the act of hunting. Similarly, this system allowed us to test behaviors as prototypes, as propositions, without the prohibitive expenditure of energy and risk that would be necessary were all such prototypes tested in the world. Such were the short-term benefits of this trick of being able to be dead while living.

I describe displacement this way (actually I prefer the term *abstraction*, because it implies withdrawal from) in order to contrast it, meaningfully, with the degree of displacement described by memory. What was intended to be surrogate reality, a blackboard on which man might work out strategies for survival, came to compete with the real world for our attention. In early man, and still in primitive man, there are connections between symbols and their visceral referents; however, as civilization advances, that connection became attenuated. For rational man, it has snapped. We might still see the connection between symbol and old brain in the words of power of religion and magic. In some cultural niches, the reified world of symbols and logic has come to be regarded as the real world, while the displaced, animal world of emotions and reflexes is derogated as chaotic and savage.

It is because of this reversal of our priorities that we are so surprised by Washoe. While the Western, reified world provides us with order, it is at the expense of life. It can recreate experience, but because of its very nature, it can only do so displaced from experience itself. Its recreations are the product of taxidermy not nature. This cultural schizophrenia of the West is so far the most extreme displacement of thought and behavior from evolutionary roots, roots which, for the neurologist, are embodied in the old brain and for the psychologist in the unconscious. The ultimate displacement is suicide—it is the ultimate abstraction from the here and now, the ultimate victory of the mind. When carried to this extreme, we begin to distress the tensions involved in displacement.

Many mammals make decisions that demonstrate learning, and some are quite flexible; but we might see a difference between a displacement that permits an animal deliberations which are anchored in natural order and one in which the animal's thought processes are displaced to the extent that they almost bypass, or at least are pitted against, that natural order. Even in *Homo sapiens*, displaced thought processes can operate in harmony with, and yet still be subordinate to, the old brain. In a primitive cosmology, we see natural order limiting the hegemony of the displaced, surrogate brain. But the idea of displacement runs counter to natural harmony, and at some point along the spectrum of displacement leading from the lower mammals through the New York literati to Jonathan Swift's Laputan logicians, displaced thought processes actually begin manifestly to disrupt natural harmony.

Displacement is the time frame that made necessary the construction of man's separate reality of symbols and logic. Without displacement there can be no self-consciousness. As displacement attenuated the connection between our thought processes and the immediate natural continuum, it made necessary the development of the personality and such constructs as the ego to negotiate between the world of the forebrain and the world of the old brain. Our ancestral memory of usurping nature's authority is embodied in that mythological constant called Original Sin; and, as we usurp more of the old brain's authority and retreat further into our surrogate world, so does our unrequited need for the natural, integrated solace and meaning provided by nature surface in that malaise called alienation. We can also understand the philosophical problem of the mind/body dualism in terms of the competition between the new and old brains. In short, we can explain much of modern man's behavior and many of his problems in terms of an ever-widening gulf between the world of displacement and the world of our evolutionary behavioral heritage. Time has become malignant for man; this malignancy is the product of cultural evolution but it is permitted by the architecture of the brain. (It can be argued that time has not yet become malignant for aboriginal peoples—but, as Hockett would say, the seeds are there.)

In the discussion of Washoe's critics, I cited Gordon Hewes's speculation that perhaps the deep structure of language is the ability to program motor actions propositionally and indicated that this pointed to an explicit relationship between technology and language. Now this idea has been broadened to suggest that not only technology and language but the whole separate reality of the personality and higher mental functions ballooned in response to pressures for displacement. In studying the chimp, the most intriguing question becomes, how far has this separate reality been permitted to bloom in our closest relative? To what degree has the chimp been forced to reify its surroundings, and has the degree to which the chimp can displace itself also spurred the concomitant development of a chimp personality? It has been well established that chimps have a degree of self-consciousness. Tool-making abilities, and now language abilities are also beginning to be discovered and educed. Moreover, primate literature is filled with accounts of the captive ape's powers of concentration. All of these suggest that the chimp is capable of demonstrating some of the dividends of displacement, but they leave a teasing question about what constraints limit the chimp's time frame. Fouts's attempts to explore some behavioral aspects of displacement will be a first step toward establishing how far along the road the chimp is. However, given the scope of behaviors affected by displacement, it will be only a very small step.

12. Future Plans

While at the moment there is little cross-fertilization between the institute's Ameslan experiments and its other research projects, ultimately Lemmon and Fouts hope explanations of Ameslan will dovetail with the study of social development. Lemmon's field is maternal behavior, and he anxiously awaits the birth of an infant from an Ameslan-using mother (hopefully Washoe) to begin collecting data on how Ameslan will effect mother-infant relationships. The most important question, of course, is whether or not the mother will actively teach her infant to sign.

The acquisition of Ameslan allows for direct study of the cognitive functions in the chimpanzee that have hitherto only been indirectly accessible. When Fouts manages to get chimpanzees talking regularly among themselves using Ameslan, Lemmon hopes to free a colony of Ameslan-speaking chimps in a fifty-acre enclosed area together with a herd of sheep in order to encourage and observe cooperative predation. Eventually, Lemmon would like subtly to foist a primitive economic system on semi-autonomous, language-using chimps and, in so doing, perhaps retrace some of the steps that might have occurred in human evolution.

I spoke to Lemmon about these plans. He described for me some of the ways this might be achieved using, for instance, electronic devices that required signing behavior before the chimps might have access to food or other treats. He describes this project as no more than a gleam in his eye at the moment, and, indeed, it is difficult to judge how realistic a gleam it is. Our roots are in a world where chimps do not use language and we are ill-equipped to judge future research in a world where chimps do.

It is difficult to assimilate events in the exploration of the language abilities of chimpanzees, because, to assimilate them, we need a radically different model of animal and human behavior. It is not like envisioning putting a man on Mars, which requires the imagining of a future technology. Rather, one has to go back into one's mind and erase all the notions about the animal mind that have occurred in the rational West—that, by using reason, man can usurp nature's authority over his actions while animal behavior is inextricably imprisoned in nature's design. The problem is that these notions are central to a world view by which Western man explains reality, and in erasing these notions, we are destroying a perspective from which to judge the language abilities of the chimpanzee. The existing Ameslan projects have been soberly conceived, executed, and assessed; and yet they are absurd, given the traditional assumption that only man has language. These experiments are anchored in an empirical method that gives us a framework within which to judge the chimp's behavior; however, as we shall see, the empirical method itself reflects certain assumptions about animal and human behavior.

The problem is aggravated in discussing future research; any such discussion presumes that the observer has some chart to guide his judgment about the probabilities of some future project. In this case, we have just been told that the original research upon which we have to base our judgment has also proved invalid the chart which was to be our guide. I found myself in this puzzling situation when Lemmon and I discussed such projects as using the chimpanzee to retrace some of the steps that might have occurred in human evolution. It's enough to dissolve one's sense of reality.

13. Sarah

Before moving on to a discussion of the cultural climate that produced the Ameslan-speaking chimpanzee, we should mention a chimp named Sarah who speaks a language entirely different from Ameslan. She is a little older than Washoe and has spent the better part of her life in Santa Barbara, California, where she has studied language under Dr. David Premack. I began reading about her as I drove in a Volkswagen camper from Oklahoma to Reno, Nevada, after my first meeting with Fouts and his pupils. During the days, I would slowly plough through hot plains or struggle toward cooler elevations, and as I drove I would sift through my recollections of the articles I had read the night before about Sarah. Her world is entirely different from Washoe's.

THE CHIMPANZEE IN THE TEMPLE OF LANGUAGE

While Washoe's use of Ameslan seemed to display the essence of the communicative act, I had difficulty fitting Sarah's performance into my image of language, a difficulty that perhaps resulted from an obstinate resurfacing of the same flawed world view which, over decades, allowed scientists to observe the chimpanzee demonstrating abilities central to the acquisition of language and still to maintain that the ability was unique to man. Better than Washoe, Sarah demonstrates how closely language abilities are tied to those abilities that have given the chimp its reputation as a tool-maker, tool-user, and problem solver.

Premack writes bluntly about Sarah and attacks any illusions we may entertain about the special nature of language. At one point he compares its acquisition to the same process by which a trained pigeon learns to peck a particular key. His unsentimental appraisal seems all the more ruthless, because his success with Sarah seems, at least partially, to justify his assumptions.

In educating Sarah, Premack differed from the Gardners on almost all counts. While they chose a gestural medium of communication in their experiment, Premack opted to use a graphic medium. Sarah and her tutors communicate by writing messages to one another. The Gardners used an existing sign language, because it facilitated their comparison of Washoe and children, and because they felt the problems of inventing a synthetic language were formidably dissuasive; Dr. Premack invented a synthetic language of tokens. Rather than attempting to determine whether the chimp has language, the Gardners felt a comparison of child and chimpanzee in language acquisition would be a more meaningful study; Dr. Premack argued for precisely the opposite postion. As a result of these differences, Washoe's performance answers questions that might be raised in denigration of Sarah, and Sarah does the same for Washoe.

For instance while Dr. Premack's language, being written, lends itself more easily to testing of syntax than does sign language, it is not a language easily integrated into the chimp's life. As one comparative psychologist observed, "Sarah obviously cannot use her plastic forms in a spontaneous manner or in novel situations unless she carries them with her in a large bag on her back in much the same fashion as the Laputa scholars of *Gulliver's Travels*." Washoe's use of sign language is characterized by just such spontaneity, which, in turn, makes it all the more difficult to explore her syntax methodically.

Sarah's language consists of arbitrarily shaped and colored plastic tokens. The language is tailored to suit the exploration of what Premack calls the EXEMPLARS of language—"The things an organism must do in order to give evidence of having language." Premack, in keeping with the fashion, has formulated his own list of design features for language. He describes his exemplars as merely a list of topics. They are: words, sentences, the interrogative, the conditional, the meta-linguistic use of language to teach language, and dimensional concepts like color, shape, and size. Premack makes no claim that his list is exhaustive or that all the exemplars are "of the same logical order." Some, says Premack, open out into classical themes like "displacement," and others like "sentences" are so broad that Premack confined himself to selected aspects of the topic. Still, Premack's list of exemplars has required Sarah to do something like reading and writing. Indeed, the selected aspects of the topic "sentences" to which Premack confined himself turn out to be word order and hierarchical organization—the aspects of human speech that Bellugi and Bronowski described through "reconstitution"—that "evolutionary hallmark of the human mind." Although this was a pilot project, and although Sarah was almost five when her training began, she showed herself capable of demonstrating each of Premack's exemplars. Her performance makes Fouts's project seem all the more feasible, because in demonstrating Premack's exemplars, Sarah also fulfilled several of Hockett's seven properties.

Like Ameslan, Premack's medium has duality—a grammar and

the equivalent of phonemes. The tokens satisfy the criterion of arbitrariness because Premack has purposefully made them arbitrary. The fact that token messages educe appropriate behavior from Sarah indicates that the language has specialization. The relative disadvantages of Premack's token language begin to surface when one applies criteria like interchangeability and cultural transmission to Sarah's use of the medium. Recall that interchangeability means the organism is equipped both to send and receive messages. The token language however, seems to be used in two distinctly different ways by Sarah and her mentors.

Dr. Premack's reports leave the impression that what is a medium of communication for her mentors is, from her point of view, a series of multiple-choice problems. Sarah does both send and receive messages, but I was troubled whether her use of the medium indicated interchangeability in the sense that Booee and Bruno demonstrate when they use Ameslan to communicate with one another. Because she was raised apart from other chimps, Sarah, of course, could not demonstrate cultural transmission.

Premack and Sarah communicate with each other by writing messages on a magnetic board. The plastic tokens have a metalized backing, and the messages are written top-to-bottom, Chinese fashion. At first Premack taught Sarah words by manipulating her desires for treats; she would have to write "give Sarah apple," using the proper tokens in order to get an apple. Then Premack taught her the token "name of." From this point he taught her new words merely by placing "name of" between a token and its object.

To test whether Sarah understood the symbolic nature of the tokens, Premack had Sarah, on different occasions, describe an object and the token for that object. Premack arbitrarily selected the shapes and colors for each token; "apple," for instance, is a small blue triangle. Then Sarah was asked to describe what was represented by the token; she named characteristics such as roundness and redness, which she had earlier ascribed to the apple, and which are not characteristics of the token itself. This association indicates that Sarah, too, is capable of a degree of "displacement."

Premack also used tokens meaning "color of" and "size of" to teach Sarah characteristics of objects signified by various tokens. In this case, not only was Sarah demonstrating a capacity of displacement, because the objects discussed were only symbolically present, but, he claims, she was also demonstrating that she could use concepts like "color of" and "size of" in a productive way. Productivity is the capacity to generate new and different sentences from a basic vocabulary. Premack feels that Sarah's ability to recognize and state that a large person and a large rock are similar in largeness, or that a green leaf and a green liquid are similar in greenness, indicates that she can productively apply these concepts.

According to conventional wisdom concerning animal nature, when confronted with a green leaf and a green liquid, Sarah should not be able to see that green applies to both, because to do so requires that she look past surface phenomena to the building blocks—greenness—that make up this particular message. To see her environment in terms of building blocks and to use those building blocks in new combinations, Sarah, like Lucy and Washoe, had to summon the ability that Bellugi and Bronowski call "reconstitution."

Premack taught Sarah the interrogative by exploiting her ability to classify objects, in this case according to the concepts "same" or "different." Eventually Sarah was taught to remove the token representing a question mark when it occurred in a phrase and replace it with the missing element (see figure 2).

Sarah learned to apply the concepts "same" and "different" to linguistic constructions. For instance, when asked to relate the sentences "apple is red? Red color of apple," she decided that the sentences were "same"; however, when asked to relate "apple is

Figure 2. Sarah learned the interrogative by replacing the token that meant "question mark" with the token for either "same" or "different." From Ann James Premack and David Premack, "Teaching Language to an Ape." Copyright © 1972 by Scientific American, Inc. All rights reserved.

red? Apple is round," she judged them "different." Occasionally Sarah would answer questions about the relationship of two objects by using the two words "no-same" rather than the one word "different."

Premack again resorted to exploiting Sarah's particular tastes in order to teach her the conditional—the "if . . . then" type of sentence. At first she was taught that if she made one choice she would receive something she coveted, but if she made another she would not. For instance, Premack would give her a choice between an apple and a banana, and if she chose the apple she would be given a prized piece of chocolate. Premack used these relations to teach her the symbol for the conditional (see figure 3). Presented with the series of sentences "Sarah take apple? Mary give chocolate Sarah," she had to substitute the symbol for the conditional in order to get the chocolate. Then she was presented with a series of such "if then" pairs of sentences with the choices mixed up so that sometimes if she took the banana she would get the chocolate and other times she had to choose the apple to get the fruit. After a series of frustrating failures, Sarah learned to read both sentences carefully. Eventually she could correctly interpret such pairs of sentences as "Mary take red if-then Sarah take apple" (the if-then conditional is represented by a single token in Premack's language) and "Mary take green if-then Sarah take apple," in which she had to watch Mary's choice; and sentences such as "red is on green if-then Sarah take apple" and "green is on red if-then Sarah take banana," in which she had to observe correctly the relative positions of two colored cards.

In contrast to the Gardners' experience with Washoe, Premack had an easy time teaching Sarah the concept "no." Again, he would first pose a question such as "What is the relationship of red to apple" or "What is the relationship of red to banana," and Sarah had to remove the question mark and replace it with "color of" or the two tokens "no color of" (see figure 4).

Finally, Premack notes that Sarah has been able to master com-

177

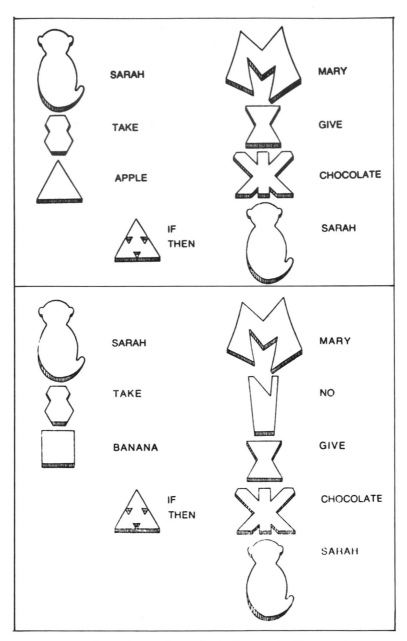

Figure 3.   To learn the conditional—the "if . . . then" type of sentence —represented by a single token, Sarah had to choose carefully in order to get a reward.
From Ann James Premack and David Premack, "Teaching Language to an Ape." Copyright © 1972 by Scientific American, Inc. All rights reserved.

pound sentence structures. First she was taught two sentences: "Sarah insert apple pail" and "Sarah insert banana dish." Ultimately Premack deleted the repetitions of the words "Sarah" and "insert" to yield the sentence "Sarah insert apple pail banana dish." To read this sentence properly, Premack believes that Sarah had to understand the hierarchical nature of sentences, that the word "insert" "is at a higher level of organization and refers to both 'apple' and 'banana' "—something she would never be able to do if, as Bellugi and Bronowski assert, the chimpanzee were only able to link words in strings. Were a child to perform similarly, says Premack, "we would not hesitate to say that he recognizes the various levels of sentence organization; that the subject dominates the predicate and the verb in the predicate dominates the objects."

In a summary of Sarah's performance, Premack cites Piaget's dictum that teaching language to an animal consists largely of mapping that animal's already existing knowledge. Thus, Premack held little hope that he would be able to teach Sarah sentences that did not map her pre-language experiences. He doubted, for instance, that Sarah could learn the conditional if she did not already understand the relationships that comprise it. The same is true of "same-different," the dimensional concepts, the interrogative, the negative, and the compound sentence. Accordingly, Premack tested Sarah's knowledge of these concepts using non-linguistic devices before he attempted to map these relationships in his token language. Sarah was about five when her training began, and in eighteen months she achieved the level of competence of a child of about two to two-and-a-half years old, although, Premack notes, in her knowledge of the conditional she was ahead of a child of that age. As of now, Premack has no idea what the ceiling of the chimp's abilities will be.

Roger Brown reviewed Sarah's performance as well as Washoe's. He noted that if Premack's claims for Sarah's mastery of such forms as the compound sentence and the conditional were valid, then Sarah had demonstrated abilities far beyond Washoe or anything the child does in Level I. However, Brown was not so sure that Premack's data on Sarah meant what Premack felt that it meant.

Premack is a behaviorist. He feels that the most obvious limitation to teaching a chimp language is man's ingenuity in breaking complex actions down into their behavioral constituents and then creating the appropriate training program to inculcate the action, piece by piece, into the animal. Brown is not convinced that this is enough. For instance, he notes that B. F. Skinner, in a famous experiment, managed to teach two pigeons to play Ping-Pong. However, while what the pigeons did looked like Ping-Pong, it really was nothing like Ping-Pong. The pigeons, of course, did not keep score, they did not try to mislead one another; in short, they did none of the things that distinguish Ping-Pong as a game rather than an arbitrary series of movements. Similarly, says Brown, Sarah's mastery of the compound sentence was a carefully contrived feat and not the particular application of a general gram-

Figure 4. Sarah learned the negative concept by replacing the interrogative token with either the tokens "color of" or "no color of."
From Ann James Premack and David Premack, "Teaching Language to an Ape." Copyright © 1972 by Scientific American, Inc. All rights reserved.

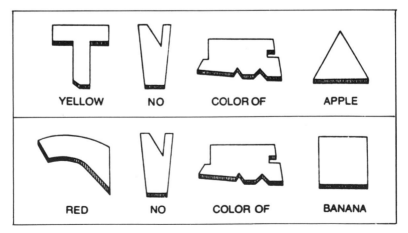

matical structure. In *A First Language*, Brown writes, "Processing a sentence which comes to you as simply one from among infinite possibilities of a language seems to be a very different matter from processing that sentence when it arrives as the crowning problem in a pyramid of training which has made one familiar with most of the components involved and put them in a state of readiness." Brown believes that Sarah operates under critical limitations concerning the scope of her application of the grammatical forms she has been taught. Her feats, says Brown, are not communication but "a set of carefully programmed language games." She does not do anything except when asked, she performs with the same steady 75 to 80 per cent accuracy regardless of the complexity of the behavior involved, and she is only confronted with one type of language problem at a time. On the other hand, even in the most casual conversation people, and the Ameslan-using chimps, have to deal with a confusing assortment of grammatical structures. Finally, Brown is not convinced that Sarah is not cued to the correct response by the experimenters. While Premack has taken pains to prevent cueing in testing, Brown wonders whether her original learning of the proper response to questions might have involved non-linguistic cueing, and that increasing familiarity with the basic problems with which she was confronted permitted her gradually to commit to memory a vocabulary of correct responses out of the desire for rewards.

Premack methodically attempted to anticipate these and other criticisms that might be leveled against Sarah: whether the questions she answered were really questions, whether Sarah really understood the compound nature of the sentence, or whether her correct interpretation of the sentence "Sarah place apple pail banana dish" was based on a strategy that involved some less sophisticated ability; in other words, whether Sarah was not indicating language ability, but was in fact performing tricks like a trained pigeon in order to get rewards. For instance, he posed the possibility that, in correctly reading the compound sentence,

Sarah was following some rule which said, "Apply the container word to the fruit word immediately above it." To test this potential criticism, Premack has invented a compound sentence that would confound this rule. He also notes that any alternative strategies Sarah might use could well involve rules as sophisticated as those which could generate hierarchical sentence structure.

However, apart from a scientist's concern for controlling variables in his experiments, Premack really is not interested whether people think Sarah is performing a trick or demonstrating language. Sarah's capacity to symbolize was unquestionably demonstrated by her feature analysis of the word for apple, a small blue triangle, as representing a red, round, stemmed object; yet, Premack does not feel that there is any magic to this process of symbolization. He describes the mind as a device for internal representation and asserts that because the mind is this kind of device, every response to a stimulus is a potential word. "The process by which a response becomes a word," says Premack, "is no different than the one by which a pigeon learns to peck a key when it is lighted," and concludes that the procedures that will train a pigeon to do this will also produce words. Thus, instead of attempting to exonerate Sarah from the charge that she is merely performing tricks, Premack asserts that there is no difference between learning to perform a trick and learning a language!

Premack admits that both the medium and the methods he used rendered Sarah's language somewhat different from normal speech. Sarah could study the sentences once they were written on the metalized board, something impossible in normal language because of the evanescent nature of the signals. Moreover, Premack notes that "the difficulty of any task can be graded by controlling the number of alternative words available to the subject at any moment in time." Unlike Washoe, who must search through her entire vocabulary when formulating her statements, Sarah, at her leisure, can select *le mot juste* from the alternatives her trainers place in front of her. Premack's use of the word "task" is also telling, because it stresses the difference between Sarah's relationship to her token language and Washoe's relationship to Ameslan. From Sarah's point of view, language might consist of a series of discontinuous feats of deduction she performs for her trainers in order to get treats. As mentioned earlier, it is difficult to imagine Sarah reaching for tokens in order to engage in the idle chatter of the Ameslan-using chimps in Oklahoma. It is also difficult to imagine Sarah spontaneously resorting to the token language to express her emotions the way Washoe and Lucy have done with Ameslan. In this respect, the token language is closer to matching tests and other tasks researchers use to test pure intelligence than to language as it is subjectively experienced. Premack eschews all interest in the question of the subjective meaning the animal attaches to its communicative acts, but it is here that the ambiguity of whether or not the animal understands what it is doing becomes most teasing.

I once read an interview with Elisabeth Mann Borghese, wife of the Italian philosopher and daughter of Thomas Mann, in which she discussed her attempts to communicate with dogs and chimpanzees. She taught her dog Arlecchino, a setter, to take dictation at a specially constructed typewriter. He would press the keys of this typewriter with his nose. His vocabulary was sixty words and he worked with seventeen letters. Although in most cases the dog only took dictation, Mrs. Borghese reported that he did make up a few things on his own. Once when she asked the dog where he wanted to go, Arlecchino, who loved to ride, typed "car." On another occasion, he didn't feel like typing and resisted all entreaties to get him to take dictation. After yawning and stretching out for a while, Mrs. Borghese recounted that the dog lifted his nose and, on his own, typed "a bad bad dog."

I could not help wishing that Premack would report one such incident to indicate that Sarah had personalized her token medium of communication as Washoe and Lucy had also done with Ameslan.

THE CHIMPANZEE IN THE TEMPLE OF LANGUAGE

The difference between Sarah and Washoe reminded me of an ongoing debate among linguists. On the one side is Noam Chomsky, who revolutionized the study of syntax with his theories of deep structure and transformational grammar. However, while deepening our understanding of syntax, Chomsky has been accused of exaggerating its structural aspects so greatly that he has lost sight of the primary purpose of language, which is communication. Clearly, if one supports Chomsky's view, then Sarah's performance provides persuasive evidence of the chimp's capacity for learning language. But if, on the other hand, one chooses to emphasize the communicative function of language (as some of Chomsky's own students have done), then Sarah's performance seems deficient compared to Washoe's.

Still, the syntactic aspects of language cannot be ignored. Besides Premack's experiment with Sarah, a famed primatologist at the Yerkes Regional Primate Center in Georgia recently began another experiment to probe the chimp's syntactic abilities. Duane Rumbaugh has taught a young female chimp named Lana to communicate by writing "sentences" on a typewriter hooked into a computer. As in the case of Sarah, instead of letters, symbols stand for certain objects, actions, and attributes (the language is called Yerkish), and Lana has already learned to write interrogative and declarative sentences in proper word order. Eventually it may be Lana who will answer Roger Brown's questions about what level of sentence complexity the chimp might generate and comprehend.

Lana's typewriter permits a spontaneity that is absent in Premack's token language. Like his use of the word "task," the mechanical aspect of Sarah's language reflects Premack's cold view of behavior in general. The brittleness of his invented token language and the stringent analytical purity of his communicative tasks—the qualities that so firmly establish the chimp's abilities in the various areas essential to language—tend to detract from the drama and immediacy of his chimp's achievements. Premack does not feel that there is any drama to what the chimp is doing, but I feel that he is wrong. For, were there not drama in the idea of the chimp's having access to language, it would mean that we never previously attached any importance to language's uniqueness to man. This is not true. We have an immense investment in the idea that man is an animal wholly alienated from the rest of nature: we have bet the world in this idea.

14. Conclusion to Part One

Why does anyone care whether or not Washoe has language? Psychologist Roger Brown asks this question at the beginning of his critical comparison of child and chimp. Brown feels that we want the chimp to learn language for perhaps the same reason we care about space travel. "It is lonely being the only language-using species in the universe. We want a chimp to talk so that we can say: 'Hello, out there. What's it like, being a chimpanzee?'" Brown's flippant answer is a near paraphrase of a remark by Carl Jung. Jung once wrote about the necessity of finding another creature with whom man can converse if he is ever to find out what it is to be human.

In *The Undiscovered Self*, Jung wrote that man remains an

enigma to himself because he lacks the means of comparison necessary for self-knowledge. "He knows how to distinguish himself from other animals in point of anatomy and physiology," wrote Jung, "but as a conscious, reflecting being, gifted with speech, he lacks all criteria for self-judgment. He is on this planet a unique phenomenon which he cannot compare with anything else. The possibility of comparison and hence of self-knowledge would arise only if he could establish relations with quasi-human mammals inhabiting other stars."

Perhaps, then, the thrill of speaking to Washoe arises from the intimation that here is a "quasi-human mammal" with whom we might establish relations and come to understand better what it is to be human. But why have we, up to now, ignored or downgraded any evidence of "human" behavior in other animals? If there is a thrill in the idea of speaking with another creature, there is also a threat, and although he considers himself above the fray, Roger Brown recognizes that threat. Before expressing his desire to ask "What's it like, being a chimpanzee," Brown wrote, "Once again, and for the third time this century, psychology has a home-raised chimpanzee who *threatens* to learn language." There's the rub. If we had wanted to talk to a chimp, we could have all along —the techniques for teaching a chimp to talk are really uncomplicated. All that is needed is patience, an acquaintance with sign languages, and the desire to speak to the chimp. But we really did not want to talk to a chimp, and, although this might sound strange, perhaps we really have not wanted to find out what it is to be human. Perhaps, too, we still do not want to think of ourselves as being animals ourselves, even though alternative explanations are becoming increasingly unconvincing.

Washoe and her chimpanzee colleagues are now forcing us to face that link which we have been successfully avoiding or obfuscating since we overturned Josephus's account of the meaning of the myth of the Fall. In the confrontation between Washoe and her critics we might see the interface of this confrontation be-

187

tween Western thought and ape. Washoe poses the greatest threat to the integrity of the Western vision of reality since Darwin. Western thought has been giving ground, adjusting to the existence of the apes since they were first discovered; however, in admitting physical similarities with the primates, we have been commensurately refining the notion of the uniqueness of human behavior to preserve the traditional Western notion that an unbreachable abyss separates animal and man. The behavior used to maintain this distinction has been language.

Part Two
Rehabilitating the
Reputation of
the Animal Mind

15. The Nature of Scientific Change

This book began with Josephus's description of a developing world view in which possession of the *word* gave man the moral authority to do with the beasts as he pleased. I noted that this world view was woven in an arid region where man's biological alienation from the animal world would dramatically reinforce the growth of a self-image in which man would come to view himself as intrinsically superior to the rest of nature. To the jungle peoples living in proximity to our primate relatives, man's biological isolation was less obvious, and the world view of the jungle peoples had to account for their neighbors who seemed to be part man, part animal.

Take for instance the Oubi, a West African tribe living in what is now called the Ivory Coast and Liberia. For centuries they have lived side by side with forest chimp bands. According to Oubi mythology, in the beginning, when God created men, he told the Oubi's ancestors, who included the chimps' ancestors, that it was the lot of man to work. The chimps, according to myth, were the smart ones—they refused to work. God punished them by making them ugly. *Gue*, the Oubi word for chimp, means "ugly man." As compensation for their punishment, the chimps were given music (possibly derivative from tribesmen hearing chimps drumming on trees). They are felt by the Oubi to be religiously superior, and killing a chimp is a taboo in Oubi culture.

The Oubi recognized the behavioral and ancestral communality of man and chimp long before Darwin shocked Europe with his first tentative suggestions that such a connection might exist. The Oubi do draw a distinction between chimp and human communication although they attach no moral prerogative to that distinction as we do. The Oubi are animists. French psychologist Mirelle Bertrand, who told me about the Oubi's relationship with the chimp, spent some time with them. In an animistic society such as theirs, the foreigner, like Dr. Bertrand, has to be especially careful because he or she is likely to be blamed for any misfortunes, such as a leopard attack, that might result from the foreigner's transfiguration or witchcraft.

We would call the Oubi primitive, although they have some agriculture; and, if we retreat even farther into the jungles of Africa, Malaysia, South America, or New Guinea, we find hunting and gathering tribes—and even some tribes who do not hunt, but only gather—and here the assumed importance of human, as opposed to animal, language begins to fade into insignificance.

When Western man discovered his ape relatives, he had to account for them just as had the Oubi. Some explorer-scientists endorsed the spirit of the Oubi viewpoint and accepted them as evidence of our communality with nature, but for the most part, the thrust of our involvement with the apes has been to attempt to use them to verify ancient Western distinctions between human and animal—such as the Platonic distinction between rational soul and animal soul. To this end, a major investigative effort in the behavioral sciences has been to find some critical faculty present in man that the apes lacked. That faculty, it was decided, was language. Then language was further broken down by men like Charles Hockett in hopes of isolating its quintessentially "human" characteristic. The traditional distinction between language and animal communication has admirably supported the Platonic distinction between rational soul and animal soul, which, in turn, has preserved the integrity of a mythology created by people who did not know about apes.

However, in the history of our scientific dealings with the apes, we might see other processes at work aside from the desire to vindicate these fundamental Western premises supporting the uniqueness of the human intellect. We might also see a gradual process of adjustment, as an intellectual tradition ill-equipped to deal with the apes sought in some way to assimilate them within the Western framework or adjust the Western framework to their realities. From the earliest contact with apes, there have been Westerners who have seen that, in spirit, the Oubi view of the chimp had more truth than a tradition which credited no kinship between man and other animals. And so, just as the behavioral sciences produced people out to dispute any behavioral interpretation of evolution, science produced people like the Gardners, who were convinced that there was some overlap of animal and human behavior, and who were willing to truly test the Western assumption that there was none.

We were never entirely comfortable thinking of ourselves as intrinsically different from the animals, although we willingly plundered the earth as our right due to our intrinsic superiority. It became increasingly difficult to believe that a creature who behaves in much the same way man does is the most glorious creation in the universe.

Just as in Western philosophy there is a continuum of argument about the uniqueness of language, so in Western mythology and imaginative literature, there is a continuum of figures who could talk to the animals, figures like Melampus of Greek mythology or Kipling's Mowgli, the Jungle Boy. In the preliterate and illiterate West, such figures are expressive of some yearning to bridge our alienation from the natural world, while in the more sophisticated literate societies such myths are a staple in children's reading and serve to keep the young happy until they mature and learn that it is more profitable to look at nature as raw material for exploitation than to look at it as something with which to communicate. Still, it has been a Western dream to talk to the animals, a dream that first began to filter to the wakeful scientific world with Darwin.

Even the adults in the most hard-boiled materialistic society retain a yearning to talk with some other creature: Roger Brown's commenting that "it's lonely being the only language-using primate in the universe" and Carl Jung's asserting that until we find some intelligent being with whom we can communicate and compare our intellect we will not really know what it is to be human. The price of our self-imposed isolation from nature is our identity, a feeling of place in the universe. Long having convinced ourselves that there is nothing non-human on this planet with whom we can communicate, we are financing extravagant explorations of the heavens in hopes of finding some other intelligent life in the universe. Ironically, the belief that we cannot communicate with other animals and the attendant belief that nature is only a collection of various resources intended for man's exploitation have permitted the development of technology and the amassing of sufficient wealth so that we can seriously attempt to scan the heavens for intelligent life. Our desire to undertake this search is predicated on the assumption that there is no other intelligence here on earth.

In an essay on the origins of pollution, historian Arnold Toynbee argues that monotheism freed Western man from the obligation to worship nature. An animist like the Oubi cannot abuse nature essentially because he is ruled by it. One cannot abuse what one worships. On the other hand, Western man has been taking "unlimited liberties with nature because we have been thinking of her in monotheistic terms, as unsacrosanct 'raw material.' " Carrying this line of thought a little further, it becomes evident that the monotheism Toynbee speaks of is, in turn, a projection of man's feelings of isolation from the rest of nature. This isolation is itself a byproduct of displacement—a function of our Western confusion between the surrogate world of the mind and the phenomenal world in which we live.

Would it have been possible for the Oubi to construct such a monotheistic tradition confronted as they were by proof that man is not so biologically isolated as the Semitic tribes assumed? Probably not. Indeed, Toynbee concludes by suggesting that if he is to save himself from his own pollution, Western man needs to abandon his claims to behavioral uniqueness and, in effect, to endorse the primitive point of view: "Man needs to reintegrate himself into the nature of which he is, in truth, an integral part. . . ."

This reintegration of Western man and nature is necessary in order to understand Washoe as well. For the reasons detailed above, Washoe is anomalous to the traditional Western view of nature. In order to find a world view in which she makes sense, one has to return to the spirit of the prescientific world of the aboriginal peoples. If one views the world as populated by Jung's longed for "conscious, reflecting beings gifted with speech," Washoe comes as no surprise.

Since Western man discovered his ape relatives, there has been an on-going struggle to explain them without undermining the Western world view and our special privileges in nature. It was incumbent upon us to offer a better explanation than the scorned savages', who saw the ape as part of a continuum linking man and the animals. We gave ground slowly, first conceding a common ancestor, but asserting that the development of language and the human intellect had obliterated any behavioral communality with the other apes. But, the reality of the ape has proved sturdier than any of the explanations offered to dismiss him, and as the demonstrable picture of our behavioral kinship with the ape grows, our traditional Western view of things seems to diminish.

The discoveries that have undermined the Western distinctions between man and animal have been made by scientists prosecuting their investigations in a thoroughly Western way. Our confrontation with the apodictic truth that we are in fact an integral part of nature has caused the maturing of a new world view within the old, a world view that might properly be called Darwinian, which is in accord with the realities of the ape. It proposes a scientific view of nature that is in accord with a prescientific world. There is no path between the Platonic and Darwinian worlds; they are profoundly different. In one, language is at the center of human nature; in the other, language is a chimera. In one, man can talk to animals, and in the other he drives his fellow creatures to extinction precisely because he cannot communicate with them. To travel from one world to the other requires a gestalt shift; presto, and the human content in animal communication and the animal content in human communication rise from obscurity into bas-relief. Until that switch is made, Washoe will remain profoundly disquieting for the Platonic world.

Fouts believes that in his grandchildren's lifetime chimps will be accepted as second-class humans. Should Washoe be accepted, we will be erasing a line we originally drew. However, it is probable that before we get around to rehabilitating the aboriginal view of our ape relatives, both ape and aborigine will be extinct, victims of the developmental combine born of our present flawed notions of animal and human nature, a combine whose lust for resources originally brought us back into the jungle. It would be unutterably sad to let any of these animals disappear. After so long, we have a lot to talk about. Perhaps they are the first and last creatures who can tell us who we really are.

Contrary to David Premack, then, I find the idea of a chimp with whom man can converse heavily freighted with drama. The second part of this book will deal with some of the contentions made in this brief summary. Specifically, I will attempt to show how Washoe fits within the Darwinian scientific revolution, what changes in the behavioral sciences preceded her first words, and what changes in science and in the larger world Washoe herself signifies.

By being scientific, the behavioral sciences produced an experiment which told them that their premises were false—that the world in which the behavioral sciences had been operating was not the real world. The behavioral sciences seem to be hurtling toward an insoluble ethical dilemma. In the process of discovering the real world, they are discovering that perhaps they should not have a license to operate in that world. Washoe is the emblem of that dilemma. If she can talk, what right have we to treat her like a dumb beast? Washoe was, in a sense, the product of changes in the behavioral sciences; we will see how, in gradually discovering the truths of the Darwinian universe, the behavioral sciences have evolved toward a nature of investigation, in fact toward a whole new science that will accord with those truths and that will resolve the ethical dilemma into which they were thrown.

Beyond the ethical dilemmas that seem to be emerging out of science's nature, Part Two will also explore how different notions of human and animal behavior condition the nature, the equipment, and the interpretation of the study of human and animal communication. Finally, I will attempt to unite the forces at work in producing Washoe as they signal the coming of profound changes in Western man's image of himself, changes that suffuse not just the behavioral sciences, but the continuum of science and culture.

Reno is an appropriate place to hold a conference on animal behavior. Built on gold and offering escape through gambling or divorce, the town's growth attests to the popularity of its offerings. To the arriving biologists, zoologists, neurologists, psychologists, ethologists, and others concerned with animal behavior, Reno lies a glittering incarnation, a mocking reminder that the city itself, the symbol of order and civilization, is rooted in greed and is nourished by compulsion and desperation.

Walking north from the gambling district on North Virginia Avenue, one slowly ascends and is soon surrounded by the university. The thin air, clean now that we are away from the city's exhausts, is warm in the June sun and incredibly clear. Miles away I can see blinding white snow fields near the Sierra peaks. Here, the buildings are new, verdantly bordered, and well spaced. One feels insulated from the temptations of the town below. From the vantage point of the university, Reno is reduced to a disquieting metaphor.

I am in Reno to attend the 1972 conference of the Animal Behavior Society. This year's conference has inspired particular interest among its wide-ranging constituency, because this year it is being hosted by R. Allen and Beatrice Gardner, the comparative psychologists who first established two-way communication with Washoe. The climax of this convention will be a symposium comprised of four scientists specialized in studying different aspects of behavior who have come together to explore the ramifications of Washoe's demonstrated abilities in using a human language.

According to traditional ideas of animal behavior, Washoe should not have been able to "say" combinations such as "Please give Washoe sweet-drink" using proper subject-verb-object order. Nor should Lucy be able to understand the difference between "Roger tickle Lucy" and "Lucy tickle Roger," nor should David Premack's chimpanzee pupil Sarah be able to read properly sentences like: "Sarah insert apple pail banana dish." Yet a burgeoning population of chimpanzees can understand and say these things, and a good deal more as well.

The behavior of Washoe, Lucy, and Sarah has precipitated a

crisis among those concerned with the study of animal and human communication. It is one that fits within the pattern a philosopher-scientist named Thomas Kuhn uses to describe the cycles of scientific revolution, which, Kuhn feels, has charted the course of science since antiquity. However, if Washoe signifies the coming of the scientific revolution, it is a revolution attendant to events outside of those specific scientific disciplines concerned with the study of language, and even outside the world of science.

Washoe, as the reaction of deaf people to films of her conversations dramatically demonstrates, speaks not only to comparative psychologists but to the world at large. Similarly, Washoe not only challenges present assumptions about animal and human behavior, but poses ethical questions for future research. These ethical questions in turn spill out of science to challenge theology, philosophy, and politics. In this respect, Washoe significantly diverges from the process Kuhn ascribes to change in "normal science." As revolutions do, Washoe has changed the world, but not only the world for the researcher at the limits of Western thought, but the world for the layman as well. This revolution has occurred in terms that are accessible to him. Despite the profound implications of her language abilities, Washoe was not the product of special genius, but rather of a simple shift in viewing the world. Anyone can now talk to a chimp.

Washoe can be considered from two principal perspectives. On the one hand she represents the focal point of a scientific revolution, the thrust of which might be summarily described as rehabilitating the reputation of the animal mind. In this respect, she speaks to broad questions of human and animal nature and the panoply of disciplines interested in such questions. On the other hand, the particulars surrounding her emergence offer a perspective from which to assess the nature of science itself. She speaks outward to the world and inward to science.

Washoe was not so much discovered as unlocked, and her first "words" were preceded by a fortuitous series of events that were the tumblers to the lock. The key to the present revolution and to Washoe is in those tumblers. To reconstruct them, it is necessary first to describe the pattern of scientific change of which Washoe is a part, then, the views of nature on either side of this scientific revolution, and, finally, the tumblers themselves—the specific events in this revolution that preceded Washoe and the symposium that heralds her spreading impact on the behavioral sciences.

In terms of science, the revolution Washoe heralds began 100 years ago. Washoe signals the unfolding of a Darwinian world view in behavioral sciences—Washoe's is a Darwinian world and not the Platonic world in which the behavioral sciences developed. Indeed, it is only with Washoe that we begin to see how profoundly incompatible the two worlds are. The Animal Behavior Society is also a product of this same scientific revolution, and during its convention the society was to consider the crisis Washoe has caused. In part, the symposium exemplified the process by which revolutions inure throughout the world of science, but, equally important, the history of the Animal Behavior Society itself reflects the process of osmosis by which the Darwinian view has gradually suffused through the behavioral sciences and produced the "climate" in which Washoe occurred.

SCIENTIFIC CHANGE

Science is not the enterprise we think it is. We tend to think of the course of science as an onward march toward specific truths, as cumulative, ever broadening its scope and its illumination of the realities to which its attention is turned. It is an image of science, says Thomas Kuhn in *The Structure of Scientific Revolutions*, that is impressed on every student through scientific textbooks themselves. Kuhn feels that this view of science is false; science is not cumulative, not marked by linear progress, nor is it directed toward some abstract truth. Rather, says Kuhn, the history of a particular science is characterized by revolution as successive *paradigms*—the scientific equivalents of regimes—refocus the attention of researchers within a particular discipline. Revolutionary change from one paradigm to another is not necessarily progress toward some higher truth, but the overthrow of one view of nature by another. After a scientific revolution, says Kuhn, the researcher works in a different world from his predecessors', but not necessarily in a more fully explained world. This is because, during *normal science*, scientists pursue their research under the paradigm which is accepted as containing the overarching truths that relate all the phenomena with which the discipline is concerned: The Newtonian scientist was as confident of his understanding of the universe as the Einsteinian who replaced him. Both worked in fully explained worlds. Similarly, before Washoe suggested otherwise, linguists were confident that the chimp lacked the neural organization necessary for the generation and comprehension of language.

Kuhn believes that the idea of the paradigm is essential to understanding the nature of science. A paradigm, says Kuhn, may be looked at as some "exemplary past achievement," or, in another sense, as "the entire constellation of beliefs, values, techniques, and so on shared by the members of a given community" that grows out of some exemplary past achievement. Without some paradigm to shape a discipline's view of the material with which it is concerned, all data seems equally relevant, all experiments seem equally important, and, because the members of a scientific community cannot agree on fundamentals, each scientist has to rewrite his science from the beginning to justify each experiment.

This, says Kuhn, is the state of a science during its pre-history. At some point during this proto-scientific chaos a theory emerges that explains better than its competitors one of the problems in the field, and, as this synthesis begins to attract "most of the next generation's practitioners," the older competing schools disappear. As it is in nature, a paradigm in science survives because its competitors die. From this point on, says Kuhn, the science has a paradigm and its real history begins. Different sciences acquire their first paradigms at different times; Kuhn dates astronomy to antiquity, the first electrical paradigm to Benjamin Franklin, and says that "it remains an open question what parts of social science have yet acquired such paradigms at all."

With its reception of a paradigm, says Kuhn, a group previously interested in the general study of nature becomes a specialized profession "or, at least, a discipline." The paradigm proposes a model of reality in which the scientist can have confidence. It frees the scientist from the necessity of always beginning his major works from first principles and justifying each concept introduced. It tells him what problems are important and gives him the confidence to make detailed explorations that would not even be conceivable without a paradigm to focus his attention. Once it has a paradigm, says Kuhn, normal science consists principally of a "puzzle-solving," whose end is putting the principles implicit or explicit in the paradigm to the test of reality. Indeed, says Kuhn, the very equipment researchers construct to investigate their domain embody the principles of the paradigm. Working within a paradigm the scientist knows what he is looking for. Should such tests fail to fit natural phenomena within the bounds of the paradigm, the failure is at first seen to be the failure of the scientist and not the failure of the paradigm.

Science proceeds by observing and asking questions. When the behavioral phenomenon being studied in creatures other than man is the same as the one which has been used to define the difference between human and animal nature, the fact that the observer is human cannot help but increase the likelihood that the act of observation will occlude what is observed. It may be that, to a degree, what unites the behavioral scientist's observations into a theory also shapes the aborigine's myths; in supplanting religion and tradition as authorities on our origins and nature, science eventually comes to be subtly shaped by the myth-making power it replaces. The history of Washoe gives support to this notion and emphatically confutes the idea that science is philosophically neutral. Thus, a paradigm has religious properties. Any paradigm is mythic in that it explains as yet unexplored properties, and something extra-scientific supplies the connecting tissue for a particular scientific theory.

Scientific revolutions occur when a paradigm consistently runs afoul of nature. A phenomenon, such as eccentricities in the motion of the pendulum, that resists assimilation within a particular paradigm is called an *anomaly*. Anomalies themselves do not cause scientific revolutions. They may remain aggravating, unsolved inconsistencies for decades. Over time, a discipline increasingly focuses its attention on an anomaly and unless the anomaly is explained, the discipline gradually falls into crisis. Ultimately the crisis is resolved when a scientist steps outside the traditional paradigm and offers a more economical, aesthetically pleasing explanation of the anomaly than would be permitted by the traditional paradigm. This is another major point Kuhn makes: scientific revolutions do not occur, nor are traditional paradigms abandoned, unless another paradigm appears to resolve the crisis caused by the anomaly. Only because an existing paradigm rigidly focuses the attention of scientists on what should happen does a science have a sensitive indicator that something has gone wrong when what should happen doesn't. Then a body of scientists willing to investigate a troublesome anomaly will eventually produce some young turk willing to step outside the bounds of the discipline's paradigm to explain it, and when, among competing theories, some new explanation comes to obtain on the thinking of the discipline's upcoming generations, the new paradigm is born.

In describing the process by which anomalies become evident to the scientist working within a paradigm, Kuhn recounts an experiment conducted by psychologist Jerome Bruner. Different people were exposed to gradually lengthened glimpses of a series of playing cards. Most of the cards were normal but salted among them were anomalies, for instance, a red six of spades or a black four of hearts. Even with the briefest glimpse, the subjects correctly identified the normal cards; but, surprisingly, they also identified the anomalous cards as normal. "Without any awareness of trouble," writes Bruner, "[the anomalous card] was immediately fitted to one of the conceptual categories prepared by prior experiences." Longer exposures to the cards began to produce more and more hesitation about the correct identity of the anomalous cards. For instance, exposed to the red six of spades, some would say: "That's the six of spades, but there's something wrong with it—the black has a red border." Eventually some would realize the anomaly and suddenly begin to identify correctly all the cards, while others might lose all confidence even in identifying normal cards. Kuhn notes that this same syndrome seems to apply to the process by which anomalies surface and are dealt with in science. The scientist tends to see what he expects to see. As he probes his subject matter in more detail, anomalies that he originally glossed begin to catch his attention, and either he loses all confidence in his ability to judge his material or suddenly the anomalies sort themselves into some pattern, changing his view of his material and commensurately changing his expectations.

The lesson the scientific revolution teaches participating scientists is that the world is not as it was perceived to be under the previous paradigm. After a scientific revolution, the researcher works in a world different from his predecessor. Here again, Kuhn departs from traditional concepts of scientific change.

"Many readers," says Kuhn, "will surely want to say that what changes with a paradigm is only the scientist's interpretation of observations that themselves are fixed once and for all by the nature of the environment and of the perceptual apparatus. On this view, Priestly and Lavoisier (chemists on different sides of a scientific revolution) both saw oxygen, but they interpreted their observations differently; Aristotle and Galileo both saw pendulums, but they differed in their interpretations of what they both had seen."

This view of science, says Kuhn, stems from an epistemological paradigm articulated by Descartes. Briefly, Descartes's paradigm proposes that there is a *fixed* perceptible world, which is differently perceived as it is filtered through the senses of different individuals. Kuhn feels that this paradigm increasingly is proving to be askew, but that so far no replacement has appeared. Kuhn believes that this is because, fundamentally, there exists no fixed data for successive scientists to interpret. Data itself is summoned into existence by the paradigm the data itself fills out. The very instruments of observation are conditioned by a paradigm to conform to the reality which that paradigm assumes: If one believes that the earth travels through a medium-like ether, then that expectation will condition the very instrumentation and methodology of astrophysics. Thus, rather than two scientists interpreting the same data in different ways, two scientists under different paradigms see different data. The shift from seeing one way to seeing another does not result from ponderous deliberation, says Kuhn, but comes rather as a flash of understanding, a gestalt switch that psychologist D. S. Lehrman refers to as the "Aha" experience. There is no fixed world, says Kuhn. As the Bruner experiment shows, people with the same retinal impression can see different things, and people with a different retinal impression can see the same thing. Likewise there is no neutral language; any vocabulary that describes reality also embodies a host of assumptions about its nature. The Newtonian physicist felt no less secure about his understanding of physical phenomena than does the Einsteinian now. His grand design was no less awesome.

This, in greatly truncated form, is how Kuhn explains the nature of scientific change. He relates his conception of scientific revolution to both natural selection and political revolutions. As in political revolution, the change from one paradigm or "regime" to another is seen as progress, because, among other reasons, only if it is seen as progress would the revolution be justified; but in reality, scientific change, like natural selection, reflects past necessity rather than future goals. Kuhn's conception of scientific change is Darwinian rather than Platonic.

How does Washoe fit within this scheme?

In Chapter 4 I discussed a 1970 article in *Science* that was critical of Washoe's language abilities. In this article, Jacob Bronowski and Ursula Bellugi accepted Washoe's performance as proof that the ability to "name" was not biologically unique to man. (A decade earlier Bronowski had argued that *naming* was the ability that separated animals and man). However, they then criticized her use of language on other grounds. In essence they said that although Washoe might be credited with the ability to *name*, to think symbolically, she could not demonstrate the grammatical lawfulness that evolved concurrently with the ability to symbolize. They then argued that grammar is an expression of the quintessentially human ability to factor the environment into symbolic units and then lawfully to manipulate those units through language and through technology. They call this literal and symbolic ability to take apart and put back together *reconstitution*. Subsequently, Washoe and other language-instructed chimps have done things which suggest that they do possess this ability. Washoe and Lucy proved this criticism, as well as other critical points in the article, to be premature. Given the temporality of such criticisms, it might seem that Bellugi and Bronowski were defensively splitting hairs and irrationally holding to an invalid conception of language, especially since Washoe and other chimps so quickly breached Bellugi and Bronowski's hastily erected lines of defense. Kuhn's model, however, would cast their actions in a different way.

Kuhn argues that once an anomaly appears and throws a discipline into crisis, scientists will stretch their existing paradigm in all manner of adaptations in attempts to accommodate and explain the anomaly. Paradigms are not abandoned lightly; if they were, they would lack the authority to focus research so rigidly that anomalies could be discerned in the first place. If a paradigm could be abandoned lightly, it would not be a paradigm. Kuhn feels that the very thing that makes a paradigm valuable as an overarching schemata, giving the researcher confidence to undertake expensive and minute investigations, makes its disciples seem dogmatic and tradition-bound when confronted by anomalies.

Bellugi and Bronowski were arguing in defense of an ancient paradigm of animal and human behavior. Like the participants in the Bruner experiment, they were attempting to fit an anomaly—Washoe—into conceptual categories prepared by prior experience. The irony is that both scientists, if asked, would probably align themselves with the pretender, with the Darwinian paradigm Washoe represents and whose encroachments their article was designed to balk. Both the Platonic and the Darwinian paradigms are so basic, and so subtly and broadly influence our expectations, that a scientist might believe himself operating in service of one paradigm while he or she was actually defending the other.

16. Darwin in the Temple of Plato

In *Beyond Freedom and Dignity*, behaviorist B. F. Skinner notes that while physics and math long ago moved beyond the first hypotheses contributed by Aristotle and Pythagoras, the behavioral sciences until this century were still working with models of human autonomy supplied by Aristotle and his contemporaries. Yet Thomas Kuhn says it is an open question which of the social sciences have acquired paradigms at all. It might seem that there is a contradiction here; but, in fact, both theorists are right.

Psychology seems to be in the situation Kuhn ascribes to a science's pre-paradigm infancy. Within psychology, there is a proliferation of competing schools all concerned with examining the psyche, but none agrees about what the psyche is. It is not clear that psychology has reached an accord on fundamentals, which would indicate that the science has left its pre-history. Noam Chomsky has supplied a paradigm for linguistics that philosopher/linguist John Searle believes fits within Kuhn's pattern of scientific revolution, but again it is not yet clear that linguists have confidence in Chomsky's model or whether they agree sufficiently on fundamentals to justify that assertion. However, if among the other concerns of the social sciences there has been ongoing disagreement about the nature of the psyche and the nature of language, Skinner is still correct in saying that until this century these disagreements about particulars of human nature occurred within the confines of ancient models of human autonomy.

Aristotle developed his model in *De Anima*, his treatise on the soul. In it, he distinguishes between man, who has a rational soul, and the animals, which have animal souls. Thus man has both a reasonable and an animal nature, separate from one another. Man is purposeful, while other animals are essentially automatons filling out nature's design. This distinction was originally popularized by Plato in his myth of the soul in the *Phaedrus*, and the earlier philosopher should be credited with this model. The distinction, however, crops up throughout the different strands that have been woven into the religious, philosophical, scientific traditions of the West. Indeed, the separate natures of man and the animals are a natural mythic projection, explained by the Europeans' and Mesopotamians' isolation from our primate relatives. It is the metaphysic of the West.

But because the behavioral sciences, like the hard sciences such as physics and math, trace their lineage from Greek thought, it is not misleading to characterize this model of human autonomy as Platonic. And, although it is more a philosophical and religious paradigm than a scientific one, the Platonic model has left a prominent stamp on the behavioral sciences. As paradigms do, this model has conditioned the approach, the methodology, the subject matter, the interpretation of data, and even the drawing of disciplinary lines within the behavioral sciences.

We are concerned here with a corollary to the expectations of that original Platonic dichotomy between man and the animals— that is, the expectation that man has language while the animal world is mute. Within the paradigm of autonomous man, the dichotomy between animal and human communication becomes the explanation for human autonomy itself. Recall George Gaylord Simpson's formulation: "As posture is focal for consideration of man's anatomical nature and tools are for the consideration of his material culture, so is language focal for his mental and non-material culture." In accord with this theme, Noam Chomsky feels that syntax is determined by the structure of the brain; that man is a syntactical animal. More than language in general, Chomsky feels that syntax in particular permits man's autonomy and the development of his "mental and non-material culture." In Bellugi and Bronowski's discussion of reconstitution, we can see a similar effort to account for human anatomy in terms of some nuclear linguistic-cognitive process.

It was Descartes who began the modern trend toward explaining autonomy in terms of the development of language. He used language as the distinguishing characteristic that made man different from the other animals. Language was the lens that permitted man access to a fixed conceptual world; thus, concepts were innate and languages arbitrary. Chomsky, however, turns the tables on Descartes by arguing that syntax is innate and that it accounts for the development of thought. Nevertheless, until this century, discussion of language and thought has occurred within the boundaries of the Cartesian epistemological paradigm, which is itself within the Greek paradigm of human autonomy.

If it is difficult to discuss the soft sciences in terms of paradigms, it is because, unlike the hard sciences, the need for models in the softer sciences has been adequately fulfilled by the philosophical paradigms under which they developed. There is of course an interplay between philosophical paradigms and the paradigms of the hard sciences, but the subject matter of the hard sciences is sufficiently remote from the broader concerns of philosophy to distinguish between that science's history and the intellectual history of the community. But in the case of the behavioral sciences, both science and philosophy share a crucial common interest: establishing man's place in nature. And it is in this common interest that an explanation lies as to why the behavioral sciences have for so long paid fealty to a philosophical paradigm contributed by the ancient Greeks.

During a conversation I had with Roger Fouts in Oklahoma, he related Washoe to what he called the "divine trauma," the insecurity that afflicts Western man whenever he is forced to face the fact that he is not the center of the universe. Copernicus sent the first quake of divine trauma through European consciousness when he demonstrated that the earth is not the center of the universe. Copernicus was dealing with matters of astronomy; however, in sixteenth-century Europe, any science that might be concerned with man's place in the universe, even if that concern be a matter of cartography, operated under the yoke of the paradigm which saw man as autonomous God-on-earth.

Astronomical truths such as those Copernicus discovered are ideally suited to refinements of calculation and observation, and Copernicus was merely attempting to refine the Ptolemaic, earth-centered universe. Historian Herbert Butterfield tells us Copernicus was obsessed with circularity and spheres. He was aesthetically offended by Ptolemy's eccentric orbits and found that by orbiting the planets about the sun he could resolve peculiarities within that system. Moreover, this adjustment solved a number of practical problems, such as those with the Ptolemaic calendar. Copernicus postponed publication of his findings expecting to be attacked as a heretic for his harmless bias. With Copernicus, the stresses between the internal direction of astronomy and the tolerances of the community became critical. His discovery marked the separation of the astronomical paradigm from the philosophical-religious paradigm. Astronomy had matured to the point where it could no longer accept the mythic conception of man's physical place in the universe, and that challenge to the integrity of the Western paradigm sent a spasm through Europe. At a point of contact between reality and the mythic tissue writing the intellectual/religious traditions of the West, the mythic tissue had been found wanting. Consequently, our notion of *earth's* place in the universe was demythologized and the paradigm viewing man as autonomous God-on-earth regrouped around questions of securing man's place on earth.

It should be clear that the more the science divorced itself from questions about man's place in nature and the harder (more rigorous) its methodology, the earlier demythologization would occur. Similarly, the more subjective the science and softer the methodology, the longer that science would be vulnerable to domination by a philosophical and religious paradigm of man's place in nature. If Western man views himself as the lone purposeful creature on earth and reason is his paragon of purposefulness (as Aristotle said, man's rational self is his highest self), science is, in turn, his paragon of reason, and empiricism (practical verification of hypothesis) is the foundation of his science. Thus it is that science, by being quintessentially Western, could inexorably reduce the reality secure within the embrace of the Platonic paradigm. The path from Copernicus to Washoe is marked by successive demythologizations of the world, successive reductions of the reality that could be explained by the Western model of autonomous man, and successive spasms of the divine trauma. The behavioral sciences remained longest under the power of this paradigm in part because, in their case, the line between philosophy and science is the most blurred. The behavioral sciences have had to deal with questions that were the linchpins of the Western paradigm, and, being so close to these basic Western notions about man's place in nature, they have been weighed with the full force of that paradigm's gravity. Until this century, the behavioral sciences lacked the empirical power to overcome that gravity. Now Washoe indicates that the process of demythologization is threatening that paradigm's last line of defense—that there are intrinsic differences between human and animal behavior. Washoe's shadow threatens the very center of the paradigm that originally gave birth to science.

The irony of this process is complete, because it is the central assumption of this Western paradigm that gave man the ethical license to experiment on the world and develop the sciences to the point where they would eventually invalidate that assumption. The world that permitted the growth of science—in which man is intrinsically superior to the rest of nature and, hence, is permitted to use nature as he wills—no longer exists. From Copernicus to Washoe, the facts of that world have, one-by-one, been shown to be illusion. A world view wrought in isolation from evidence of man's biological and behavioral connections with nature has not been able to assimilate evidence of those connections. In Darwinian terms, this world view is beginnnig to prove maladapted to the world it must explain.

There are other facets to the Western notion of man's place in nature that help explain the durability of this paradigm and its power over the behavioral sciences. For instance the ethics that view the world as unsacrosanct raw material at man's disposal have been extremely profitable. They have permitted Western man to construct a society based on consumption rather than conservation. The paradigm of autonomous man might be abandoned, but only at the peril of modern civilization: Our notions of human nature and language are not just dry textbook ideas; they are our excuse for plundering the planet.

The behavioral sciences also operate within constraints imposed by the political manifestations of the model of autonomous man. American and British law is built on that ancient Greek assumption that man is a rational animal, and ultimately responsible for his acts. To propose a model of behavior in which man is not viewed as autonomous is to risk being branded a totalitarian. On the other hand, physics and math run no risk of coming under political heat for the political implications of their paradigms.

The durability of the Western ethos can be credited to the fact that it has brought success and profit to people of the West. The paradigm of autonomous man has served to justify and perpetuate that mode of acting in the world. But the fact that this world view is contradicted by scientific reality indicates that its leading edge has run afoul of nature. Science's demythologization of this world view is a harbinger of its decline. The crunch will come when political and economic contradictions inherent in this paradigm begin to surface and throw the Western world into a crisis, the resolution of which is a question of survival. When events demand that Western man abandon his peculiar attitude toward nature and adopt a new way of acting in the world, a new paradigm will emerge to support that way of behaving.

We might now consider the durability of the Western paradigm on a more practical level, in terms of the scientist's everyday behavior. The behavioral sciences are concerned with the way organisms behave. The organism that is the behavioral scientist behaves as well, and he lives within and profits from the Western ethos. Behaving in a thoroughly Western fashion, such a scientist should naturally be enthralled by a model of autonomous man, and, in his work, he would willingly explicate the particular dichotomy upon which his science and his way of life are constructed. This is not surprising, nor is it then surprising that the scientific community's investigation of communication in other species for so long was subverted by this same dichotomy.

As stated above, Thomas Kuhn believes that a paradigm will shape science at every level—that it will determine fields of inquiry, the important problems, and even the shape of the science's tools of investigation. The influence of the Platonic paradigm over the behavioral sciences is most clearly visible in the way disciplinary lines have been drawn (disciplinary lines provide a good map of the world view of a science at a particular moment). The study of behavior reflects a rigid paradigmatic demarcation.

In the study of human behavior, the linguist studies language; the sociologist and anthropologist, collective behavior; the psychologist, both individual and collective behavior. Until recently, the naturalist, on the other hand, was responsible for all aspects of animal behavior. Unlike the human sciences, naturalists traditionally did not draw a disciplinary distinction between the animal's body and its mind, or its individual or collective behavior. Moreover, in order to compare animal and human sociology or animal and human communication, one had to step across disciplinary lines; and, in stepping across them, one was leaving behind a world that viewed the subject as an individual able to control its destiny and entering into a world that viewed its subjects as tools of nature. The study of animal and human behavior was thoroughly confounded by the paradigm of autonomous man.

Thus, discussion of the question of whether the chimpanzee can use language was long impeded because linguistics used the assumption that only man had language to define the limits of its field of inquiry. Linguistics could not be concerned with the question of whether the chimp was capable of using language, because such questions are outside its field, and they are outside its field only because man has language. In this instance, it is easy to see the "Catch-22" aspects of working within a paradigm. Thus any comparisons between animal communication and human language perforce stressed differences, and these differences came to be used to reinforce arguments for the discontinuity between animal and human behavior. We studied animals as if they did not have language, as if their communication fulfilled nature's purposes; we studied man as if language were a tool to fulfill his own purposes. Thus, these disparate investigations tended to perpetuate the assumptions on which they were based. The approach to animal and human communication eventually resurfaced as the *explanation* of the difference between the two—man is different from the animals because that is the way we have looked at him. At least until this century.

Kuhn argues that a scientific paradigm is not abandoned until a successor appears and begins to win over upcoming generations of scientists. The behavioral sciences have operated within a paradigm that not just supplies a model for scientific thought but that expresses and justifies the way Western man acts in the world. The successor to this paradigm will redefine not only the world the behavioral scientist studies but the way behavioral scientists and other Westerners behave.

The West attends to the world of science, and so we might expect that science will anticipate the successor to the Western paradigm. While science has implemented the ever-expanding consuming appetites of the West on the one hand, so has it increasingly threatened the central assumptions about animal and human nature that justify those appetites on the other. Because science represents the purest implementation of that Platonic paradigm, it is, among the various Western enterprises, the most sensitively equipped to perceive anomalies to that model of reality.

Earlier we noted that, within science, the hard sciences were the most precociously equipped to perceive anomalies to this model; but, while the hard sciences gradually assembled worlds of their own, the behavioral sciences languished in shamanistic service to the notion of man as a gifted rational creature with prerogatives over the rest of nature. However, as man classified the animals and creatures within his domain, homologies began to appear linking different species. With the development of these homologies, scientists saw indications that different species were not created *ex nihilo* but rather evolved from common ancestors. Man—bipedal and hairless and manifestly different from any cat, dog, or plant— might cheerfully have accepted this as a rule that applied to the rest of nature but not to himself had he not left Europe for the tropics and discovered there an entire grade of primates, which, as one moved from small to larger, looked ever more pointedly human. But, unhappily for our peace of mind, in the sixteenth and seventeenth centuries, Europe began a host of exploratory voyages that brought back not only treasure but reports of a host of animals and plants and peoples that Europe, with a philosophical framework attuned to the relatively barren flora and fauna of the north, was unequipped to explain. Two centuries later, a new philosophical framework began to gel about these newly discovered relatives.

It is ironic that in the 1860s—at the point when Europe and America were beginning a century of the most intense industrial exploitation and manipulation of nature in Western history—European culture gave birth to and nurtured through infancy a model of nature that, when fully developed, would prove this profligate growth was supported by an invalid assumption about human nature. While Europe had ignored the evolutionary feelers put out by Lamarck and others, the first edition of Darwin's *Origin of the Species* was sold out on the day it was released.

The epiphany that spawned the theory of natural selection occurred in the Galápagos Islands in 1837. In 1859 Darwin published *Origin of the Species;* and in 1871—thirty-three years after the significance of homologies between South American fossils and the fauna of the Galápagos dawned upon him—he published *The Descent of Man.* The noose was tightening on the Platonic model of human nature. Darwin had provided the basis for a paradigm that might explain both human psychology and human behavior in terms of man's continuity with the rest of nature rather than his discontinuity. Here was a model of nature and man in accord with the world Europe discovered but not with the world European philosophy had originally presumed. The Darwinian paradigm has been slow to spread through the world of science. In 1871 science accepted the physiological continuities between man and the other primates, but in 1974 the question of behavioral continuity between man and ape is still considered open. Behavior has been the last stronghold of the Platonic paradigm, but now Washoe and Darwin have entered it. Let us contrast the Darwinian world with this Platonic world to see why Washoe, profoundly anomalous to the notion of autonomous man, fits within this Darwinian world, and to see why the Darwinian world is not the world as the Westerner sees it.

It is not certain whether Darwin, like Einstein, was altogether aware of what he was starting. Similarly, many eminent Darwinians have taken a Platonic view of Washoe, which is to say that rather than focus on the communalities between Washoe's use of language and human speech, critics like the great neo-Darwinist Theodosius Dobzhansky have exaggerated the differences. That a Darwinian might take a decidedly un-Darwinian view of Washoe is not surprising, because it is not until the evolutionary view of man is fully amplified that its inimical relation to the Platonic view of man becomes apparent.

The idea of purpose is central to the idea of rational man—the idea of a man whose acts are ultimately responsible to his reason. Plato described the human soul as tripartite; the rational part fought with the appetitive part as it sought to mold behavior in accord with a higher, ideal emotion. Clearly, if man's acts are to be responses to his reason, reason must have identified some ideal behavior, some goal for human acts. Similarly, in the *Cratylus Dialogue*, Plato saw language as an instrument of thought, the purpose of which was to express *true* thoughts accurately.* According to this notion, the individual, society, and the universe are all directed toward some goal; in philosophical terms, the Platonic universe is teleological.

Seen in terms of the model of displacement, it becomes apparent

---

* The Cartesian epistemological paradigm reflects this belief as well. Descartes believed that there was an absolute *true* world that was variously interpreted by the various languages of various perceptors.

that the goal of rational man is to shift authority over behavior from the "appetitive" world of the animal brain to the reified world of displacement where all is order and stasis. Plato, the philosopher William Barrett tells us, was tormented by a vision of ceaseless change and "desired at all costs a refuge in the eternal from the insecurities and ravages of time." Rational man is motivated not to live in the immediate apprehensible world; rather, his purpose is to rise above the clamor of the here and now, to live in and to pursue the absolute truths of the world of displacement. He is concerned not with living, but with becoming.

In contrast to this, the purpose in Darwin's universe is not the achievement of higher creations, such as man, but, rather, it is survival. The Darwinian universe is not teleological but existential; its ambition is not perfect truth in a displaced world but survival in the here and now. When Kuhn discusses Darwin, he notes that opposition to Darwin in the sciences was not principally directed at the idea that man possibly descended from the apes. Instead, the difficulty for Darwin's contemporaries lay in his conception of the nature of the evolutionary process.

"All the well-known pre-Darwinian evolutionary theories," writes Kuhn, "—those of Lamarck, Chambers, Spencer, and the German *Naturphilosophers*—had taken evolution to be a goal-directed process. The 'idea' of man and of contemporary flora and fauna was thought to have been present from the first creation of life, perhaps in the mind of God. The idea of plan had provided the direction and the guiding force to the entire evolutionary process. Each new stage of evolutionary development was a more perfect realization of a plan that had been present from the start."

For this view, Darwin substituted a vision that saw evolution as a process reflecting the necessity for survival. (Kuhn's view of scientific revolution is thus Darwinian, because he sees scientific change as a process where paradigmatic survival is the goal, and not some more perfect truth.) "The belief," Kuhn continues, "that natural selection, resulting from mere competition between organisms for survival, could have produced man together with the higher animals and plants was the most difficult and disturbing aspect of Darwin's theory. What could 'evolution,' 'development,' and 'progress' mean in the absence of a specified goal?"

The key to the notion of rational man had been that while animals were responsible to nature, human reason was presumed to be part of some higher plan. If the same process that produced bugs also produced reason and language, then what became of those absolute truths to which reason was responsible? Within Darwin's universe, the world of displacement was responsible to nature and not vice versa, as his contemporaries were inclined to believe.

Darwin has inadvertently changed the notion of truth itself. If the face of the world represents past exigencies rather than the unfolding of some pre-existent design, what then is fixed? In concert with the foundering of a goal-directed universe, the Cartesian epistemological paradigm has been increasingly threatened by anomalies. This paradigm, as noted, holds that perceptual information is a constant for all men in all ages upon which different minds foist different interpretations. The notion of a fixed world in an evolving universe is an intolerable contradiction, and Kuhn notes that the Cartesian paradigm is coming under increasing attack as experimental psychology becomes more sophisticated in investigating man's perceptual organization. While the truths of the Platonic world are constructed around enduring forms, the truths of the Darwinian universe are constructed around the Heraclitean notion of a world in which the only enduring aspect is change. The Platonic world is directed toward the world of displacement; the Darwinian world lives in the urge to reproduce.

Kuhn felt that the Cartesian paradigm reflected the physical realities of Newton's dynamics. Whatever epistemological paradigm emerges to explain Darwin's universe will have to reflect the physical realities of Einstein's theory of relativity.

DARWIN IN THE TEMPLE OF PLATO

By denying the notion that nature has pre-existent goals, Darwin not only eviscerated commonly accepted philosophical beliefs about "development," and "progress" but, as I have suggested earlier, set the stage for a challenge to the ethics of the economics based on those ideas. If man, being rational, is an ethical creature, it behooves him to justify whatever liberties he takes with the rest of creation. Until Darwin, he could argue that he was endowed with the gift of reason—a behavior different in kind from other animal behavior—which granted him not merely the prerogatives but also the responsibility to reorganize and use the natural world around him in accord with humanistic principles. But if, on the other hand, selective pressures produced reason, then, in accord with evolutionary doctrine, we might expect to find that similar selective pressures in other creatures might produce adaptive strategies similar to reason. And, if evidences of reason appear in other creatures, then we must reassess the basis of our rights over these other creatures. Any such evidence calls into question the notion of the intrinsic differences between the rational mind and the animal mind that are at the heart of and are the basis for the Western way of life.

The Darwinian and Platonic worlds are indeed profoundly incompatible. If we begin to search for a life style that reflects the ethics of a paradigm with man in continuity with nature, we find it necessary to step out of the monotheistic West entirely and return to an animistic world. One has to move from a world where all magic is invested in man into one where whatever magic infuses man also extends to the rest of nature. As it branched out to explore the primitive world where evolution is a manifest reality, science began to validate the metaphysics and ethics of that primitive world.

It is only now that the ethical dimensions of the Darwinian paradigm are becoming apparent. The spread of Darwinism through the behavioral sciences has been slow, in part because scientists (quite naturally) like to consider themselves as the very exemplars of autonomous man. They are willing to credit *physical* communalities with other animals—and even certain behavioral similarities—but scientists begin to get very nervous when Darwinists begin to take a hard look at cognitive behavior. Thus, even great evolutionists can cling without self-consciousness to such Platonic notions as the mind-body duality. For instance, Konrad Lorenz—who won the Nobel prize for his pioneering work in ethology, a science directly indebted to Darwin—still takes a very Platonic view of man. He has summarized the *human* elements of man's behavior as follows: 1) reason and "insight"; 2) ethics or rational responsibility; 3) culture; 4) speech—the sine qua non for the rise and transmission of culture; 5) self-awareness; and 6) meta-curiosity, an "active, dialectic construction and dismemberment of the environment." Lorenz's list is a scientific translation of the Western metaphysic.

Nevertheless, in recent years Darwinism has begun to suffuse through the behavioral sciences. Washoe signals the unfolding of of a Darwinist world in the Platonic temple of the behavioral sciences. In confirmation of this, certain behavioral scientists have anticipated the lessons of Washoe. In Reno, I discovered that ethologists are shifting toward a methodology in accord with a Darwinist world. As in cultural revolutions so too in scientific ones, it is among the young that such change is most dramatically evident.

In this chapter I have sketched two major paradigms, one that Washoe threatens and the other that Washoe exemplifies. The difference between the two might be briefly summarized as follows: the Darwinian sees continuity between animal and human behavior, while the traditional Western metaphysic sees discontinuity. Not coincidentally these are the precise terms in which the Animal Behavior Society's symposium cast the controversy over Washoe under the title "Animal Communication and Human Language, A Discontinuity in Approach or in Evolution."

Here was an opportunity to observe the process of scientific revolution at work. The Animal Behavior Society itself had provided the context for marking the slow progress of the Darwinian paradigm through the behavioral sciences and triggered the first successful attempt to establish two-way communication with another animal.

I have so far attempted to suggest that Washoe both fits into a recurrent pattern of scientific change and, at the same time, that she heralds a revolution significantly broader than one within any particular scientific discipline. Let us now attempt to reconstruct some of the events Darwin triggered that led, a century later, to Washoe and to this symposium at the 1972 gathering of the Animal Behavior Society.

17. The Animal Behavior Society, Washoe, and a Confluence of Skinner and Lorenz

The Animal Behavior Society's meetings were scheduled to take place over four days. The conference included ten research sessions devoted to the presentation and discussion of new research, an invited address, a symposium, a field trip, films, special interest discussions, and perhaps, most importantly, informal opportunities for various researchers to talk to one another about what they were doing.

After a research session, the audience would drift down to a coffee room in the School of Journalism where discussion would start the juices flowing into such droll topics as "Aggression and submission in Hawaiian Drosophila plantibia species" or "The Use of Echolation by the Wandering Shrew, Sorex Vagrans."

From my first day at the conference, it became clear that the Animal Behavior Society, or ABS, was comprised of a different breed of scientist. For the most part the animal behaviorists were a lean and weatherbeaten lot. The more senior conferees looked like ranchers, while the more hirsute younger scientists looked like backpackers in transit (as some of them were) to the nearby Sierras. Basically they looked healthier than one might expect, given our traditional image of the scientist as a gnomish individual who pursues his investigations in sulfurous laboratories. The health of its constituency is just one dividend of the ABS's principal focus—the study of animal behavior in natural conditions. Like the society's role as an interdisciplinary forum, this particular feature distinguishes the society's membership from normal investigators of behavior. And this difference affects more than the members' appearance alone.

Patti Moelman is a typical member of the ABS. After one paper-giving session, I met up with Roger Fouts in the coffee room. We talked a little about Washoe and the upcoming symposium and then wandered out into the sunshine. A Ford Bronco screeched to a halt and out jumped Miss Moelman who came over to say hello to Roger. She had arrived at the conference directly from Death Valley where she had been studying the wild burro for the past eighteen months. Miss Moelman had long golden hair, a splendid tan, and looked altogether healthy. The three of us talked a bit about living in Death Valley, and eventually I asked her why she was interested in animal behavior. "A lot of us are in animal behavior," she replied simply, "because we don't like cutting up animals." This, in a nutshell, sums up the difference between the new breed of animal behaviorists and their predecessors. These scientists would rather observe than, to use Francis Bacon's word, "torment" nature to determine its secrets.

Until only recently, the study of animal behavior has been based, surprisingly, on observations of animals in zoos and in laboratory situations. While scientists concentrated on dissection, vivisection, and Skinner-box manipulations, the study of animals in the wild was usually left to amateurs. Studies of aggression and territoriality, for example, have been based on observations of caged animals, reflecting the erroneous presumption that animals cooped in cages behave the same way they do in the wild. Recently, anthropologist David Pilbeam examined examples of baboon aggression that have been used as cornerstones in theories of primate nature. He discovered that baboon troops in the wild savannahs provided no evidence of such behavior. Until the last decade, most research was being predicated on the following assumptions: the animal world is pre-programmed; animals are machines filling out roles assigned by nature; animals are useful to science largely as subjects for experiments to further the understanding of human problems, but which, for delicate political and religious reasons, could not be carried out on humans. (One participant in the symposium advanced this very same view.) In summarizing the position, anthropologist Harvey Sarles argues that these idea grew from the behavioral sciences' original orientation, which was to cure human problems rather than to understand nature.

The right to vivesect animals in order to discover cures for human ailments derives from the belief that nature exists in service of mankind, as Toynbee suggested in discussing the monotheistic notion of nature as "unsacrosanct raw material." We can use nature as we wish, because, in effect, it cannot tell us not to. Washoe's achievements would seem to shatter this rationalization. We can of course still say that man is smarter than the chimpanzee, but it is becoming difficult to cling to the idea of intrinsic differences between man and chimp. Thus, in proving that the chimpanzee is capable of something similar to language, the Gardners created through their work an ethical dilemma that undermined the ethical justification for their own original manipulations of Washoe.

It should be evident that this ethical dilemma would not confront Patti Moelman and those who share her beliefs about the study of animal behavior. She and other naturalists seem to have anticipated, emotionally more than rationally, what Washoe demonstrates—that our justification for taking liberties with nature is on shaky scientific and moral grounds. Patti Moelman and Jane Goodall brought their feelings toward other animals to the study of science. Long before she received any formal scientific training, Jane Goodall preferred the company of animals, and this same bond seems to apply to many researchers who are willing to spend long months in the wilds.

Jane Goodall and Patti Moelman are not the first scientists to spend extended periods of time observing animals in natural conditions. In the early part of this century, a Dutch South African, Eugene Marais, spent many months living in close proximity to a tribe of baboons. From his observations he wrote *The Soul of the Ape* ("soul" here is used in the African sense, meaning mind). Marais was amazed by the sociability and problem-solving powers of the baboons. In this book, he suggested that, along with the other primates, man possessed two memories, a "phyletic" memory, which is similar to an "instinctive" memory of the lessons from collective primate history, and another, more important, "causal" memory, which enables the individual to learn from his unique experiences. Marais's book was radical, because it drew no arbitrary line between man and the other mammals; rather, he said that "both these types of mentality exist in different degrees of activity in all the higher mammalia." Marais only distinguished across species by noting that non-primate mammals were dominated by hereditary memory while primates were dominated by causal memory. Marais's writing receives an attentive reading today, but he lived and died in virtual obscurity. It was his misfortune to be a Darwinian before people accepted that Darwin's theories could be applied to questions of not only man's origins but also his behavior.

Marais was a precursor of a new science whose roots have a

particular focus in Darwin's writings—ethology, the biology of behavior. A relative newcomer among the behavioral sciences, ethology can trace its brief history to an 1879 study by Darwin entitled *Expression of the Emotions in Man and Animals.* In it, Darwin proposed two radical ideas: 1) that there was a biology to man's behavior; 2) that just as there are physiological correlates relating different species, there might be behavioral correlates as well. The field that grew out of this study might be described as the behavioral *distillation* of natural selection.

Even though ethology is based on perfectly reputable scientific foundations, its early contributors seemed motivated by an emotional or unconscious acknowledgment of kinship with other mammals, a feeling the laboratory scientist must suppress if he is to be effective in his particular explorations. Nobel prize-winning ethologist Niko Tinbergen noted this when he said that most information on animal sociology—a field ignored by the traditional paradigm—has come from people with the love and patience to spend months studying animals in natural settings. As Allen and Beatrice Gardner describe their own attitude, "Our religion is that there must be some overlap between man and the animals." It is this evolutionary perspective which the Animal Behavior Society expresses and which is manifest in its weatherbeaten constituency. What we see in the history of the ABS is the behavioral sciences shifting their attention from the laboratory to the field.

The idea of the ABS originated out of the desire of some naturalists to study aspects of behavior that were not of immediate focus in zoology. Reacting against limitations imposed by the way disciplinary lines were drawn, a group of zoologists sought to involve psychologists and anthropologists in studies of animal behavior, and, conversely, they felt that the human sciences might also profit from exposure to the methods of the naturalists. Founded in 1967 in Montreal to create an interdisciplinary group, the ABS was structured along the lines of the British Animal Behavior Society with which it is still informally allied.

The ABS emerged to serve as midwife to the restructuring of the behavioral sciences along Darwinian lines, and in this role its most important function was as a medium for interdisciplinary communication. In true Darwinian spirit, the ABS resolved the mind-body split; those who studied behavior in terms of the mind (e.g., psychologists) were ready to speak to those who studied behavior in terms of the body (e.g., biologists, zoologists). Disciplinary lines define the world view of a science at a particular time, and, especially in the behavioral sciences, they embody assumptions about the behavior being investigated. By impeding the flow of any information that might challenge those assumptions, disciplinary lines tend to perpetuate a fixed body of ideas, locking their constituents inside a particular paradigm. Previous to the ABS, communication across disciplines in the behavioral sciences occurred primarily through informal contacts and through the molasses-like medium of scientific journals. People specializing in inter-disciplinary studies still tend to be regarded as researchers who lack the talent to make it within one particular field in the same way that researchers in the behavioral sciences in general are thought to be people without candlepower to make it in the hard sciences such as physics or math. Because of these prejudices, a biologist might overlook pertinent research coming from a softer science like psychology, and both biologist and psychologist might scorn the student specializing in interdisciplinary studies. Thus, different disciplines ignored other perspectives on their subject matter and even evolved contradictory notions about the same behavior in their self-imposed isolation. And, naturally, a discipline such as linguistics would tend to exaggerate its own contributions to the understanding of its subject matter.

Working in self-reinforcing isolation from the latest breakthroughs in other fields, schools of thought like the Skinnerian behaviorists or the Chomskyan linguists tended not to recognize information from other disciplines that might have controlled or tempered the development of their theories. This myopia was not altogether the result of willful blindness, but was instead, as Kuhn would say, a natural consequence of working within different paradigms. If a paradigm is so powerful that, for a time, the scientist sees regularity where there is anomaly within his own field, it is even more difficult for him to assimilate information gathered in the "different world" of another discipline—unless he has already stepped outside the paradigm of his home discipline. This cross-fertilization is what the ABS signifies—a wholesale abandonment of traditional disciplinary dogma on the part of scientists from a number of disciplines; and it is this phenomenon that led to Washoe.

Washoe is one of the first fruits borne by the Animal Behavior Society, having benefited from the society-fostered rapprochement between two bitterly antagonistic schools of behavior—ethology and behaviorist psychology. Their antagonism is especially interesting because both schools in odd ways are rooted in Darwin. In fact, Roger Fouts has described Washoe as a meeting of Konrad Lorenz and B. F. Skinner: joining together the laboratory and the field. The separate histories of ethology and behaviorism show how disciplines sharing a common origin can radically diverge by working in self-imposed isolation.

Ethology was little more than an attitude toward behavior until Lorenz began his studies of the birds and animals native to his home on the Danube. Lorenz acknowledges ethology's debt to Darwin and dates it as a science from the studies of Charles Otis Whitman (1899) and Oskar Heinroth (1911). In independent studies, they discovered that certain actions recur among species with as much constancy as gross physical characteristics—that is, certain things an animal does identify it not only as a part of a species but also as part of a genus or order, and do so as reliably as the animal's bodily structure. To the ethologist, then, an animal's selective history is evident in its behavior as well as in its physical structure. Just as there is a biological history to the peacock's fan, so is there a biology to the courting ceremony in which it is used.

The behaviorists, on the other hand, seized on another aspect of Darwinism, namely the way in which behavior is shaped by the environment. This school of psychology is generally dated from Pavlov's studies of the conditioned reflex, and John Watson used Pavlov's work as a starting point to found behaviorism in America. In the 1930s and 1940s, behaviorism glorified man as a creature whose every action occurs as a result of learning, or, to put it another way, he was a creature utterly free from a genetic heritage to his behavior. Later, in the 1950s, B. F. Skinner began his modifications of behaviorist theory at Harvard. Rather than glorify man as nature's lonely creature of learning, Skinner held that learning in man is no different than learning in the pigeon and, in either case, that learning is merely the shaping of behavior by the environment in which the animal lives. Because behaviorist techniques and controls tempered with ethological insight into the chimp's physiology had a good deal to do with the success of Washoe, it would do well to explore this rapprochement.

The Darwinist elements of Skinnerian behaviorism are evident in its lack of distinction between animal and human behavior and in its environmentalist bias (behaviorism is concerned solely with what an organism *does* and not with the cognitive functions that precede the act). But behaviorism has even stronger anti-Darwinist roots. Earlier I mentioned Skinner's lament that while physics and math long ago moved beyond the first hypothesis of Aristotle and Pythagoras, the behavioral sciences were still working with models of human autonomy supplied by Aristotle and his contemporaries. Skinner was quite right in saying the behavioral sciences had languished under this paradigm; however, in a sense, psychology almost kept pace with physics: the stimulus-response paradigm within which behaviorism operates reflects the physical world of Newton's dynamics. Newton's dynamics, in turn, operate in a world of enduring matter, the word of Cartesian epistemology, which reflects not an evolving universe but a Platonic one.

Psychology has had a long-standing desire to explain learning in terms of mechanics—in terms of the motion of unchanging particles. In attempting to describe rational thought in terms of the same principals that govern the motion of planets, Galileo had suggested that man conceived of natural events in terms of mechanics, and the history of classical mechanics has been the search for some unchanging particle that suffers no change save in location. Seeking to apply physics to psychology, David Hume popularized the Law of Association, which is founded on contiguity: "Ideas cling together in mind as complex compounds, because they have been together in time in a man's experience. For the same reason, idea suggests idea in trains of imagination or thinking." * Hume claimed that the Law of Association was to psychology what the Law of Gravitation was to physics.

To this mechanical paradigm were added the elements of motivation (pleasure or pain), some physiology (the reflex arc), some neurology (Broca showed the relationship between behavior and specific brain areas), and then, in the last part of the nineteenth century, some experimentation. The Law of Association underwent some modifications, and, in the early twentieth century, underwent a final modification by Edward Lee Thorndike, a comparative psychologist influenced by Darwin. In its final form the Law of Association's lineal descendant is the S-R paradigm: learning is the setting up of a bond between a given stimulus (S) and a given response (R). This paradigm in turn was variously explicated. Ultimately, Watson became aware of Pavlov's conditioned reflex and decided that conditioning was the sole principle of learning; conditioning was nothing more than association by contiguity in time. Thus, behavioral psychology works back to

* Horace English, *Historical Roots of Learning Theory.*

Newtonian physics and the idea of the motion of unchanging particles. But just as the particulate universe founders on uncertainty, so does its psychological expression in the S-R paradigm prove illusorily simple.

The problem is this: while experimental psychologists can point to results that have accrued through operating within the S-R paradigm, both the stimulus and the response have more a mythic than a physiological reality. It is difficult to explain a stimulus in terms of a particular theory, given the uniqueness and complexity of each stimulus and each response. Just as Gestalt psychology has been threatening Cartesian epistemology, so has it been threatening the S-R paradigm; in fact, Gestalt psychology began as a reaction to the atomistic basis of the S-R paradigm. While the behaviorist is concerned with an individual stimulus, the Gestalt psychologist attends to *relationships*. Recall Jerome Bruner's experiments with anomalous playing cards. They demonstrated that a local stimulus can change without affecting perception. To the Gestalt psychologist, learning occurs as an organism fills out relationships in terms of its genetic predispositions.

Still, behaviorism was successful to some degree in getting animals to do things we would not expect them to be able to do. And behaviorism's importance to Washoe becomes more evident if we contrast behaviorism with ethology. If ever there was a school of thought that projected the realities of the laboratory onto the realities of nature, behaviorism was it. To the behaviorist, biology was an accessory after the facts; an organism was a tabula rasa at birth, and its life thereafter was the product of various reinforcements. Based on the probabilities that related particular input to output, the behaviorist study of activity ignored the causal chain of events that led from one to the other. Thus, the behaviorist assumed a posture toward behavior that was precisely opposite to the ethologist's.

The ethologist assumed that selective pressure shaped an organism's gross physical characteristics as well as its behavior and confirmed his assumptions through observations of related species of animals in the field; but the behaviorist tended to ignore any predispositions created by the animal's selective history, because it appeared that, through proper reinforcements, the technician in the laboratory could overrule constraints imposed on behavior by eons of selective pressures. Through conditioning, researchers could get cats to jump at the sight of mice, and, in the hermetic world of the laboratory, it did in fact appear that a properly constructed reinforcement program could get any animal to do anything. Where the ethologist was interested in understanding how the animal lived on its own terms, the behaviorist was interested in manipulating the animal to suit human purposes. Behaviorism was perhaps the purest expression of a cure-oriented science. From its manipulations in the laboratory grew a concept of social engineering that was seen as the solution to man's social ills, and its deterministic and mechanistic view of behavior seemed to justify such engineering. Behaviorism had a ready-made answer to the ethical question of man's right to manipulate the animal world: man was not the manipulator, but was merely an intermediary filling out some larger evolutionary design; and his manipulations were conditioned by his environment, not by some fiction like free will. To the behaviorist, man and animal were no different from one another; and if man had any justification to manipulate the rest of the world, it was only to maintain environmental order.

Although the behaviorist did acknowledge Darwin in looking at man as a product of evolutionary pressures and not as a being intrinsically superior to the rest of the animal kingdom, he was actually an anti-Darwinist, because he ignored the very questions of what made a guinea pig a guinea pig and what made a person a person. Darwin believed that just as a creature's shape reflects its selective history, so does its behavior—that learning occurs within gentically conditioned corridors. In limiting their interest in an organism to the probabilities that relate input to output, the behaviorists ignored the question of change and clung to a static model of nature. Founded in mechanics, behaviorism, according to one prominent critic, acted as if there were no such thing as evolution. Thus, in this branch of psychology, the Darwinist aspect of environmental pressures was essentially overpowered and transformed by the traditional epistemology embodied in the laboratory where behavior was investigated.

The behaviorists made many enemies, perhaps foremost among them has been Konrad Lorenz. Skinner lamented the backwardness of psychology when he noted that the Western philosophical paradigm had hamstrung the development of the behavioral sciences. But, argues Lorenz, in Skinner's zeal to close the gap between psychology and the hard sciences, he developed a method that caricatured physics rather than adapted it. Whereas the physicist resorts to using probabilities only when common sense and normal investigative methods offer no guide, the behaviorist uses such methods as a primary means of inquiry. Like Swift's Laputan who used a sextant to measure a man for clothes, so do the behaviorists ignore common sense observation in favor of blind mathematical interpretation of the relationships between input (some reinforcement) and output (some response). Lorenz says the behaviorists are able to preserve this blindness only by skillfully avoiding manipulations that might run afoul of specific limitations imposed on the animal's behavior by its "nature." For instance, a lot of psychological theorizing has been based on the maze-solving abilities of the common rat. It has been discovered, however, that this rat is predisposed genetically to find its way around on a horizontal plane, but would appear to be a dolt if the mazes required the rat to solve vertical puzzles.

Lorenz goes on to say that "the programmatic restrictions of behaviorist research preclude participation of any consideration of structure or of causal chains of events. . . . Avoidance of the evolutionist viewpoint makes it impossible to consider adaptation. . . .

235

In other words, the behaviorists' program excludes practically all the questions which biological science is asking; one is tempted to say all problems which are really interesting to us as live creatures and human beings." He feels that, by excluding questions of adaptive significance, the behaviorist loses the perspective by which health can be distinguished from illness. Lorenz feels that the reason the behaviorist in conducting his experiments negates all that which makes a person a person or a cat a cat is a totalitarian desire to ignore individuality as an excuse to manipulate and "engineer" masses of people in the manner Huxley describes in *Brave New World*. He writes: "As D. S. Lehrman has recently pointed out, 'it is not only the subject which is denatured by behaviorist psychology; the experimenter himself is not permitted to be entirely human.' An epistemological lobotomy, which prevents an intelligent man from using the normal cognitive functions nature gave him, does indeed constitute an act of dehumanization."

Behaviorism, to Konrad Lorenz and to many others as well, is the ultimate laboratory nightmare. But even though behaviorism and ethology were polar opposites, they still needed each other. Ethology observed how the animal operated within its environment but suffered from lack of controls; it was a science poorly equipped to prove what it saw. On the other hand, ethology might bring the behaviorists out of the laboratory and show them the interrelationships between an organism and its environment. While the animosity between behaviorism and ethology makes it extraordinary that a rapprochement would occur, it did; and the essence of that rapprochement is evolution. "That's the idea that dominates the ABS," says geneticist Jerry Hirsch, "the idea of the organism and the environment evolving together."

The behaviorists have now abandoned their rigid environmentalist position and have come closer to the position of the ethologists, while the ethologists, like Lorenz, have shown how, over time, an instinct might be said to be "learned," which partially vindicates the behaviorists.

Indeed, the Animal Behavior Society has fulfilled its purpose in contributing to this rapprochement and in quickening communication between the disciplines. Whereas a few years ago if you asked a psychologist what biology was, he might answer "the nervous system," through contact with ethologists, the behaviorists are now beginning to get a feel for how the animal acts in its environment. On the other hand, the behaviorists have contributed to ethology a rigorous control of variables. Psychological techniques have useful applications in the study of animal behavior, particularly in such areas as conservation. One man has attempted to develop ways to adversely condition the coyote against eating sheep and thus assuage sheep ranchers who, out of exaggerated fears, have been devastating the prairie with cyanide guns and traps. This man is using straight Skinnerian techniques. Conversely, ethology has some practical applications to human problems; for instance, researchers have been studying retarded children using the ethological method, which might be summarized as "Don't ask questions just look." They discovered that retarded children distributed themselves differently from normal children. Why they do this has not been fully explained, but it is something that had gone unnoticed through decades of non-ethological observation. Roger Fouts has discovered that by using the techniques he employs to teach chimpanzees sign language, he has been able to break through to and communicate with certain autistic children. "The question," said Hirsch, "is why haven't comparative psychologists been doing this all along? They have had the techniques."

So far the most dramatic fruits of this rapprochement have been the breakthroughs in communicating with chimpanzees. Ethology contributed the insight that enabled the Gardners to sidestep the chimp's difficulty in controlling its voice and to exploit the homologous manual dexterity in chimp and man. And the behaviorists contributed the necessary empirical techniques to implement such a comparison.

The Gardners operated within the S-R paradigm and within

the *behaviorists'* assumption that language is a behavior (if an animal *does* what is called language, it has language). But their work and Fouts's is more convincing than David Premack's Sarah because Washoe's and Lucy's use of language seems to reflect a type of *gestalt* insight rather than a conditioned response. Washoe initiated new behaviors *spontaneously*, and the Gardners also seemed pleased with that spontaneity, perhaps reflecting a distinctly un-behaviorist bias toward insight. Similarly, Lucy seemed to discover the difference between "Roger tickle Lucy" and "Lucy tickle Roger" in a flash of understanding—the "aha" experience that is the essence of gestalt perception. On the other hand, Sarah seems to perform with about the same accuracy regardless of the complexity of the problem. Roger Brown finds this evidence of Sarah's lack of insight troublesome, and I do too. In fact, upon reflection, what is so convincing about Washoe and Lucy is their performance of precisely those behaviors that are inadmissable within the behaviorist paradigm. These indicate that the chimps were integrating Ameslan into some developing gestalt *displaced* from the act of communication and were not just being programmed to perform a complex gestural dance.

Still, to a degree, Premack also represents this softening of the behaviorist position. In explaining why he attempted to teach language to a chimpanzee, he says he does not rule out the possibility of teaching language to a relative of man more remote than the chimpanzee. But he felt that the results would be less ambiguous if his attempts were directed at the chimp, whose "evident brightness" indicated that its perceptual organization was closer to man's system of classifying sensory data. Thus, Premack admits the possibility that biology limits the behavior an animal can learn (he does not attempt to teach a chimp a spoken language). However, Premack aligns himself with traditional behaviorist thinking in comparing learning a language to a pigeon's learning to peck a key. He also argues that the chimpanzee's language ability may only be limited by the "astuteness of the training program," and affords the notion that the differences between responses with and without meaning are not radical ones. With the proper training program, Premack implies, any animal can learn language.

Because the nature of Premack's language investigation involves problem-solving, natural questions arise: Would his work have as much impact were it not for the presence of Washoe to assuage peoples looking for the more dramatic and subjective phenomena we associate with language? Would attention have been paid to either investigation were it not for people who were ready to accept the implications of these experiments—e.g., the Animal Behavior Society—and to assimilate experiments that were heretical to traditional disciplinary dogma? The Gardners' and Premack's work occurred when it did as a result of evolution's eroding traditional assumptions about behavior; there was now a body of scientists willing and equipped to believe that a chimp might demonstrate the rudiments of language. A population of scientists willing to accept a phenomenon will eventually produce someone who is willing to investigate it.

The breakthrough involving Washoe was produced not by prodigious mental effort, but by the felicitous use of long-standing psychological tools and a simple shift in seeing everyday reality. The behaviorist, blind to the peculiarities of the chimp, would have failed as had many past attempts to teach a chimp to "speak"; similarly, the ethologist, lacking behaviorist controls and techniques, would probably have failed to convince anyone that he had established two-way communication with a chimp even had he attempted such an investigation in the first place. However, most important, there is now a scientific and public constituency ready to accept the validity of Washoe's behavior. I am convinced that informal two-way communication between man and various animals has occurred in the past but that evidence of animal language abilities has been ignored because the instances lacked scientific credibility and because there was not a public ready to believe such communication was possible. The Animal Behavior

Society could confer such credibility, and now it had to consider what it had wrought.

INTO THE SYMPOSIUM

Just as an executive session of the ABS was about to commence, I saw a man and a woman sitting in the back of the room, the man gray-haired and genial-looking, the woman dark-haired and intense. After the meeting I introduced myself to R. Allen and Beatrice Gardner, and we began a series of brief, well-punctuated conversations.

Allen Gardner fits very comfortably into academic surroundings. He wears a moustache, and smokes a pipe, and projects the archetypal academic image.

Roger Fouts had warned me that the Gardners are very wary of outsiders, and he was right. After talking for a few minutes it became clear that, at least for the first conversation, Allen Gardner viewed me as one of those implacably truth-warping journalists who misquotes events of significance into insignificance. The Gardners gave a number of reasons for their caution. Above all, they were wary of the possibility that their research and Washoe would be abused—through misinterpretation, through exaggeration, through oversimplification, and through being caught up and consumed by the faddism that is omnipresent in American life and that attaches itself to and trivializes certain phenomena: "We don't want the importance of Washoe to become obscured by a lot of ill-informed publicity." Consequently, the Gardners attempt to exert maximum control over what is written and said about Washoe, and their caution extends to distrusting what they themselves might say in an unguarded moment that could distort something they had previously defined carefully in print.

Seemingly so well insulated from hucksterism and faddism, Allen Gardner has first-hand knowledge of the shifting, consuming patterns of hysteria in American life. One of his brothers invented the Nebbish, the very monument to mass tastes, and another brother is screenwriter Herb Gardner, who wrote "A Thousand Clowns."

Apart from their fears about ill-informed publicity in the non-scientific community, the Gardners have also suffered barbed criticism from linguists, anthropologists, and fellow psychologists. Some attacks have been scholarly, but their work has aroused emotional responses as well. Their behaviorist bias toward species-blurring naturally raises the hackles of specialists who have devoted their lives to studying chimpanzees. An icthyologist once asked me how I would feel if I had spent decades studying the chimp and then saw fame and fortune fall to someone having only a cursory knowledge of the creature with whom they were dealing. Later I spoke to a psychologist who told me that a good deal of resentment of the Gardners stems from the fact that they were relatively unknown before Washoe—i.e., they had not properly cut their teeth within the scientific community. But by far the largest group of critics is comprised of scientists whose theories and statements on language and human behavior are now invalid as a result of Washoe. A distinguished ornithologist told me that linguists were "laughing" at Washoe. I asked him why, and he brought up the arguments advanced in the Bellugi and Bronowski article. This storm of controversy and misinformation is the reason the Gardners eschew all consideration of Washoe's impact on the outside world.

If the Gardners themselves were reluctant to explore the extra-scientific implications of Washoe, they nonetheless had a champion in Harvey Sarles. Leaving the Gardners, I strolled outside and gravitated downhill toward the Student Union for a cup of coffee. There discussing the next day's symposium were two of its participants, Sarles and Norman Geshwind, who invited me to join them. Sarles is an anthropologist-linguist from the University of Minnesota. He is tall and large-boned, sports a bushy moustache, and appears casual, even diffuse. Geshwind is the leading American neurologist concerned with the specialization of the human brain for language, and he is quite the opposite of diffuse. He is stocky and conveys an aura of tenseness and extraordinary intellectual control. Looking at Geshwind, one wondered whether this dynamism has burned off his hair, rather than his baldness being the result of some more mundane inherited trait.

Sarles is a gadfly. He has turned his anthropological training inwards to study communication across disciplines. He is an admirer of Thomas Kuhn, and he is acutely sensitive to the mythologies constructed by different disciplines to justify their fields of inquiry, the individual beliefs the scientist displays in approaching his subject matter, and the overall ethos in which scientific investigations occur. Besides exploring the "cure" orientation of the behavioral sciences, Sarles has analyzed the mechanisms governing interdisciplinary communication, the respect and lack of respect accorded to information moving across disciplines, and the whole constellation of irrational, non-scientific influences that condition such information transfer. Of all the people at the conference, it was Sarles who most profoundly explored the implications Washoe held for the future of scientific inquiry and the judgment she pronounced upon the past performance of the behavioral sciences.

Allen Gardner speaks about Sarles almost as if he were his daemon, exploring questions in which Gardner himself did not want to become enmeshed. Once, during a conversation with Allen Gardner, I referred to something Sarles had written. Gardner said, "Anything you quote by Sarles is fine with us. We think what he is doing is great; we're behind Sarles one hundred per cent." Sarles's purpose at the next day's symposium would be to place in context Washoe and the remarks of the three other scientists.

It was expected that Geshwind would fill the role of critic during the symposium. He is a dedicated empiricist and has preferred to reserve judgment on the language abilities of the chimp until he has had the opportunity to study the chimp brain. Geshwind and a fellow neurologist first established that there were anatomical asymmetries in the human brain associated with language, asymmetries so subtle that they became apparent only after the pair had examined hundreds of brains. Geshwind is not one to leap to conclusions on fragmentary evidence.

The three of us talked a little about Washoe and some of the questions her performance raised. During our conversation in the coffee shop, I noticed that Sarles was making some form of signal to me and occasionally rephrasing my questions. I was a little confused, and later I asked him what he was up to. Sarles, ever the interdisciplinary communicator, had been trying to guide my questioning to what, from a neurologist's point of view, would be central issues, and was also attempting to translate what I was saying into a vocabulary that would be more meaningful to Geshwind than the somewhat literary terms I had been using.

The other member of the symposium was to be Peter Marler, a British-born naturalist from the Rockefeller Institute in New York. Marler is considered a respected researcher of animal communication, or "animal callist," as people in this field are termed.

On the surface it looked as though the Animal Behavior Society had succeeded admirably in bringing together the expertise and different points of view demanded for a discussion of the topic: "Animal Communication and Human Language: A Discontinuity in Approach or in Evolution?" During the days preceding the symposium, the questions it posed were discussed with great intensity; indeed, the event itself was the focus of so much attention that at times it seemed obscured by the noumena of the interest it inspired. The symposium would offer a glimpse of the process by which a new idea, radical in terms of traditional dogma about behavior, pervades the scientific world—in this case an idea that reflected the spreading of evolution through the hostile behavioral sciences.

The night before the symposium the Gardners showed some films of Vicki, the subject of an earlier attempt to teach a chimp to speak. Keith and Virginia Hayes had raised Vicki as part of their family while living in Florida in the early 1950s. They had attempted to teach the chimp a spoken language, but although Vicki drove herself into paroxysms of frustration attempting to mimic words, she was never able to reproduce more than a few with any regularity. When the Gardners first saw the films, they noticed that Vicki was intelligible with the sound track turned off. She could form the words with her mouth, but for some reason she could not properly control her supralaryngeal tract. It was then that the Gardners began thinking that perhaps the chimp might learn a non-spoken language.

The home movies showed Vicki gaming and learning in the Hayes's yard. There was one shot of her vigorously performing some carpentry with a hammer and nail. "I can tell you the source of that behavior," joked Allen Gardner. "There's always a lot of repair work in a house with a chimp." It was a nice image, Vicki hammering purposefully away, because the chimpanzee in the temple of language is really Darwin wreaking havoc in the temple of Plato.

18. The Symposium

Animal Communication and Human Language:
A Discontinuity in Approach or in Evolution?

Beatrice Gardner chaired the symposium before a packed auditorium. In her opening remarks, she admitted that the topic before the symposium was controversial. Jokingly, she said that the dimensions and absurdity of some of the controversy over Washoe had caused her and her husband to look back wistfully on the action taken by the Paris Linguistics Society in 1866: After being swamped with papers on the origins of language, the society pronounced the subject taboo, because they felt that such speculations were not subject to empirical verification at that time. Mrs.

Gardner then noted the composition of the panel and the one obvious omission—the absence of a bona fide linguist who had been publicly critical of Washoe. "We dismissed from consideration psycholinguists and linguists," said Mrs. Gardner with unconcealed anger, "because their methods of proving what they know to be true and dismissing other evidence as trivial or obvious make me and other animal behaviorists bristle with indignation." Through its previous posture toward language and Washoe, the linguistic community had eliminated itself, in Mrs. Gardner's eyes, from any meaningful discussion of the topic at hand. If there was a dissenting opinion in the auditorium, it was not voiced now. She then introduced the speakers.

The order of the speakers was to be Peter Marler, Allen Gardner, Norman Geshwind, and finally Harvey Sarles. Each was to make a presentation, and afterwards there was to be a discussion of the four talks. The presentations would center on four different topics as each speaker approached the riddle of human behavior in a chimpanzee from a different perspective; however, one speaker would often confirm ideas brought up as speculations by another. It was as though the four were naïve masons, each unconsciously filling out some larger design.

Allen Gardner listed his topic as "The Comparative Psychology of Two-Way Communication." He began by recounting the general methods and precautions he and his wife had taken in collecting data on Washoe and describing their elaborate double-blind procedure in particular. "Once we had collected sufficient data, we decided to consult the nearest linguistic text," Gardner said, adding sardonically, "Because we had respect for other disciplines and because we were naïve, we expected to find a definition of language." They found, instead, that linguistics was "rooted in scholasticism" and that it used an inverted empirical method, in which, "as Chomsky said, 'experiments are found to prove the result.'" Comparison of Washoe's performance with that of children was hampered, Gardner felt, because there existed no rigorous methods for gathering data on language acquisition in infants. To substantiate this claim, Gardner chose to respond to psycholinguist Roger Brown's critical comparison of Washoe's first utterances with those of children. So that Gardner's rebuttal might be more meaningful, let us, as we proceed, briefly reiterate Brown's 1970 criticism of Washoe.

Brown, like Bellugi and Bronowski, felt that there was "something missing" from Washoe's combinations of signs that is present in the child's. He felt, for instance, that a baby's statement "mommy lunch" shows more evidence of structural meaning than a similar statement by Washoe, such as "baby mine." In Brown's view, the baby's mother correctly interprets "mommy lunch" as being a telegraphic form of a more complex statement when she replies, "That's right, mommy is having her lunch"; when the infant says, "Fraser coffee," again, her mother recognizes her intent in responding, "Yes, that's Fraser's coffee." Thus, the baby is displaying the rudiments of a syntax that would develop later.

Allen Gardner felt that these telegraphic interpretations are somewhat ambiguous. After citing these examples of Brown's, Gardner observed, "Why little Eve doesn't mean 'Fraser is having her coffee [in the second example],' I guess you have to be a linguist to know."

Next Gardner looked at the data Brown had used to substantiate his claim. Brown had contended that infants rarely reverse the word order in statements like "mommy lunch," whereas Washoe did. Citing the data Brown presented on children, Gardner contended that researchers testing children accepted word combinations he and his wife would have dismissed as reverses had they been made by Washoe. Brown had claimed that out of thousands of statements, children had made less than 100 reverses. On the contrary, said Gardner, an examination of the data shows 42 reverses out of 205 examples. "Not bad," commented Dr. Gardner, "but worse than Washoe."

On another test, children were asked to select pictures to determine whether they understood the difference between "cat bit dog" and "dog bit cat." The children were correct about half the time, which Gardner said was better than chance but considerably worse than Washoe, who performed at about 90 per cent. Thus, using Brown's argument and the data against Washoe, Gardner felt that he could make a pretty good case to show that humans do not have language and that chimps do.

Gardner's point in making these comparisons was not to discredit children or Roger Brown, whom he later called a "friend among psycholinguists." Instead, Gardner hoped to point out that, since it is known that children do acquire language, perhaps this knowledge has spawned an empirical laziness in attempts to collect and quantify data on how the child does it; but, on the other hand, the belief that the chimp cannot acquire language has caused denigration of the comparative data on how the chimp does it. In comparing Washoe's scores in language acquisition with the child's, Gardner asserted that the discontinuity between animal and human communication existed in approach, but, judging from the evidence, that it did not exist in evolution. "If you realize," he concluded, "that we have limited ourselves to hard data, you come to realize, and on the basis of hard data alone, the chimp appears to be better than humans at acquiring language." Of course, with better data, humans will be shown to be better at acquiring language. "But," he added, "by then we too will have more data—and on many more chimps."

Peter Marler chose as his topic "Signal Diversity and Strategies of Development." Marler chose to address the question of whether there is continuity between animal communication and human language in terms of one aspect of speech—vocal learning. This aspect of language is so basic that, although it is a "key aspect of the emergence of language as we know it, it is in many respects so elementary as to be trivial to students of man." In his discussion, Marler sought to show that 1) vocal learning occurs in creatures other than man; 2) certain aspects of ecology can cause a species to resort to vocal learning as an adaptive strategy; and 3) specific mechanisms are involved in the development of vocal learning in both man and other creatures.

Referring to Sarah and Washoe, Marler said, "These studies demonstrate to my satisfaction that the potential for much of what makes up human language is present in the chimpanzee, using signs or tokens as vehicles." He also agreed with Premack and the Gardners that the operating principles of language are more important than the particular vehicle used for signaling. But since the essentials of language appear in other animals, Marler intended to shed light on how speech—our particular medium—developed in man.

First, Marler spoke briefly about vocal learning in the context of the study of the child's speech development. In investigations of the mechanisms leading to the development of competence with syntax and grammar, there were two main lines of research: one on the universals among languages used by adults and the other on the development of speech in children. Both approaches mistakenly think of the newborn child as a tabula rasa, which is the behaviorist view. Rather, said Marler, the child brings to "the task of speech development strong predispositions, which serve to guide development in certain directions." Marler was, of course, suggesting that speech is the result of more than cultural reinforcement alone; it has biological prerequisites as well. The most elementary prerequisite, said Marler, is the capacity to alter the sounds one emits as a result of exposure to auditory models.

In supporting his argument, Marler then explored vocal learning in other creatures. The natural place to start looking would be among our fellow primates; Marler noted, however, that primates are particularly limited in vocal learning. It was among birds that Marler discovered fellow creatures whose vocal learning occurs "as a key process in their natural development." Marler had found vocal learning in two distantly related bird groups, perching birds and parrots, and perhaps in hummingbirds and toucans as well. He noted that learning affected some sounds in the bird's individual repertoire but not others.

Having found his comparative subject, Marler then set about to determine what aspects of "vocal functioning" help explain why learning occurs in some groups but not others. And why it affects certain sounds in the individual repertoire but not others. To do this, Marler briefly returned to the consideration of primates, in particular, to the Bundongo Forest in East Africa where he had recorded the sounds of two species of *Cercopithecus* monkey.

The blue monkey and the red-tailed monkey live in close proximity to one another in the rain forest and are so closely related that they can be considered descendants from a common ancestor. In examining the adult male calls and the alarm calls of these two species, Marler noticed that, in the course of evolution, the alarm calls have remained very similar, while the calls of the adult males have "diverged markedly." Marler believes this can be explained by the calls' separate functions.

Of 129 sightings of blue monkeys listed in Marler's field notes, he recorded the presence of red-tailed monkeys in the same tree or groups of trees in almost half of these instances. The two species are vulnerable to the same predators—man, leopard, and eagle; on many occasions, Marler noted monkeys of one species responding to alarm calls of the other. Therefore, Marler feels, the alarm calls diverged slowly, owing to "the mutual advantage of interspecific communication of danger."

The adult male calls, on the other hand, function to rally groups within a species prior to movement and to maintain distance between groups of the same species. If the male calls of the two species were similar, chaos would result, thus, the two male calls have been selected for divergence in the course of evolution. The point is, says Marler, that the degree of need for signal diversity will be evident in the strategies for behavioral development. But because, in the case of monkeys, this need is not particularly great, signal diversity can be achieved without resorting to more drastic adaptive strategies, one of which is learning. On the other hand, the need for greater signal diversity is evident among those birds that learn their song.

Whereas the *Cercopithecus* has but a few relatives sharing a common ancestor, among song birds there may be as many as fifty related species evolving and living in the same habitat. Again, as in the case of the monkeys, the alarm calls are similar across species, but, says Marler, in the case of the male song, "extreme selective pressure from signal diversity can call for more drastic revisions of developmental strategy, leading eventually to a great increase in the dependence on learning." The needs of reproduction and territoriality within the species placed a premium on maintaining a specie's distinctness from its neighbors. It was the pressures for signal divergence in the face of what Marler calls "rampant speciation" that, he thinks, ultimately required learning as a strategy whereby the male song could keep pace with change.

Marler further noticed that in species where vocal learning occurs, dialects occur as well; even within dialect groups there are individual differences in male songs. Thus, when signal diversity calls for learning, diversity occurs not only across species but within species. "We are beginning to think now," said Marler, "that dialects in bird song . . . serve a function in restricting gene flow between local populations, maintaining a degree of coherence of local gene pools and perhaps permitting adaptations to local conditions."

Marler feels that, under certain conditions, dialect may serve the same function for man. Over time, a society adapts to its local conditions, and, suggests Marler, in primitive times there may have been some advantage toward perpetuation of that adaptation through restricting the flow of people from population to population by means of, among other things, dialects. "In earlier times," he suggests, "human tribal differences in ecological niches must have been almost as distinctive as differences between full species in other organisms."

Marler's remark that signal diversity, when it occurs as the result of learning, occurs at all levels and that it has a group-defining purpose at each level (species, group, individual) calls to mind the obvious group-defining functions of slang, which seems to occur spontaneously even among the most deculturized, middle-class communities. Dialect perhaps indicates the process of speciation beginning all over again. In time, both in man and birds, the isolation fostered by dialect might allow a particular adaptation to local conditions to become enshrined in the organism's genes. In the course of evolution, what Marler calls the "adaptive gradation" of species tends to simplify itself as a dominant competitor drives its close competing relatives into extinction, leaving gaps between it and its nearest successful relative. Perhaps extinction will result among rampantly speciated perching birds; many people feel that this is what has already happened to the apes and quasi-humans who filled out the adaptive grade between man and the chimpanzee. Thus, the question arises: What role did dialect and vocal learning play in giving one group of early men a competitive edge if language, in fact, had the origins and functions that Marler hypothesizes?

Having established that vocal learning does occur in other animals, and having suggested that in both birds and men it may have originally intruded as a drastic behavioral strategy to accommodate extraordinary selective pressures from signal diversity, Marler then began to consider the actual mechanisms of development that are involved. In both birds and men, Marler noticed, learning from an adult model is necessary, and "when it occurs, . . . we tend to find dialects as a result."

Although learning is necessary, Marler continued, "there are also marked constraints on this learning both in time and on what models will be copied. Some birds seem to learn throughout their entire lifetime." Here Marler mentioned goldfinches and other carduelines; however, in other birds, like the white-crowned sparrow, learning occurs from ten to fifty days of age. Thus, says Marler, when there are critical periods, these occur early in life, as in the case of the human child.

Then, Marler the ethologist considered the behaviorist notion of the organism as a tabula rasa at birth. He noted that the white-crowned sparrow, when presented with a choice between song sparrow song and white-crowned sparrow song, will choose its own species. This selectivity exists, he believes, to prevent the bird from learning the song of another species. In some cases—in the white-crowned sparrow, for instance—the ability to know its own song seems to be part of its make-up. In other species where this selectivity occurs, different mechanisms exist. As an example, Marler cited the red-winged blackbird, which can be tricked into learning two different songs in captivity, something it does not do in the wild. Marler feels this may be because, in the wild, the young bird responds to the plumage of the male of its own species.

Just as Marler feels that the notion of the organism as a tabula rasa is inappropriate in both birds and men, he also doubts the notion of classical reinforcement as applied to vocal learning: "There seems to be something intrinsically reinforcing in producing sounds that match the memory of sounds heard in the past in a particular context."

He notes that some birds, not dependent on learning, can develop a song in isolation, provided they can hear their own voice, but that they cannot do so when deafened. This led Marler to think that perhaps between the stages of dependence on learning and independence from outside influences there is some intermediate step during which the animal learns by matching its noises against what Marler calls an "auditory template." This animal, dependent on feedback, is then "well placed to make the further step to learning from external sources." Thus, Marler hopes that experiments with infant monkeys will determine whether this intermediate step exists among primates, which, he says, "would make the eventual flowering of vocal learning in man more understandable."

As a final parallel between men and birds, Marler mentioned the discovery that in some birds where vocal learning occurs, there may be left-side dominance in the chaffinch and canary brains with regard to vocalization. In these birds, the left-side hyperglossus is dominant in the production of sounds. Although Marler mentioned this as a footnote, it had an electrifying effect on his audience, because, as Norman Geshwind sought to demonstrate later, left-side dominance is regarded as the most palpable evidence of the specialization of the human brain for language. Indeed, Geshwind's talk seemed to confirm Marler's hypotheses about the origins of vocal learning. Marler suggested, in summary, that there was continuity between animal communication and human language in two areas—vocal learning and left-side dominance—where it was previously thought there was discontinuity.

Norman Geshwind, a neurologist, had studied the brain. He made it clear that he had no stake in religious conceptions of its nature, he knew what he had investigated, and he knew what others had investigated. Also, he readily admitted ignorance of questions he had not investigated. Geshwind began by saying that he believed there is no good definition of language. He feels that language is not a unitary thing, as the word "language" implies; in fact, different aspects of it are handled by different portions of the brain. Rather, Geshwind thinks of language as a collection of disparate abilities, which developed in the course of evolution, but not at the same rate. As the brain changed, man gradually built up the repertoire of abilities we call language.

Having established his bias, Geshwind then launched into his topic. He first noted that man is the only animal in which brain structure for language has been studied. The most obtrusive feature of this specialization is what is called lateral dominance, where one hemisphere of the brain shows itself to be superior in carrying out a particular function. Geshwind mentioned that while there was evidence for dominance in those birds that learn their song, so far no evidence for dominance had been found in any other species. In the human brain, the left hemisphere is dominant in both the production and comprehension of language. In those people he has examined whose language ability has been impaired (aphasics), 97 per cent have suffered brain damage in the left hemisphere. The two hemispheres also play different roles in functions other than language; the right hemisphere, said Geshwind, seems to be more musical, better at fine perceptual tasks, more emotional. Finally, the lateralization of the brain also affects left- or right-handedness.

Geshwind then moved into a discussion of the anatomical asymmetries that coincide with left-hemisphere dominance in the production and comprehension of language. He did not describe in detail the roles of the various areas, because he was intent on establishing that the left hemisphere and the language areas in the left hemisphere of the brain *are* anatomically different from their mates in the right hemisphere. It was only after intensive study of many human brains that these differences became apparent.

The left side of the left hemisphere is, on the average, one centimeter larger than the comparable area in the right hemisphere, which, Geshwind asserted, means that the left hemisphere has an enormous numerical superiority in nerve cells. This superiority is present at birth—a significant feature, because it is felt that some areas of the brain associated with language are not fully matured until some weeks after birth.

Here again Haeckel's dictum offers a guiding hand. If the history of the development of the individual recapitulates the evolutionary development of the species, then the order in which body and brain mature before and after birth can be taken as an indicator of the order in which events occurred during the evolution of the species. For instance, Geshwind said, the angular gyrus, which is important in the evolution of language, is *late* maturing in the baby, implying that it is responding to relatively recent evolutionary events.

Geshwind then moved to the anatomical differences between specific areas in the two hemispheres: the sylvian fissure is larger on the left than on the right; Heschl's Gyrus is a triangular area within the area of associative cortex on the left, but is a small torpedo-shaped area on the right; Wernicke's Area is larger on the left, and so on. Geshwind pointed out that from the neurologist's point of view, human communication is founded on a series of adaptions that have distorted the size and shape of different areas within the left hemisphere of the human brain—the pressures that produced language in man have also pushed the brain out of shape.

If some areas are damaged in an adult, different aspects of language are impaired; however, if the damage to the left hemisphere occurs when the individual is a child, the right hemisphere seems to be able to fill in and the child usually recovers. The brain is characterized by dominance, says Geshwind, and not by strict division of functions; thus, rather than a unity behavior, language is a repertoire of abilities.

The changes in the human brain have not been made without related costs. Lateralization has been matched with a concomitant loss of ambidexterity. Moreover, says Geshwind, the brain, in nature's terms, is a terribly expensive piece of equipment; in man it consumes a fourth of cardiac output. Given its costs, Geshwind believes that no animal has more brain than it uses—our brain is as large as it is and is organized the way it is because it had to be, in order for our ancestors to survive.

Finally, Geshwind posed the questions of why the changes that characterize the left hemisphere occurred, and why they did not occur in both hemispheres. At some point in evolution, he feels, man was under extraordinary selective pressures for change, and —perhaps just as in the case of the chaffinch where pressures from signal diversity produced vocal learning and lateral dominance—

nature found it too difficult to keep pouring "new machinery" into man's brain to meet the demands of change and duplicate that machinery in both hemispheres. The fateful selective decision was made, at least on the short term; the necessity of making the animal smarter, or, to put it another way, more flexible, outweighed the disadvantages of his lopsided brain.

Because of Washoe, Geshwind looks forward to seeing whether there is any evidence in the chimpanzee of the peculiar asymmetries that characterize the human brain.

Harvey Sarles anchored the symposium with the topic, "The Search for Comparative Variables in Human Speech"—the search for attributes of human speech that might be compared with similar properties in animal communication. Sarles, in effect, continued to explore in human context such themes as dialect in animal and human communication, themes which Peter Marler had introduced from the naturalist's point of view. Marler had said there were continuities between animal and human communication, which, like the presence of dialect and vocal learning across species, were so basic that they had ceased to be of interest to those concerned with the study of human communication. Sarles reaffirmed Marler's assertion that these continuities existed; but, he added, they were significantly more extensive than Marler, in his modest way, had hinted. Sarles agreed, too, that these aspects of communication lay outside the ambit of linguistics and attempted to explain the discontinuity in approach to communication that has allowed the linguist to ignore these comparative variables in speech, which naturalists like Marler focus on. But where Marler had apologetically noted that his points of comparison between animal and human communication were so basic as to be "trivial," Sarles viewed these same ignored aspects of speech as the "loudest and most obvious part of the speech stream" and said they conveyed perhaps as much information between speakers as the words themselves. He detailed the inadequacy of linguistics to deal with the information contained in this somatic and bulky area of speech and, finally, proposed some methods that would benefit the study of communication across species.

For Sarles, the symposium was an opportunity to deliver a manifesto. He seized on what he believed were the topic's theological as well as its scientific implications: the study of language across species has had the characteristics of a self-fulfilling prophecy; the approach to animal and human communication later resurfaces as arguments for disparity between the two; and theological tenets thinly disguised as science have been born of this type of inquiry and have contributed greatly to man's ignorance about himself and to his blindness toward his fellow creatures. Sarles used the symposium as an opportunity to give methodological shape to the revolution Washoe embodies.

Sarles called the ignored, non-linguistic, somatic aspects of speech, "para-language." It consists of signals such as tone-of-voice, facial expression, and even more broadly shared habits like the meaning assigned to relative physical positions, the stances, and relationships of two speakers. If language is looked at as a behavior consisting of "movement, vibrations, and tensions," rather than, as Chomsky tends to view it, as a package called "grammar," the importance of these para-linguistic phenomena becomes more evident.

However, language has not been looked at in this way; the approach to communication across species has been encumbered by distorted perspectives. Researchers motivated to establish the uniqueness of human communication have seized on supposedly differentiating factors, such as "grammar," and have ballooned them in importance to obscure all other attributes of speech.

Sarles then posed a number of questions about language: Would grammar be the first thing another species would notice about human communication? Or would another species do as we do in investigating animal communication, first being struck by the broadest contextual meaning of communication and assigning lesser importance to the subtleties and innovations introduced by the group or individuals concerned?

Tone of voice, for instance, has meaning across species; dogs and other animals react to this and not necessarily to the literal meaning of the message. Sarles noted that in the course of linguistic fieldwork among Tzotzil-Mayan speakers in Southern Mexico, he could tell whether the speakers were friends, husband and wife, enemies, superior talking to inferior, and many features of the message itself long before he understood the aspects of the language with which linguistics would be concerned. Sarles became sensitized to aspects of human communication that are so much a part of the speech stream they are largely ignored. Similarly, when he returned to a psychiatric clinic where he was doing research, he noticed that he could tell by their tones of voice who his colleagues were talking with on the telephone. At the least, says Sarles, this "loudest" part of the speech stream—meaning the part of the speech stream that would first be understood by an outsider —was carrying information about the relationships among the speakers.

Yet there is little study of para-language in human beings; consequently, little is known about those features of speech which man most likely shares with other animals. "Except for a few rather cryptic statements about emotions and context," said Sarles, "there is no theory concerning the status of para-language. Consider that tone of voice—a sine qua non of speech—has remained in the demilitarized zone of linguistic thought!" Sarles then addressed himself to the origins of our distorted approach to animal and human communication and why problems of comparing paralinguistic phenomena across species have remained in linguistics' "demilitarized zone."

The basic discontinuity between the naturalist's and the linguist's approaches to animal communication is evident, says Sarles, in their opposite methods. Even so, the naturalist's methods in studying animal communication, at times, seem to reflect the linguist's assumptions about the animal's limitations and serve to enhance the differences between the animal's call and the human's word. "It is an implicit gospel in liguistics," said Sarles, "that study should proceed *from* structure to context." While Sarles feels that the socio-contextual aspects of communication are the "loudest," the linguist, in his approach to communication, assumes just the opposite. By studying a message as independent of—or, at best, only "sensitive" to—context, the linguist leaves the impression that the message-sender and his message are relatively independent of the circumstances surrounding the sending of the message and minimizes the importance of context. By allowing that language is "context-sensitive," linguists, says Sarles, do little more than pay lip service to context. In contrast, Sarles notes, studies of animal verbalizations proceed "fairly directly *from* context and meaning to structure—approximately the opposite to how human language studies proceed." Thus, while the linguist exaggerates the flexibility of the message and the autonomy of the speaker, the naturalist proceeds as though the animal was bound to context, or "undisplaced," and minimizes the importance of message variations introduced by the animal.

It is the naturalist, Sarles believes, who has his priorities correct in examining communication. He does concede that the problems of applying "callist" procedures to the study of human language would be formidable; but, he points out, if "callist" methods could not be used to examine the structure of human language, which we "know" to be complex, how could the naturalist be expected to discover complexity and variation in animal communication, which he suspects to be simple? Thus the opposite approaches of the two disciplines tend to exaggerate the differences between animal and human communication. In doing so, they reveal the assumptions on which they are based.

In Sarles's view, the naturalist and the linguist use opposite approaches in studying communication because they are rooted in different traditions and pay homage to different world views—

the naturalist lives in the evolutionary world of Darwin; the linguist, in Western philosophical traditions rooted in Plato and Aristotle. In looking at the spectrum of animal and human communication, the Darwinian expects to see continuity and relationships, while the linguist discusses the origins of language in terms of "emergence and saltation (discontinuity and jumps)." If biologically we see continuity, asked Sarles, where did discontinuity come from? In reply to this question, he described two "fairly distinct" theories of human language origin—a sentence theory and a word theory—which roughly represent continuous Platonic and Aristotelian traditions.

"In the sentence-grammar theory, man was created uniquely," said Sarles. "This is a true creationist/saltation theory, and its proponents—including most modern linguists—rightfully deny the possibility of doing useful comparative work." They *rightfully* deny comparisons because, if one believes that man was created uniquely, it is useless to compare his behavior with mere animals. "Within this theory," continued Sarles, "a sentence is an idea or thought—in effect, only humans can have and understand them. Such theories have a kind of biologistic essence to them, since Chomsky and others have claimed that the neuronic rules for generating thoughts is innate in humans. Learning is not terribly interesting in this pre-wired view." Sarles went on to say that Skinner, who looks at all learning in animals and humans as the result of conditioning, posed a threat to the idea that the apparatus necessary for language was unique to man. In the resulting "nature-nurture skirmish" over Skinner's ideas, linguistics sided with nature, but, said Sarles, with nature "super-hardened along certain species' lines." Such maneuverings suggest interesting parallels with international diplomacy, especially so since they serve to protect the influence of a set of ideas. The idea of man as a being outside nature is rooted, says Sarles, in Plato's distinction between the rational soul and the animal soul.

If the sentence theorists "demilitarized" the field of comparative study of animal and human communication, Sarles claims the "word theorists," on the other hand, have always been impressed by "cross-species similarities." The idea of continuity between the animal's grunt and the human's word "has been in the air for a long while. In common parlance, animals sign, men symbol." Even so, word theorists still look at this continuum as progressive, and, said Sarles, "in these origin-of-men ideas, the *naming* of objects has been the crucial issue." It is here that Washoe and Sarah deal their most devastating and most irrefutable blows, because both of them quite clearly can *name*. Consequently, some word theorists now acknowledge that the cognitive abilities and competencies underlying the ability to *name* are not so different in man and chimp as was believed. Jacob Bronowski was one "outstanding" word theorist. With Ursula Bellugi, he authored the critical and, it turned out, premature review of Washoe that was published in *Science*. Sarles notes that, as that article revealed, Bronowski has abandoned *naming* as a dividing line between animal and human and has "retreated to a creationist-grammarian position in response to the Gardners' and Premack's work on chimpanzees." Word theory then has been abandoned to Darwin, while some of its proponents have retrenched with the sentence theorists. Yet even here, Washoe and Sarah raise questions about how long linguists will be able to keep this area demilitarized.

The different assumptions governing studies of animal and human communication can clearly cripple at the start any attempts to compare the two. Instead of investigating whether human communication conveys contextual information in the way animal communication does, Sarles asserts that the question of comparability centers around whether animal verbalization has structure, words, sentences, etc. Similarly the argument against animal language has been based, not on direct evidence but rather on the claimed lack in lower species of such human things as "soul, rationality, logic, intelligence, consciousness, and purposefulness." We don't deny that we share some language features with animals, says Sarles; the ploy is to overturn the question and say that those features do not constitute language.

The gingerliness afflicting comparisons of animal and human communication also extends to biologists approaching human language from the study of animal behavior. "In my experience," said Sarles, "many biologists have overly accepted the extra-natural definition of man contained in current linguistic formulations and have not yet demanded the same rigor of themselves in looking at humans that they apply in observing other species."

Even the tools we have constructed to examine speech have served to obscure verbal phenomena that might be compared across species, said Sarles. "The Helmholtzian spectrographic analysis of human speech has been essentially the analysis of those sound features which make up *words*," he said. "It has been restricted, I believe, to a very small number of speech variables—those which can distinguish one word from another. It has been a minimal analysis."

Sarles feels that research into communication at every level has served to "enhance the human features of language and to conceal or to mystify those verbal features which are continuous or homologous across species." The study of communication across species has largely served to buttress and give a sheen of scientific credibility to the mythology of human language, and, as is the case with myth, when the huge disparity between animal and human communication is questioned, it turns out that animal and human are so grossly different because we approach them as being grossly different. Here Sarles raised an intriguing question: Could another species discover that we have language with the tools we use to investigate animal communication?

As a result of his experience with the aforementioned Tzotzil-Mayan speakers and his benign eavesdropping on his psychiatric colleagues, Sarles has significantly broadened his view of human communication. As a result, he has become sensitized to and even a little self-conscious about the body movements, facial expressions, tones of voice, and smells that accompany his conversations with various people, wondering what commentary these extra-linguistic phenomena offer on the message itself and Sarles's relationship to whomever he was speaking. At one point, Sarles mentioned that he had dreaded having to confine his body in a lecture hall during this four-hour symposium and that he had looked forward to his chance to speak in order to express himself physically as well as verbally. Here some titters arose from the more scholastic groups in the audience, perhaps in nervous anticipation of what manifestation this physical expression might take. However, there was no cause for alarm. Sarles merely meant expressing himself through normal foot tappings and gesticulations; one message these were conveying was that Sarles was nervous about his relationship to this audience.

But Sarles's manner and movements conveyed much more: His bushy moustache, relatively long hair, and casual-but-not-hippie manner of dress aligned him with the liberal wing of the University of Minnesota faculty. His attempts to exploit the slang as well as the scientific connotations of words like "vibrations" strengthened the impression that he was attempting to associate himself in part with the counter-culture, although the self-conscious tone with which he used these terms indicated that Sarles hedged his commitment to this life style and perhaps was merely acknowledging his debt to the world-view from which he drew some of his ideas. Just as Norman Geshwind's relaxed, controlled manner of speaking and walking about the stage—and even his comfortable paunch—communicated that he felt equal, if not superior, to his audience, Sarles's diffident stoop, his tentative and slightly stagey delivery, and nervous gestures communicated that he respected the authority of his audience and perhaps was not completely confident of his own authority. It would have been interesting to contrast Sarles's "lecture voice" in this auditorium with the voice his students in Minnesota hear. This, of course, is precisely the type of contrast Sarles himself is attempting to study.

By the above, I have, to a degree, contextualized Sarles's remarks, something every journalist does in conveying the setting and atmosphere of a story. Without such a context, reportage is lifeless and confusing. The journalist thus acknowledges the importance of the para-linguistic phenomena that Sarles feels the linguist ignores. Often, as in the case of a White House briefing, the journalist attends more to para-linguistic phenomena such as sweating or tenseness, than to the words being said, which indicates that the journalist, like Sarles, feels that they are the "loudest" part of the speech stream, that their commentary on a message often submerges the message itself. However, not only journalists but everybody "listens" to these para-linguistic phenomena to "understand" what is being said. When someone is talking to us and we want to know what "he is trying to say," we look for clues in his tone of voice and manner. Linguistics, by being in a sense overly rational, has "dehumanized" itself in the same way Lorenz feels behaviorism has dehumanized itself—reason has schooled the mind not to trust data and priorities as sifted and organized by common sense, which, after all, is the basis for scientific induction.

"Having dismissed the bulk of human speech from human linguistics," said Sarles, "we may well have missed or misinterpreted speech variables in other species." He feels that just as there are many Harvey Sarleses, according to whom he is talking, it is also "extremely likely that other animals also vary in their verbal production according to their relationships and context with others of their own groups." Sarles believes that animal communication is not so wooden and mechanical as it is studied to be, and he has begun to formulate a program to investigate para-linguistic phenomena in animals and in men. He credits the perspective for such an investigation to ethology.

Sarles feels that the natural approach to the comparison of animal and human communication should be to look for continuity. The concepts of genetics are mechanisms to account for continuity, and are felt to do so, says Sarles, even though huge variations can exist within a population of a given species. Sarles, like Lorenz, feels that the chief contribution of ethology to biological theory is in stressing the fact that "behavioral features exhibit continuity and heretibility." Sarles appropriately calls this context bio-behavioral thought.

"I believe," said Sarles, "that a bio-behavioral orientation should help us to recast progressively derived theories of human language development—the sort which claim that man has what some animals have, plus some additional features—and attempt to ask how linguistic continuity might operate among humans and others." Peter Marler had earlier proposed that dialect was one feature of linguistic continuity which operated in humans and others. In suggesting how questions of continuity in communication might be posed, Sarles brought up an even broader aspect of speech—facial expression. He proposed that facial expression functions much like words, and that its development is remarkably similar to the development of dialect. He attempted to show that the development of the entire body is shaped by the demands of communication.

When asked the question, "How do faces get to look the way they do?" Sarles says that the first response is to say that the skeletal tissues are genetic and that the soft tissues of the face are probably related to the skeletal tissues in a direct way. This idea, he said, has been proved wrong, rather, "bone itself is a dynamic tissue. It depends for its structural integrity and continuity on its soft tissue relationships and its weight-bearing functions (body integrity being a major problem in space exploration and in prolonged bed-ridden illness). During development, the very continuity of one's looks depends directly on the contrast maintenance of muscle tonus." Without this tonus, he continued, the facial structure would be altered considerably.

Sarles went on to say that the facial muscles themselves take their shape through a form of imitation. "Human anatomists call them *mimetic*," Sarles said. This means that the external facial muscles are sensitive to, and can transfigure, movements in other people's faces; during early childhood, particularly in the mother's face. "Facial tonus," said Sarles, "is socially involved, if not socially derived." It is learned much as a word is learned.

Sarles looks at the face and face-shaping as dynamic, processional, and an integral part of a person's being, not mere "changes played out upon a permanent skeletal matrix." The individual facial expression is an evanescent signal, which, if it is abstracted from its ongoing context, appears to be very much like a word. Sarles feels, however, that this approach to both the word or the facial expression would "be the most literal, dullest, least subtle approach to language, communication, and meaning that I can imagine."

Sarles added that it would be more profitable to look at language and facial expression in dynamic terms. "Behaviorally," he said, "speech is a continuous, constantly changing set of muscularly generated vibrations." In understanding speech we are "constant speech analyzers" factoring the sound stream into an immense array of variables. In the course of development we attempt (whether consciously or unconsciously is irrelevant) to get our children to analyze sounds as we do. "In general," Sarles stated, "there is as much continuity in speech-analysis and production as in faces. I believe that both these aspects of communication function as *dialects*, because they are basically muscular, and because a large number of features of muscular tonus, tensions, and movement habits are shared in populations. Dialects are internal muscular habits in much the same ways as faces are more external muscular habits."

Sarles believes that the whole body of an individual contributes to a message being said. To eliminate from consideration accompanying gestures, facial expression, and tone of voice is to chop from the message major portions of its meaning.

The problem concerning dialect and facial expression for Sarles is not describing what they are, but describing the behavior in terms of what it is about. At this point Sarles turned and nodded toward Marler and said, "Here, non-human linguists have been clear and, I believe, in advance of human linguists." Sarles's tone in referring to animal callists as non-human linguists indicated that he wanted to stress his belief that a first step to a productive comparison of communication across species is to erase the arbitrary dividing line between the callist and the linguist.

The animal linguists' strength, according to Sarles, is that they have started their study with what the call is about and proceeded from there *to* acoustic behavior. This approach, in Sarles's thinking, has allowed them to avoid the trap that snares the linguist who, in constructing alphabets to describe the acoustic behavior that forms words, omits a large portion of speech constancies and contrasts. To illustrate this point, Sarles referred to a record by Stan Freberg called "John and Marcia." The acoustic behavior—the record—consists of only two words: she says "John," and he says "Marcia."

"Phonemically," said Sarles, "they repeat the same words about a dozen times—nothing else." Yet they tell the story of an entire love affair. The story is clearly not told phonemically—by the sound contrasts the linguist uses to describe the speech stream—rather, says Sarles, the story lies in the social variables conveyed by the sound contrasts and also in what he called the *narrative* variables, "including a peculiar sort of history and relationship between words, within the context of this story." Sarles mentioned another record in which acoustic contrasts told the story, a French record entitled "*Je T'aime.*" "Nobody missed the point of that record," he said. "It was banned in every country in which it was played."

Sarles discovered the importance of the non-phonemic aspects of the speech stream while he was working on the sound track of a filmed interview of a psychiatric patient. In order to compare similar appearing movements, he had cut and respliced the film several times. Words that had sounded normal in the normal unfolding of the film, began to sound peculiar as they appeared out of context. Sarles began to think that the reason they sounded peculiar was because he had interrupted the *ongoingness* of the speech stream. When written, the words looked the same in or out of context, but the sounds that made up the words were clearly carrying and conveying much more information. He began to experiment.

He discovered that the sound stream, besides carrying information about context and relationships, also carried information about the length of the utterance. A sense of continuity, a pre-signalling of what is to come, was conveyed by the sounds across sentences. Sarles feels this may explain why people rarely interrupt at inappropriate points within the speech stream.

He compared two strings of words. One string was short, while the other contained the same words as the first string and then some more. He discovered that the words shared by both strings would be spoken louder in the longer string, indicating to the listener that the second string is going to be longer.

He also discovered that if a word like "pencil" is repeated, it gets quieter and quieter. Sarles feels this suggests that when words or calls are really the same in a structural sense and their repetition does not convey new information or organization, their amplitude falls greatly. This implies that, in animals and men, when a message is repeated several times at the same volume, there is a reason for it, even if the reason is non-linguistic.

Sarles believes that it is only when we begin to search for comparative extra-linguistic phenomena in animal communication that we begin to find out how complex animal languages are. If we continue to try to prove that there is nothing animal in human communication, we will merely continue to use science as a type of kangaroo court to give a veneer of scientific credibility to prejudices about human nature—what Sarles calls "novel, biologized myths."

"I have tried to suggest a potentially rich direction for doing comparative work in verbal behavior," Sarles concluded. "This is to reexamine and rethink the ideas which had led to current theories about the human language; to show that a very narrow, restrictive set of variables has been thought to characterize all of human language. I am convinced that human speech is a much more intricate process than it has been thought to be, and one which is potentially studiable. I think the comparison of human language and animal communication suffers from misconception, not from discontinuity!"

So ended the formal part of this symposium intended to explore the question raised by Washoe's and Sarah's performance in language—whether the difference between animal and human communication is characterized by a discontinuity in approach or in evolution. All over the auditorium people began expressing themselves in para-linguistic ways, at this point principally through applause.

The symposium was followed by a short, almost apologetic question and answer period. George Barlow, the biologist, wondered why scientists should bother with theological questions such as the uniqueness of man. Marler replied that he felt that it was a question of ethics and not theology. Sarles felt that the question entailed both ethics and theology, and that scientists were commanded by intellectual honesty to confront the religious and philosophical traditions which had fostered the notions of discontinuity between animal and human behavior and warped scientific inquiry in the process. "Chimps know [that man is an animal]," said Sarles, "bees know it, every other species knows it; and it's time we face it!"

19. Aftermath

On the day following the symposium, some members of the ABS took a field trip to Pyramid Lake. Anoho Island, just off the north shore of the lake, is a bird refuge, and the lake and surrounding land are protected. The lake is the center of an Indian reservation, which is home to Piaute and perhaps also a few Washo Indians, for whom Washoe County and hence Washoe are named. Although the lake is protected, irrigation projects, which are greening the desert in nearby Fallon, have siphoned off much of the inflow to the lake from the Truckee River. Over the past fifty years the needs af Fallon have denied Pyramid its only protection against the sun. The lake has shrunk; it has become alkaline and desolate. Gone are most of the Lahontan trout, prized by the Piaute as sustenance. Few things now live in the lake's gemlike waters; the greening of the desert has spelled the death of Pyramid Lake.

The lake is bordered by arid hills and rock formations. The Animal Behavior Society drove like a caravan around the littoral. As we passed some huge, bulbous boulders, biologist George Barlow remarked, "They look like dinosaur turds."

"Coprolite?" suggested someone else picking up on his archeological joke.

We parked on the north shore and walked down toward an abrupt pinnacle that rose from the edge of the lake. Browsing among the rocks and brush, the naturalists were in their element. One woman apprehended, identified, and released a poisonous snake. Meanwhile, a cluster of scientists scaled the pinnacle and discovered the abandoned nest of some raptor. They attempted to determine its identity from the evidence of the dried bones of its prey and a few feathers. Far away an eagle spiraled, possibly outraged by the unlawful intrusion into a neighbor's home.

These scientists have been schooled by the same society that had doomed the lake, but their relationship to the land and their familiarity with its ecology was more akin to the spirit of the Piaute and Washo Indians than to the developmental combine that had brought about both the Indians' and the lake's decline.

This kinship, evident in both the style and the interests of these scientists, was the most significant aspect of this conference. The Animal Behavior Society is not large in numbers, but, borne on a Darwinian tide, it is influential beyond its numbers. It is a powerful creative force, as upcoming generations of scientists spill out of laboratories and into the field. The symposium was not a landmark event like the Wilberforce-Huxley debate, although Washoe, to whom the symposium was addressed, is a more powerful impulse toward the spread of evolution than any debate. Instead, the symposium was indicative of the process by which anomalous events seep throughout science. The symposium had enabled four scientists from four disciplines to look inward and, with the aid of the light cast by Washoe, sort through the assumptions on which they operate.

The symposium had set out to explore whether the difference between human language and animal communication was the result of saltation in evolution or an illusion resulting from an approach to animal and human communication that assumed such saltation. In other words, the topic was whether Washoe demanded the abandonment of the traditional paradigm or, if not, whether she could be explained by distinctions derived from that paradigm. The dispute over Washoe could not be summarized more concisely: The Gardners never argued that Washoe could do everything a person does in using language; rather, they sought to determine whether there was "overlap," continuity, between animal and human communication, which an evolutionary view of behavior would suggest. Washoe is anomalous—not to the notion that there are differences between animal and human communication, but to the notion that these differences are essential, rather than differences of degree.

Harvey Sarles and Allen Gardner had argued that the problem was one of approach; but, of course, the symposium could not settle this question any more than the Wilberforce-Huxley debate might settle the question of man's origins. On a practical level, the Gardners are open to the charge of stacking the panel in favor of their bias; but, more important, as can be seen from Kuhn's description of scientific revolution, questions such as these are answered not so much by what people argue as they are by what new generations of scientists choose to believe. In this light, the symposium was important because it indicated a trend.

Indeed, Washoe has made the behavioral sciences reassess their core assumptions concerning animal and human behavior. Perception of anomaly is the first stage in scientific revolution, and the reaction to Washoe described in Chapter Four indicates that Washoe was perceived as an anomalous threat from the time the Gardners first published accounts of her progress in learning

Ameslan. The symposium indicates that certain behavioral scientists were sorting out their perceptions of and assumptions about their subject matter, rather than, as is the case during paradigm defense, describing Washoe in terms of the traditional paradigm. Rather than interpreting Washoe in terms of a discontinuity in evolution, as in Chapter Four, scientists like Sarles were using Washoe as evidence that the differences between animal communication and human language might be the result of a paradigm-determined *approach*. In Sarles's talk a new gestalt might be seen tentatively arranging itself around Washoe.

Sarles himself looked at the function of the symposium in these terms and was quite pleased with what he thought it had accomplished. He felt that the symposium had redirected attention to the *problem* in comparing animal and human communication, and to the communalities in animal and human communication that various disciplines might explore (as, for instance, Marler's and Geshwind's talks suggested) should they solve problems of approach. When scientists become conscious of the assumptions behind an approach, it indicates that they have stepped away from the paradigm that conditions that approach. Sarles believes that only by finding a common approach to animal and human behavior will the behavioral sciences be able to isolate what it is that accounts for the manifest differences between man and chimpanzee. The symposium on Washoe, he feels, took a step toward implementing that common approach and has helped to set the stage for an exploration of what a common approach to behavior shows to be distinctive about man. From an evolutionary perspective, man does look different from the other animals, but not in the same way he looks different when seen in terms of the Platonic paradigm.

20. Washoe and the Moon Shot: Dionysus and Apollo

Earlier in this book, I suggested that, among the various behavioral attributes which have been ascribed to language, perhaps *displacement* is the most useful for considering the behavioral differences between man and other animals. In that section, I described a scenario in which demands for change led to the evolution of a displaced, surrogate world of symbols and logic that enabled a threatened primate to revise its behavior faster than normal genetic encoding permitted. Demands that man restructure his behavior along lines suitable to a technological society produced a competition as our new brain sought to bring more and more behavior within the perimeter of its surrogate world, and, consequently, it usurped the authority of the old

275

brain. I also described how the degree to which our behavior has come within the thrall of this surrogate world might serve to mark differences not only across species but among human cultures as well. This does *not* suggest that there are any differences in intelligence among diverse cultures, as there are between man and ape, but it does suggest that diverse cultures reflect the different degrees to which the world of displacement has encroached on the authority of the world of nature. This is evident in the constraints different cultures impose on the way intelligence is *employed*, and also in the way they view man's place in nature. In this sense, the more conservative the society, the less behavior will be subject to rational appraisal.

In concluding this book, I would like to consider how this competition between nature and the world of displacement has become manifest, first, as it is reflected in the traditions that produced the moon shot and, then, in whatever changes in that competition the emergence of Washoe portends.

I use the word "traditions" here because I would like to broaden the consideration of the paradigms previously discussed in order to relate them to the cultural heritage they reflect. In his postscript to the *Structure of Scientific Revolutions*, Kuhn notes that he uses the word "paradigm" in two senses: "On the one hand," he writes, "it stands for the entire constellation of beliefs, values, techniques, and so on shared by the members of a given community," while, on the other, he uses it to refer to some "exemplary past achievement," one element of the constellation of beliefs of the community that serves as the basis for the solutions to remaining problems in normal science. I have previously tried to show that, among the behavioral sciences, the "community-of-beliefs" idea of a paradigm is exaggerated, because the line between philosophical and scientific paradigms is considerably more blurred in the behavioral sciences than it is in the hard sciences. Now I would like to show how the Platonic paradigm, and several of its subparadigms, reflects the ambition to live amid what

Nietzsche called Apollonian order, an ambition achieved at the expense of Dionysian fulfillment and wisdom.

The paradigm of man as a rational animal is linked with Plato; however, this model of human autonomy occurs in many tributaries of Western thought. Plato is credited with proposing the idea of rational man because he was the lens through which that commonly shared belief entered the philosophical and scientific thinking of his time. Greek thought was stimulated, and Greek self-consciousness heightened, by exposure through trade and conflict with a variety of different cultures—Persian, Egyptian, Phoenecian, Semitic—and the Greeks were in an advantageous position to ruminate on and appraise the science and thought of the Mediterranean and Near-Asia. This heady cross-fertilization focused Greek attention on the wonders of the human intellect, just as the Gardners' enriched environment focused Washoe's attention on the utility of gestural communication. There is little wonder that classical Greece should have become fascinated with the world of the mind. However, the religious manifestation of rational man derived from sources wholly independent of Plato. Since the interplay of the religious and intellectual manifestations of that paradigm has so powerfully conditioned our image of man's place in nature, it is important to deal with these religious roots before returning to the scientific aspects of this Western paradigm.

Those scientific achievements upon which Greek eyes feasted were products of the adaptive genius of neighboring peoples forced to gouge an existence out of a rugged habitat, peoples forced to usurp nature's hand through agriculture and animal domestication who lived without the providential security of the jungle canopy. The Old Testament served to explain this harsh existence; it also gave man the ethical license to develop the technologies necessary to his survival.

Just as the rigors of temperate and desert climates summoned our adaptive genius, so did the inhospitality of these regions eliminate any other primates who might have reinforced man's communality with nature and limited the liberties man took with his environment. Isolated from manlike animals, man forgot he was an animal, and thus, conveniently, at a time and place when strategies for survival demanded that man ethically displace himself from the animal kingdom in order to have the license to manipulate it, there was no form of life around to temper that license and limit either the audacity of his manipulations or the grandeur of his self-image. The Greeks readily saw that necessity was the mother of invention; but necessity is also the mother of ethics, and, as Toynbee points out, monotheism freed the hand of the ancient Hebrews and encouraged the development of agriculture, herding, and rural technology. The desert tribes projected a cosmos in accord with the needs of a people who were forced to manipulate, and not just harvest, nature's bounty. This is the purpose of the myth of the Fall. Genesis contains a legal brief of man's rights in nature: "Let us [says God] make man in our image, after our likeness; and let them have dominion over the fish of the sea, and over the birds of the air, and over the cattle, and over all the earth, and over every creeping thing that creeps upon the earth." In addition, the Bible had to account for, and thus absorb, anxiety resulting from man's alienation from nature, because, if man was not an animal, then his relationship with them, or rather his estrangement from them, had to be explained. Part of the answer was offered in the creation myth; we were a Xerox copy of God, and He summoned into existence both us and our plaything, the earth, to brighten His life. What we lacked, but God possessed, was self-consciousness—the knowledge of good and evil—and the gift of eternal life. We could think, but a God-like autonomy (represented by the temptation of the forbidden fruit), though within our grasp, was religiously proscribed. The condition of pre-Fall humanity might be likened to an acceptance of natural authority. However, once accessible, the ambition to be God, to possess knowledge and autonomy, proved irresistible. We fell, and cursed with knowledge, there was no way to re-enter Eden.

One element in the account of the Fall that has changed during successive editions of the Bible is the notion that, before the Fall, man could speak with the animals: ". . . all the living animals had one language at that time . . . [before the Fall]." Josephus's account mythically related man's alienation from nature to the evolution of a language incompatible with that of other animals, but it contained an implicit moral problem: explaining man's dominion over creatures with whom he could communicate. This may account for the absence of this explicit statement in later editions (it remains implicit; after all, the serpent *tells* Eve to eat the fruit).

Josephus's account of Genesis is also more explicit than later accounts about the lot of man before and after the Fall. When God, perceiving Adam's guilty conscience over his transgression, confronts Adam, He details the life that He had planned for Adam and Eve and contrasts this with what lies ahead of them as a result of their usurpation: "I had before determined about you both, how you might lead a happy life, without any affliction, and care, and vexation of soul; and that all things which might contribute to your enjoyment and pleasure should grow up by my providence of their own accord, without your own labour and pains-taking; which state of labour and pains-taking would soon bring on old age; and death would not be at any remote distance: but now thou hast abused this my good-will, and hast disobeyed my commands; for thy silence is not the sign of thy virtue, but of thy evil conscience." And then later, "But God allotted him punishment, because he weakly submitted to the counsel of his wife; and said the ground should not henceforth yield its fruit of its own accord, but that when it should be harassed by their labour, it should bring forth some of its fruits, and refuse to bring forth others." Thus God describes the transformation from an innocent hunting and gathering existence amid the providential bounty of the forest to the agricultural and herding existence pursued by the Semitic tribes whose lot the Bible explained.

Later editions of the Old Testament strengthen the link between man's sin of usurpation and the necessity of this sin for the development of agriculture if he is to survive in his fallen state. In the Revised Standard version, God says that, because man ate of the tree ". . . of which I commanded you, 'You shall not eat of it,' cursed is the ground because of you; in toil you shall eat of it all the days of your life." Man's usurpation transformed nature from a patron into an adversary against which reason must be employed in toil if man is to survive. If awareness displaced man from Eden, once so displaced, it was this awareness which was necessary for man's survival. Hence the Semitic tribes outfitted themselves and Western civilization with an ethical system that granted man the authority to use the world as he wished. The secret of man's power over nature was that act of usurpation which originally caused his expulsion from Eden—the act of displacing himself from God's authority and presuming a Godlike autonomy.

The ancient Greeks shared with the ancient Hebrews a biological isolation from any primate links between animal and man, and were similarly unrestrained in their glorification of human intellect, which distinguished human nature and placed man above the other animals. For the Greeks, as for the Hebrews, the idea of man as a rational being attained pre-eminence because there was no other creature to stop it from doing so. Plato did not create the idea of rational man any more than one bearded prophet wrote Genesis. What both the Old Testament and Plato did was to articulate *gestalts* that interpreted man's peculiar biological isolation and adaptive strengths. But whereas Genesis pictured knowledge as a tool that had cursed man with expulsion from the Garden, the Greeks saw knowledge as a refuge from time and the passions of nature. The Platonic man wanted to live in the world of thought, in the displaced surrogate world of order and stability.

Greek tragedians were sensitive to this ambition. In *The Birth of Tragedy*, Nietzsche describes the Apollonian and Dionysian stresses that characterized Greek tragedy from Sophocles to

Euripides. These stresses circumscribe the competition between what, in this book, have been termed the surrogate world of displacement and the world of nature embodied in man's behavorial heritage. Nietzsche recounts how Greek thought, under the influence of Socratic skepticism, increasingly repressed the Dionysian, the animal side of life, in favor of constructing an ideal life in terms of the world of displacement.

Euripides, originally the most skeptical of the Greek tragedians, saw the dangers and futility of denying the animal side of life, and, says Nietzsche, wrote his spellbinding drama *The Bacchae* as a penance. Euripides saw the pretension that man-is-not-an-animal will not of itself make the animal part of man's nature disappear. Instead, when denied expression, the Dionysian aspect of life turns subversive and threatening. In the *Bacchae* the skeptical King Pentheus's rationalistic view of the world is distorted by these subversive animal passions into a fun-house mirror, and eventually he has his head torn off by his own subjects. Neither Pentheus nor the Socratic can live in his head. Reason operates in displacement from the world, and not vice versa.

If man could form his opinions through understanding rather than under the gun of necessity, the notion of rational man might have been entombed with Euripides, but it was not for several centuries that the dangers of the *Bacchae* began to become sufficiently *manifest* to force us to consider its lessons. Only now are we beginning to realize that the profitable image of rational man contains serious costs as well. And so, let us skip from Euripides and the Apollonian/Dionysian tension to the Apollo moon program of today, in which the Apollonian ideal of the ancient Greeks to live in the world of displacement began to be fulfilled, and the Dionysian dangers of that ambition have begun to become manifest.

In Chapter 17, I offered a brief précis of the history of the S-R paradigm and its relationship to the notion of the particulate universe. In that précis, the origins of that paradigm are dated from Galileo's mechanics and the notion that thought might be conceived as the motion of unchanging particles. This idea of a particulate universe recurs, like the idea of rational man, throughout Western thought. It was Leucippus, a Milesian thinker of about 400 B.C., who first proposed the notion that matter is composed of atoms, which sort into different patterns that are visible as the objects of nature; but, again, the idea was in the air before Leucippus gave it shape. The Apollo moon program of today offers a metaphor for the advantages and limitations of looking at the universe this way, and for the connection between the notion of a particulate universe and the Platonic paradigm of man's place in nature.

The Apollo moonshot has been seen as the crowning technological achievement of Western civilization, the ultimate conquest of nature, and the consummate defiance of gravity and the implication that man is a prisoner of earth. The ambitions to conquer nature and defy gravity are rooted in the belief that man is not a part of nature, that he is responsible to something higher, displaced from nature's laws. Nature is "unsacrosanct raw material," an aggregate of particles whose movements follow physical laws. The particles that form the building blocks of the world are discrete, they are bound; there is no communication between the particle and the medium through which it travels, just as there is no communication between the rational mind and the world on which it performs its manipulations. A space probe embodies this belief, that there is a division between matter and medium. The rocket is a particle—something that moves through space with no change save in location. The communication between the capsule and its medium is minimal; the space capsule is a discrete environment violating another environment. The advantages of looking at nature as unsacrosanct raw material are perfectly summarized by the fact that this attitude enabled us to get to the moon. The disadvantages in looking at the universe this way are that we cannot get very much farther. Space probes much beyond the moon begin to run afoul of problems of space and time and energy: the enabling concepts of Western technology and of a consuming attitude toward nature impose limitations on the degree of our displacement from earth.

In a sense, Western technology fulfilled itself in putting a man on the moon, because perhaps it was observations showing that the movements of the moon were different from those of the other stars that first jolted man to think that the heavens might not be one cohesive tissue, that there were discrete bodies floating around in a vacuum called space. Perhaps this is what spurred us to think in three dimensions, instead of remaining content with a two-dimensional flat earth and flat sky. Perhaps three-dimensionality is a function of displacement, and man in reaching the moon has reached the origins of Western technology. If our first sinful infatuation with the world of displacement was rooted in the need to see ourselves as distinct from the rest of nature, then the one sympathetic body in the heavens around which our notions of distinctiveness might gel would be the moon, distinct from the tissue of the night sky just as we thought ourselves distinct from the animal kingdom.

If we overturn this need to see ourselves as distinct from nature, it becomes evident that the special hallmark of Western thought has not been clearsightedness but, rather, selective blindness. By being blind to the continuities between animals and men, we could look at men as intrinsically superior to animals. While the primitive may look at nature as a cohesive tissue, we have been proud that we can see past nature's mask to the discrete particles of which it is comprised; but here again we must be selectively blind, because, as quantum physicist Werner Heisenberg discovered, if we look even closer at these particles their discreteness begins to become illusory. The electron, that fundamental particle, cannot be isolated in time and space. If fixed in space, one has to sacrifice fixing its direction and speed;

if fixed in speed and direction then one cannot explain its position in space. It eludes description in terms of a vector.

The dilemma is a uniquely suitable problem for Western thought, because, while reason is equipped to slice up reality, we have always had difficulty putting this mince back together again. I suspect this failing is a property of symbolization and logic itself. To examine the world abstractly, one has to withdraw from it, to displace oneself from the phenomenon to be examined. The nature of displacement demands that some aspect of a phenomenon be sacrificed—reality must be fixed on some continuum. Discreteness is in the nature of reason, because, without discreteness, displacement and reason would not be possible. The uncertainty of Heisenberg's electron reflects the uncertainty of reason itself. Heisenberg's electron reflects the problems of a system of thought and a model of the universe founded on discreteness' attempting to quantify an irrationally founded and undiscrete universe. Heisenberg's electron is mythic; it reflects the properties and limitations of reason itself. The discrete, particulate universe ultimately founders on the very keystone of its adaptive strength—displacement.

When we look at the world as a cohesive tissue of which we are a part, we are loath to tear or disrupt one part of that tissue for fear of the effects on the whole and on ourselves. However, when the universe is viewed as composed of moving particles, which are in turn compartmentalized in ever grander aggregates, such aboriginal restraints are overcome. But if one is safe in the belief that disruption of some particles need not necessarily redound adversely on all other particles and oneself, one wants to discover the key to the movement of those particles and thus to influence the course of events. Looking at the world this way frees us to influence successfully certain events in the world. The technologies reflecting the notion that the universe is particulate have permitted us to set foot on that numinous lunar particle. Yet, in attempting to reach the moon, to displace ourselves from nature, and in attempting to reconstitute nature to conform with the verities of the world of displacement (which is, after all, what materialism is all about), we have been consuming and gradually exhausting the resources of the world in which we must live. Foisting a particulate grid upon nature, we have not seen the connections between particles that are obscured by the grid, and, not seeing the connections between particles, we have violated those connections, rending and mutilating the cohesive tissue that lies obscured beneath that particulate grid. In trying to create a world displaced from the prison of time and nature, we have wounded nature and ourselves.

To illustrate this, let us return to the metaphor of the spaceship. The spaceship is a stable environment. Great energy is expended maintaining this stability in the face of the extreme environmental stresses that affect the capsule. To say that modern civilization attempts to reconstitute the world of displacement is to say that it attempts to reconstitute the environment in terms of the stability and order of the world of the mind. Man's desire to conquer nature is to create islands of stability, insulated, just as the spaceship is insulated, from the stresses of nature around it. To create and maintain a world of stability in an evolving universe demands vast amounts of energy. We can see that the energy waste of a consuming society is directed toward the demands of maintaining a displaced, stable world in a passionate universe whether that displacement be from tropical temperatures via air conditioning or from basic animal functions such as food gathering via supermarkets. Profligately we consume the world in which we live to attempt to create an environment that reflects the world in which we think.

But, while traditionally we have thought of such a life style as ideal, we are now learning that, though ideal, it is also unnatural. We are becoming aware that we cannot live in the displaced world. We are slowly becoming conscious of the tattered connective tissue obscured by the grid through which we factor the world.

On board Apollo 14 was astronaut Edgar Mitchell who, while aboard the capsule circling the moon, conducted experiments in ESP. He has since devoted his life to psychic research. Thus, on a space flight embodying the aspirations of Western technology, an astronaut disdained the bias of the particulate model of the universe that got him into space and attempted to look beyond arbitrary particulate divisions to the interconnections that lie beneath those divisions. In a capsule embodying a discrete, alienated universe, an astronaut was looking for evidence that nature was not as empty as the structure and mission of the moon shot assumed it was. Displaced from nature, man ultimately becomes lonely.

The abyss we presume to separate the space capsule from earth mirrors, in fact, stems from, the abyss we presume to separate man from the other animals. Mitchell reveals man trying to bridge his self-imposed isolation from his world and offers us a metaphor for the process Washoe represents. Washoe, schooled with the psychological manifestation of the particulate paradigm, shows science rediscovering the continuities that lead from animal to man and, in so doing, rediscovering the connective tissue that has lain obscured beneath the grid we have foisted on nature. Washoe is one of many indicators that Western culture has matured to the point where it has confronted, and begun to run afoul of, its own original assumptions.

This trend relates a number of seemingly disparate phenomena. Evolution—the notion that the environment and the organism evolve together as a seamless unity—is seeping through the behavioral sciences. In ethology, we see a reënchantment with the continuities between animal and human and the beginnings of a style of science in ethical accord with a universe in which man evolved from the same ancestors as the other mammals. Similarly, Russian scientists have been investigating the possibility that organisms are surrounded by "auras," a phenomenon that would blend the organism and its environment. Psychic research is beginning to attain some respectability in the skeptical West.

While scientists are talking to chimps, ordinary people have for a few years been talking with their plants. Here, the idea is that the visceral elements of communication have meaning not just across species but across phyla, an idea that revitalizes organisms almost universally perceived to be "unsacrosanct raw material." People are increasingly disavowing synthetic foods and drugs and applauding the virtues of natural foods and cures. Among the young there is an undercurrant pantheistic spirit reflected in the growth of the conservation movement, the repopulation of rural areas, and a Dionysian celebration of nature and the senses.

The point is not to suggest the validity of these various phenomena, but to suggest that they are expressive of a shared intuition of the inadequacy of the rational world and are also expressive of the shared need to re-establish communication with nature. The Platonic distrust of nature is being replaced with a distrust of rationality and technology.

In the behavioral sciences, Harvey Sarles calls this movement the return to biology. He feels that the return to biology for explanations of man's behavior reflects a pessimistic age in which man turns to biology for excuses for his failure to fulfill the ideals set by reason. However, while this return to biology reflects an awareness of the failing notions of rational man, I think it is not motivated by a sense of retreat so much as it reflects the first stirrings of a new view of man's place in nature. One cannot condemn as sinful man's failure to live up to the ideals of reason. Over the years reason has constructed a straitjacket for human behavior into which only an android could fit comfortably, while the rest of the population is saddled with a sense of failure and forced into various neurotic adaptations. The return to nature is more than an excuse for our failure as rational animals. Moreover, the paradigm of rational man could not be abandoned were there not a successor to it to redefine the world. I have described the scientific manifestation of that successor as a Darwinian paradigm. It is rooted in nature rather than in the world of displacement, and it is a paradigm in accord with Washoe, who offers evidence of our behavioral continuity with nature. It remains to be seen when the culture forecast by this Darwinian paradigm will appear.

Bibliography

BARRETT, WILLIAM. *Irrational Man*. New York: Doubleday, 1958.

BRONOWSKI, J. S., and BELLUGI, URSULA. "Language, Name, and Concept," *Science* (1970): 168, 699ff.

BROWN, ROGER. *A First Language: The Early Stages*. Cambridge: Harvard University Press, 1974.

———. "The First Sentences of Child and Chimpanzee" in *Psycholinguistics: Selected Papers*. New York: Free Press, 1970.

CHOMSKY, NOAM. *Language and Mind*. New York: Harcourt, Brace, Jovanovich, 1968.

DARWIN, CHARLES. *The Expression of the Emotions in Man and Animals*. London: J. Murray, 1872.

ENGLISH, HORACE. *Historical Roots of Learning Theory*. Garden City, N. Y.: Doubleday & Co., 1954.

289

BIBLIOGRAPHY

GARDNER, R. ALLEN and BEATRICE. "Teaching Sign-language to a Chimpanzee," *Science* (1969): 165, 664–672.

———. "Two-Way Communication with an Infant Chimpanzee," in *Behavior of Nonhuman Primates*, eds. A. Schrier, et al., vol. 4. New York: Academic Press, 1971.

GESHWIND, NORMAN. "Intermodal Equivalence of Stimuli in Apes," *Science* (1970): 170, 1249ff.

———. "The Organization of Language and the Brain," *Science* (1970): 1970, 940–944.

GOODALL, JANE. "A Preliminary Report on Expressive Movements and Communication in the Gombe Stream Chimpanzees," in *Primates: Studies in Adaptation and Variability*, Phyllis Jay, ed. New York: Holt, Rinehart and Winston, 1968.

———. *In the Shadow of Man*. Boston: Houghton Mifflin, 1971.

HEWES, GORDON W. "An Explicit Formulation of the Relationship between Tool-using, Tool-making, and the Emergence of Language," in *Abstracts, American Anthropological Association, Annual Meeting*. New York: American Anthropological Association, 1971.

———. *Language Origins: A Bibliography*. Boulder, Colo.: University of Colorado Press, 1971.

———. "Primate Communication, and the Gestural Origin of Language," *Current Anthropology*, vol. 14, nos. 1–2 (1973).

HOCKETT, CHARLES F. *A Course in Modern Linguistics*. New York: Macmillan, 1958.

KUHN, THOMAS S. *The Structure of Scientific Revolutions*. Chicago: University of Chicago Press, 1970.

LENNENBERG, ERIC H. "Of Language, Knowledge, Apes, and Brains," *Journal of Psycholinguistic Research*, vol. 1, no. 1 (1971).

LIEBERMAN, PHILIP and CRELIN, DEMUND S. "On the Speech of Neanderthal Man," *Linguistic Inquiry*, vol. 11, no. 2 (1971): 203–222.

LORENZ, KONRAD. *Studies in Animal Behavior*. Vol. 2. Cambridge: Harvard University Press, 1971.

NOTTEBOHM, FERNANDO. "Ontogeny of Bird Song," *Science*, 167 (1970): 950–956.

PREMACK, DAVID. "Language in the Chimpanzee?" *Science*, 172 (1971): 808–822.

———. "The Education of Sarah: A Chimp Learns Language," *Psychology Today*, vol. 4, no. 4 (1970): 55–58.

BIBLIOGRAPHY

SARLES, HARVEY. "The Study of Language and Communication across Species," *Current Anthropology*, vol. 10, nos. 1–2 (1969).

SEARLE, JOHN. "Chomsky's Revolution in Linguistics," in *The New York Review of Books* (June 29, 1972).

SIMPSON, GEORGE GAYLORD. "On Sarles's View of Language and Communication," *Current Anthropology*, vol. 11, no. 1 (1970) (with reply by Harvey B. Sarles).

Index